Student Solutions Manual of Odd-Numbered Exercises and Problems

for use with

Managerial Accounting

6th Canadian Edition

Ray H. Garrison, D.B.A., CPA

Eric W. Noreen, Ph.D., CMA

G.R. (Dick) Chesley, Ph.D.

Raymond F. Carroll, Ph.D., F.C.G.A.

McGraw-Hill Ryerson

Toronto   Montréal   Boston   Burr Ridge, IL   Dubuque, IA   Madison, WI   New York
San Francisco   St. Louis   Bangkok   Bogotá   Caracas   Kuala Lumpur   Lisbon   London
Madrid   Mexico City   Milan   New Delhi   Santiago   Seoul   Singapore   Sydney   Taipei

The McGraw-Hill Companies

McGraw-Hill Ryerson

Student Solutions Manual of Odd-Numbered Exercises and Problems for use with
Fundamental Financial Accounting Concepts
First Canadian Edition

ISBN: 0-07-091530-X

1 2 3 4 5 6 7 8 9 10 CP 0 9 8 7 6 5 4

Printed and bound in Canada

Care has been taken to trace ownership of copyright material contained in this text; however, the publisher will welcome any information that enables them to rectify any reference or credit for subsequent editions.

Vice President, Editorial and Media Technology: Pat Ferrier
Sponsoring Editor: Rhonda McNabb
Developmental Editor: Christine Gilbert
Production Coordinator: Madeleine Harrington
Marketing Manager: Kim Verhaeghe
Supervising Editor: Jaime Duffy
Printer: Canadian Printco

Contents

Chapter 1
Managerial Accounting and the Business Environment

Exercise 1-1 (10 minutes)

1. Managerial accounting, Financial accounting
2. Planning
3. Directing and motivating
4. Feedback
5. Decentralization
6. Line
7. Staff
8. Controller
9. Budgets
10. Performance report
11. Chief Financial Officer
12. Precision; Nonmonetary data

Exercise 1-3 (15 minutes)

If cashiers routinely short-changed customers whenever the opportunity presented itself, most of us would be careful to count our change before leaving the counter. Imagine what effect this would have on the line at your favourite fast-food restaurant. How would you like to wait in line while each and every customer labouriously counts out his or her change? Additionally, if you can't trust the cashiers to give honest change, can you trust the cooks to take the time to follow health precautions such as washing their hands? If you can't trust anyone at the restaurant would you even want to eat out?

Generally, when we buy goods and services in the free market, we assume we are buying from people who have a certain level of ethical standards. If we could not trust people to maintain those standards, we would be reluctant to buy. The net result of widespread dishonesty would be a shrunken economy with a lower growth rate and fewer goods and services for sale at a lower overall level of quality.

Problem 1-5 (20 minutes)

1. No, Sarver did not act in an ethical manner. In complying with the president's instructions to omit liabilities from the company's financial statements he was in direct violation of normal ethical conduct. He violated both the "Integrity" and "Objectivity" guidelines of a code of ethical conduct. The fact that the president ordered the omission of the liabilities is immaterial.

2. No, Sarver's actions can't be justified. In dealing with similar situations, the securities regulators have consistently ruled that "…corporate officers…cannot escape culpability by asserting that they acted as 'good soldiers' and cannot rely upon the fact that the violative conduct may have been condoned or ordered by their corporate superiors." (Quoted from: Gerald H. Lander, Michael T. Cronin, and Alan Reinstein, "In Defense of the Management Accountant," *Management Accounting*, May, 1990, p. 55) Thus, Sarver not only acted unethically, but he could be held legally liable if insolvency occurs and litigation is brought against the company by creditors or others. It is important that students understand this point early in the course, since it is widely assumed that "good soldiers" are justified by the fact that they are just following orders. In the case at hand, Sarver should have resigned rather than become a party to the fraudulent misrepresentation of the company's financial statements.

Problem 1-7 (20 minutes)

1. If all automotive service shops routinely tried to sell parts and services to customers that they didn't really need, most customers would eventually figure this out. They would then be reluctant to accept the word of the service representative that a particular problem needs to be corrected—even when there is a legitimate problem. Either the work would not be done, or customers would learn to diagnose and repair problems themselves, or customers would hire an independent expert to verify that the work is really needed. All three of these alternatives impose costs and hassles on customers.

2. As argued above, if customers could not trust their service representatives, they would be reluctant to follow the service representative's advice. They would be inclined not to order the work done even when it is really necessary. And, more customers would learn to do automotive repairs and maintenance themselves. Moreover, customers would be unwilling to pay as much for work that is done since customers would have reason to believe that the work may be unnecessary. These two effects would reduce demand for automotive repair services. The reduced demand would reduce employment in the industry and would lead to lower overall profits.

Group Exercise 1-9

Students' answers will depend on the specific experiences they had while working.

Group Exercise 1-11

Experience with the textbook Web site should be discussed.

Chapter 2
Cost Terms, Concepts, and Classifications

Exercise 2-1 (15 minutes)

1. Product; variable
2. Opportunity
3. Prime
4. Period
5. Product; period; fixed
6. Product
7. Conversion
8. Period; variable
9. Sunk
10. Fixed; product; conversion

Exercise 2-3 (15 minutes)

Cost	Cost Behaviour	
	Variable	Fixed
1. Small glass plates used for lab tests in a hospital..	X	
2. Straight-line depreciation of a building		X
3. Top management salaries.............................		X
4. Electrical costs of running machines.............	X	
5. Advertising of products and services*..........		X
6. Batteries used in manufacturing trucks........	X	
7. Commissions to salespersons......................	X	
8. Insurance on a dentist's office		X
9. Leather used in manufacturing footballs.......	X	
10. Rent on a medical centre...........................		X

* This particular item may cause some debate. Hopefully, advertising results in more demand for products and services by customers. So advertising costs are correlated with the amount of products and services provided. However, note the direction of causality. Advertising causes an increase in the amount of goods and services provided, but an increase in the amount of goods and services demanded by customers does not necessarily result in a proportional increase in advertising costs. Hence, advertising costs are fixed in the classical sense that the total amount spent on advertising is not proportional to what the unit sales turn out to be.

Exercise 2-5 (15 minutes)

1.

	Prevention Costs	Appraisal Costs	Internal Failure Costs	External Failure Costs
a. Repairs of goods still under warranty				X
b. Customer returns due to defects				X
c. Statistical process control........................	X			
d. Disposal of spoiled goods			X	
e. Maintaining testing equipment		X		
f. Inspecting finished goods		X		
g. Downtime caused by quality problems.............			X	
h. Debugging errors in software			X	
i. Recalls of defective products				X
j. Training quality engineers......................	X			
k. Re-entering data due to typing errors			X	
l. Inspecting materials received from suppliers...		X		
m. Audits of the quality system........................	X			
n. Supervision of testing personnel....................		X		
o. Rework labour			X	

2. Prevention costs and appraisal costs are incurred to keep poor quality of conformance from occurring. Internal and external failure costs are incurred because poor quality of conformance has occurred.

Exercise 2-7 (30 minutes)

   1.

ECCLES COMPANY
Schedule of Cost of Goods Manufactured

Direct materials:
Raw materials inventory, beginning	$ 8,000	
Add: Purchases of raw materials....................	132,000	
Raw materials available for use......................	140,000	
Deduct: Raw materials inventory, ending	10,000	
Raw materials used in production		$130,000
Direct labour		90,000
Manufacturing overhead:		
Rent, factory building....................................	80,000	
Indirect labour...	56,300	
Utilities, factory...	9,000	
Maintenance, factory equipment....................	24,000	
Supplies, factory	700	
Depreciation, factory equipment	40,000	
Total overhead costs		210,000
Total manufacturing costs.................................		430,000
Add: Work in process, beginning		5,000
		435,000
Deduct: Work in process, ending......................		20,000
Cost of goods manufactured		$415,000

2. The cost of goods sold section would be:

Finished goods inventory, beginning.................	$ 70,000
Add: Cost of goods manufactured	415,000
Goods available for sale	485,000
Deduct: Finished goods inventory, ending.........	25,000
Cost of goods sold...	$460,000

Exercise 2-9 (15 minutes)

1. Quality
2. Quality of conformance
3. Prevention costs, appraisal costs
4. Internal failure costs, external failure costs
5. External failure costs
6. Appraisal costs
7. Prevention costs
8. Internal failure costs
9. External failure costs
10. Prevention costs, appraisal costs
11. Quality circles
12. Quality cost report

Problem 2-11 (30 minutes)

Name of the Cost	Variable Cost	Fixed Cost	Product Cost — Direct Materials	Product Cost — Direct Labour	Product Cost — Mfg. Overhead	Period (Selling and Admin.) Cost	Opportunity Cost	Sunk Cost
Rental revenue forgone, $40,000 per year							X	
Direct materials cost, $40 per unit	X		X					
Supervisor's salary, $2,500 per month		X			X			
Direct labour cost, $18 per unit	X			X				
Rental cost of warehouse, $1,000 per month		X				X		
Rental cost of equipment, $3,000 per month		X			X			
Depreciation of the building, $10,000 per year		X			X			X
Advertising cost, $50,000 per year		X				X		
Shipping cost, $10 per unit	X					X		
Electrical costs, $2 per unit	X				X			
Return earned on investments, $6,000 per year							X	

Managerial Accounting, 6th Canadian Edition

Problem 2-13 (30 minutes)

1. Total wages for the week:

Regular time: 40 hours × $24 per hour...................	$ 960
Overtime: 5 hours × $36 per hour..........................	180
Total wages	$1,140
Allocation of total wages:	
Direct labour: 45 hours × $24 per hour	$1,080
Manufacturing overhead: 5 hours × $12 per hour ...	60
Total wages	$1,140

2. Total wages for the week:

Regular time: 40 hours × $24 per hour...................		$ 960
Overtime: 10 hours × $36 per hour		360
Total wages		$1,320
Allocation of total wages:		
Direct labour: 46 hours × $24 per hour		$1,104
Manufacturing overhead:		
Idle time: 4 hours × $24 per hour	$ 96	
Overtime premium: 10 hours × $12 per hour	120	216
Total wages		$1,320

3. Total wages and fringe benefits for the week:

Regular time: 40 hours × $24 per hour...................		$ 960
Overtime: 8 hours × $36 per hour..........................		288
Fringe benefits: 48 hours × $8 per hour		384
Total wages and fringe benefits		$1,632
Allocation of wages and fringe benefits:		
Direct labour: 45 hours × $24 per hour		$1,080
Manufacturing overhead:		
Idle time: 3 hours × $24 per hour	$ 72	
Overtime premium: 8 hours × $12 per hour	96	
Fringe benefits: 48 hours × $8 per hour..............	384	552
Total wages and fringe benefits		$1,632

Problem 2-13 (continued)

4. Allocation of wages and fringe benefits:
   Direct labour:
       Wage cost: 45 hours × $24 per hour $1,080
       Fringe benefits: 45 hours × $8 per hour............ <u>360</u> $1,440
   Manufacturing overhead:
       Idle time: 3 hours × $24 per hour 72
       Overtime premium: 8 hours × $12 per hour 96
       Fringe benefits: 3 hours × $8 per hour............. <u>24</u> <u>192</u>
       Total wages and fringe benefits.......................... <u>$1,632</u>

Managerial Accounting, 6th Canadian Edition

Problem 2-15 (30 minutes)

Note to the Instructor: Some of the answers below are debatable.

Cost Item	Variable or Fixed	Selling Cost	Administrative Cost	Manufacturing (Product) Cost Direct	Manufacturing (Product) Cost Indirect
1. Depreciation, executive jet	F		X		
2. Costs of shipping finished goods to customers	V	X			
3. Wood used in furniture manufacturing	V			X	
4. Sales manager's salary	F	X			
5. Electricity used in furniture manufacturing	V				X
6. Secretary to the company president	F		X		
7. Aerosol attachment placed on a spray can produced by the company	V			X	
8. Billing costs	V	X*			
9. Packing supplies for shipping products overseas	V	X			
10. Sand used in concrete manufacturing	V			X	
11. Supervisor's salary, factory	F				X
12. Executive life insurance	F		X		
13. Sales commissions	V	X			
14. Fringe benefits, assembly line workers	V			X**	
15. Advertising costs	F	X			
16. Property taxes on finished goods warehouses	F	X			
17. Lubricants for machines	V				X

*Could be an administrative cost.

**Could be an indirect cost.

© McGraw-Hill Ryerson, 2004

Problem 2-17 (30 minutes)

1.

Name of the Cost	Variable Cost	Fixed Cost	Product Cost: Direct Materials	Product Cost: Direct Labour	Product Cost: Mfg. Overhead	Period (Selling and Admin.) Cost	Opportunity Cost	Sunk Cost
Frieda's present salary of $4,000 per month							X	
Rent on the garage, $150 per month		X			X			
Rent of production equipment, $500 per month		X			X			
Materials for producing fly swatters, at $0.30 each	X		X					
Labour cost of producing fly swatters, at $0.50 each	X			X				
Rent of room for a sales office, $75 per month		X				X		
Answering device attachment, $20 per month		X				X		
Interest lost on savings account, $1,000 per year							X	
Advertising cost, $400 per month		X				X		
Sales commission, at $0.10 per fly swatter	X					X		
Legal and filing fees, $600								X

Problem 2-17 (continued)

2. The $600 legal and filing fees are not a differential cost. These legal and filing fees have already been paid and are a sunk cost. Thus, the cost will not differ depending on whether Frieda decides to produce fly swatters or to stay with the computer firm. All other costs listed above are differential costs since they will be incurred only if Frieda leaves the computer firm and produces the fly swatters.

Problem 2-19 (60 minutes)

1.

MEDCO, INC.

Schedule of Cost of Goods Manufactured

Direct materials:

Raw materials inventory, beginning	$ 10,000	
Add: Purchases of raw materials	90,000	
Raw materials available for use	100,000	
Deduct: Raw materials inventory, ending	17,000	
Raw materials used in production		$ 83,000
Direct labour		60,000
Manufacturing overhead:		
Depreciation, factory	42,000	
Insurance, factory	5,000	
Maintenance, factory	30,000	
Utilities, factory	27,000	
Supplies, factory	1,000	
Indirect labour	65,000	
Total overhead costs		170,000
Total manufacturing costs		313,000
Add: Work in process inventory, beginning		7,000
		320,000
Deduct: Work in process inventory, ending		30,000
Cost of goods manufactured		$290,000

Problem 2-19 (continued)

2.

MEDCO, INC.
Income Statement

Sales		$450,000
Less cost of goods sold:		
Finished goods inventory, beginning	$ 10,000	
Add: Cost of goods manufactured	290,000	
Goods available for sale	300,000	
Deduct: Finished goods inventory, ending	40,000	260,000
Gross margin		190,000
Less operating expenses:		
Selling expenses	80,000	
Administrative expenses	70,000	150,000
Net operating income		$ 40,000

3. Direct materials: $83,000 ÷ 10,000 units = $8.30 per unit.
    Depreciation: $42,000 ÷ 10,000 units = $4.20 per unit.

4. Direct materials:
    Unit cost: $8.30 (unchanged)
    Total cost: 15,000 units × $8.30 per unit = $124,500.
    Depreciation:
    Unit cost: $42,000 ÷ 15,000 units = $2.80 per unit.
    Total cost: $42,000 (unchanged)

5. Unit cost for depreciation dropped from $4.20 to $2.80, because of the increase in production
    between the two years. Since fixed costs do not change *in total* as the activity level changes, they

will decrease on a unit basis as the activity level rises.

Problem 2-21 (60 minutes)

1.

VALENKO COMPANY
Schedule of Cost of Goods Manufactured

Direct materials:
Raw materials inventory, beginning .... $ 50,000
Add: Purchases of raw materials................. 260,000
Raw materials available for use................. 310,000
Deduct: Raw materials inventory, ending .. 40,000
Raw materials used in production $270,000
Direct labour .... 65,000 *
Manufacturing overhead:
Insurance, factory 8,000
Rent, factory building 90,000
Utilities, factory.................................... 52,000
Cleaning supplies, factory.................... 6,000
Depreciation, factory equipment........... 110,000
Maintenance, factory 74,000
Total overhead costs 340,000
Total manufacturing costs .... 675,000 (given)
Add: Work in process inventory, beginning .. 48,000 *
723,000
Deduct: Work in process inventory, ending .. 33,000
Cost of goods manufactured $690,000

Problem 2-21 (continued)

The cost of goods sold section of the income statement follows:

Finished goods inventory, beginning	$ 30,000	
Add: Cost of goods manufactured	690,000	*
Goods available for sale	720,000	(given)
Deduct: Finished goods inventory, ending	85,000	*
Cost of goods sold	$635,000	(given)

*These items must be computed by working backwards up through the statements. An effective way of doing this is to record the form and known balances, and then work toward the unknown figures.

2. Direct materials: $270,000 ÷ 30,000 units = $9.00 per unit.
   Rent, factory building: $90,000 ÷ 30,000 units = $3.00 per unit.

3. Direct materials:
   Per unit: $9.00 (unchanged)
   Total: 50,000 units × $9.00 per unit = $450,000.

   Rent, factory building:
   Per unit: $90,000 ÷ 50,000 units = $1.80 per unit.
   Total: $90,000 (unchanged).

4. The unit cost for rent dropped from $3.00 to $1.80, because of the increase in production between the two years. Since fixed costs do not change *in total* as the activity level changes, they will decrease on a unit basis as the activity level rises.

Problem 2-23 (45 minutes)

1. A percentage analysis of the company's quality cost report is presented below:

	Year 2			Year 1		
	Amount	Percentage*	Percentage*	Amount	Percentage*	Percentage*
Prevention costs:						
Machine maintenance	$ 160	3.5 %	27.1 %	$ 215	5.2 %	22.3 %
Training suppliers	15	0.3	2.5	5	0.1	0.5
Design reviews	95	2.1	16.1	20	0.5	2.1
Total	270	6.0	45.7	240	5.8	24.9
Appraisal costs:						
Incoming inspection	22	0.5	3.7	45	1.1	4.7
Final testing	94	2.1	15.9	160	3.9	16.6
Total	116	2.6	19.6	205	5.0	21.3
Internal failure costs:						
Rework	62	1.4	10.5	120	2.9	12.4
Scrap	40	0.9	6.8	68	1.7	7.1
Total	102	2.3	17.3	188	4.6	19.5
External failure costs:						
Warranty repairs	23	0.5	3.9	69	1.7	7.2
Customer returns	80	1.8	13.5	262	6.4	27.2
Total	103	2.3	17.4	331	8.0	34.3
Total quality cost	$ 591	13.1 %	100.0 %	$ 964	23.4 %	100.0 %
Total production cost	$4,510			$4,120		

*Percentage figures may not add down due to rounding.

© McGraw-Hill Ryerson, 2004

Managerial Accounting, 6th Canadian Edition

Problem 2-23 (continued)

From the above analysis it would appear that Bergen, Inc.'s program has been successful, since:

- total quality costs as a percentage of total production have declined from 23.4% to 13.1%.
- external failure costs, those costs signaling customer dissatisfaction, have declined from 8% of total production to 2.3%. These declines in warranty repairs and customer returns should translate into increased sales in the future.
- internal failure costs have been reduced from 4.6% to 2.3% of production costs, which represents a 50% drop.
- appraisal costs have decreased from 5.0% to 2.6% of total production—a drop of 48%. Higher quality is reducing the demand for final testing.
- quality costs have shifted to the area of prevention where problems are solved before the customer becomes involved. Maintenance, training, and design reviews have increased from 5.8% of total production cost to 6% and from 24.9% of total quality costs to 45.7%. The $30,000 increase is more than offset by decreases in other quality costs.

2. Tony Reese's current reaction to the quality improvement program is more favourable as he is seeing the benefits of having the quality problems investigated and solved before they reach the production floor. Because of improved designs, quality training, and additional pre-production inspections, scrap and rework costs have declined. Consequently, fewer resources are now required for customer service. Throughput has increased and throughput time has decreased; work is now moving much faster through the department.

3. To measure the opportunity cost of not implementing the quality program, Bergen Inc. could assume that:

- sales and market share would continue to decline and then calculate the revenue and income lost.
- the company would have to compete on price rather than quality and calculate the impact of having to lower product prices.

Problem 2-25 (45 minutes)

	Case 1		Case 2		Case 3		Case 4	
Direct materials	$ 7,000		$ 9,000		$ 6,000		$ 8,000	
Direct labour	2,000		4,000		5,000	*	3,000	
Manufacturing overhead	10,000		12,000	*	7,000		21,000	
Total manufacturing costs	19,000	*	25,000		18,000		32,000	*
Beginning work in process inventory	3,000	*	1,000		2,000		1,500	*
Ending work in process inventory	(4,000)	*	(3,500)		(4,000)	*	(2,000)	
Cost of goods manufactured	$18,000		$22,500	*	$16,000		$31,500	*
Sales	$25,000		$40,000		$30,000		$50,000	
Beginning finished goods inventory	6,000		8,000		7,000		9,000	
Cost of goods manufactured	18,000	*	22,500	*	16,000	*	31,500	
Goods available for sale	24,000	*	30,500	*	23,000	*	40,500	*
Ending finished goods inventory	9,000		4,000		5,000	*	7,000	
Cost of goods sold	15,000	*	26,500		18,000		33,500	*
Gross margin	10,000	*	13,500	*	12,000	*	16,500	*
Operating expenses	6,000		8,000		9,000	*	10,000	
Net operating income	$ 4,000	*	$ 5,500	*	$ 3,000	*	$ 6,500	*

*Missing data in the problem.

Case 2-27 (60 minutes)

1. No distinction has been made between period expenses and product costs on the income statement prepared by Louganis. Product costs (e.g., direct materials, direct labour, and manufacturing overhead) should be assigned to inventory accounts and flow through to the income statement as cost of goods sold only when finished products are sold. Since there were ending inventories, some of the product costs should appear on the balance sheet as assets rather than on the income statement as expenses.

2.

MEDICAL TECHNOLOGY, INC.
Schedule of Cost of Goods Manufactured
For the Quarter Ended June 30

Direct materials:		
Raw materials inventory, beginning	$ 0	
Add: Purchases of raw materials	310,000	
Raw materials available for use	310,000	
Deduct: Raw materials inventory, ending	40,000	
Raw materials used in production		$270,000
Direct labour		80,000
Manufacturing overhead:		
Cleaning supplies, production	6,000	
Indirect labour cost	135,000	
Maintenance, production	47,000	
Rental cost, facilities (80% × $65,000)	52,000	
Insurance, production	9,000	
Utilities (90% × $40,000)	36,000	
Depreciation, production equipment	75,000	
Total overhead costs		360,000
Total manufacturing costs		710,000
Add: Work in process inventory, beginning		0
		710,000
Deduct: Work in process inventory, ending		30,000
Cost of goods manufactured		$680,000

Case 2-27 (continued)

3. Before an income statement can be prepared, the cost of the 4,000 monitors in the ending finished goods inventory must be determined. Altogether, the company produced 20,000 units during the quarter; thus, the production cost per unit would be:

$$\frac{\text{Cost of goods manufactured}}{\text{Units produced during the quarter}} = \frac{\$680,000}{20,000 \text{ units}} = \$34 \text{ per unit}$$

Since 4,000 monitors (20,000 − 16,000 = 4,000) were in the ending finished goods inventory, the total cost of this inventory would be:

$$4,000 \text{ units} \times \$34 \text{ per unit} = \$136,000.$$

With this figure and other data from the case, the company's income statement for the quarter can be prepared as follows:

MEDICAL TECHNOLOGY, INC.
Income Statement
For the Quarter Ended June 30

Sales..		$975,000
Less cost of goods sold:		
Finished goods inventory, beginning	$ 0	
Add: Cost of goods manufactured	680,000	
Goods available for sale..............................	680,000	
Deduct: Finished goods inventory, ending	136,000	544,000
Gross margin..		431,000
Less operating expenses:		
Selling and administrative salaries................	90,000	
Advertising	200,000	
Rental cost, facilities (20% × $65,000)	13,000	
Depreciation, office equipment	18,000	
Utilities (10% × $40,000).............................	4,000	
Travel, salespersons....................................	60,000	385,000
Net operating income		$ 46,000

Case 2-27 (continued)

4. No, the insurance company probably does not owe Medical Technology $227,000. The key question is how "cost" was defined in the insurance contract. It is most likely that the insurance contract limits reimbursement for losses to those costs that would normally be considered product costs—in other words, direct materials, direct labour, and manufacturing overhead. The $227,000 figure is overstated since it includes elements of selling and administrative expenses as well as all of the product costs. The $227,000 figure also does not recognize that some costs incurred during the period are in the ending Raw Materials and Work in Process inventory accounts, as explained in part (1) above. The insurance company's liability is probably just $136,000, which is the amount of cost associated with the ending Finished Goods inventory as shown in part (3) above.

Case 2-29 (45 minutes)

1. The key strategic decisions important to Seaman's were as follows:
   - not to sell out to Pepsi or Coke.
   - maintain their own varieties of pop.
   - expand markets outside PEI.
   - determine that the Environmental Protection Law in PEI will remain in effect.
   - modernize production and packaging.
   - premium pricing to consumers.

2. Bottling plants are high fixed cost operations. Thus the more that is produced, the lower the costs. Setups for new varieties are costly because equipment must be cleaned. Given quality maintenance personnel and the historical availability of used bottling machinery, some considerable cost savings are possible. Because Seaman's does not operate as a low cost producer, it must maintain a product differentiation from its low cost competitors. However, cost control within the differentiation strategy is important in order to maintain a reasonable rate of return on the fixed investment.

Group Exercise 2-31

1. A fixed cost is normally defined as a cost that remains constant, in total, regardless of changes in the level of activity. A variable cost is normally defined as a cost that varies, in total, in direct proportion to changes in the level of activity.

2. The relevant measure of activity for a steel company is probably the volume of steel produced. Fixed costs for a steel company include factory rent and depreciation, property taxes, many administrative costs, salaries, and periodic depreciation of equipment. Variable costs include the cost of raw materials, some energy costs, some labour costs, and some supply costs.

3. A number of different measures of activity could be used at a hospital. Some hospitals use a measure called patient-days, which counts a patient in the hospital for one day as a patient-day. Fixed costs at a hospital include the rental and depreciation of buildings, administrative salaries, utilities, insurance, and the costs of equipment. Variable costs include the costs of drugs and supplies and some labour costs.

   Universities often use credit-hours or the total number of students enrolled as the measure of activity. Fixed costs for a university include the costs of buildings, salaries, utilities, grounds maintenance, and so on. Variable costs are minimal.

   A measure of activity at an auto manufacturer might be the number of cars produced. Fixed costs for an auto manufacturer include the costs of buildings and equipment, insurance, salaries, and utilities. Variable costs include raw materials and perhaps some labour.

4. As the volume of steel produced increases, total fixed costs remain the same; the fixed cost per unit decreases; total variable costs increase; the variable cost per unit remains the same; total cost increases (due to the increase in total variable cost); and the average unit cost decreases (because of the decline in the fixed cost per unit).

Group Exercise 2-31 (continued)

5. The following graph depicts how total costs behave as a function of how many tonnes of steel are produced.

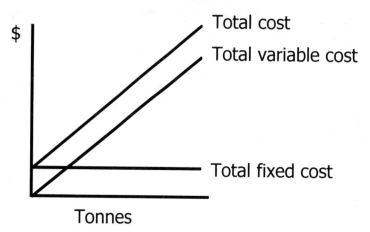

6. The following graph depicts how average costs per unit behave as a function of how many tonnes of steel are produced.

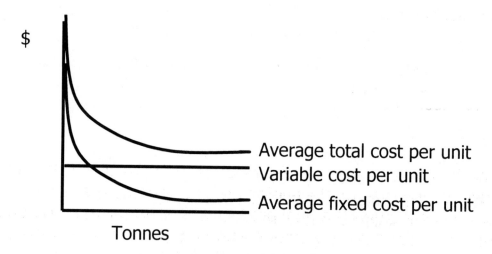

7. Once capacity has been set, total fixed costs and variable costs per unit remain the same while the average fixed cost per unit drops and the total variable cost increases as demand (output) increases.

Chapter 3
Systems Design: Job-Order Costing

Exercise 3-1 (10 minutes)

a. Job-order costing

b. Job-order costing

c. Process costing

d. Job-order costing

e. Process costing*

f. Process costing*

g. Job-order costing

h. Job-order costing

i. Job-order costing

j. Job-order costing

k. Process costing

l. Process costing

* Some of the listed companies might use either a process costing or a job-order costing system, depending on how operations are carried out and how homogeneous the final product is. For example, a plywood manufacturer might use job-order costing if plywoods are constructed of different woods or come in markedly different sizes.

Exercise 3-3 (15 minutes)

1. Predetermined overhead rates:

Company A:

$$\text{Predetermined overhead rate} = \frac{\text{Estimated total manufacturing overhead cost}}{\text{Estimated total amount of the allocation base}}$$

$$= \frac{\$432,000}{60,000 \text{ DLHs}} = \$7.20 \text{ per DLH}$$

Company B:

$$\text{Predetermined overhead rate} = \frac{\text{Estimated total manufacturing overhead cost}}{\text{Estimated total amount of the allocation base}}$$

$$= \frac{\$270,000}{90,000 \text{ MHs}} = \$3.00 \text{ per MH}$$

Company C:

$$\text{Predetermined overhead rate} = \frac{\text{Estimated total manufacturing overhead cost}}{\text{Estimated total amount of the allocation base}}$$

$$= \frac{\$384,000}{\$240,000 \text{ materials cost}} = 160\% \text{ of materials cost}$$

2. Actual overhead costs incurred.......................... $420,000
   Overhead cost applied to Work in Process:
     58,000* actual hours × $7.20 per hour............ <u>417,600</u>
   Underapplied overhead cost.............................. <u>$ 2,400</u>

   *7,000 hours + 30,000 hours + 21,000 hours = 58,000 hours

Exercise 3-5 (15 minutes)

1. Milling Department:

$$\frac{\text{Predetermined}}{\text{overhead rate}} = \frac{\text{Estimated total manufacturing overhead cost}}{\text{Estimated total amount of the allocation base}}$$

$$= \frac{\$510,000}{60,000 \text{ machine-hours}} = \$8.50 \text{ per machine-hour}$$

Assembly Department:

$$\frac{\text{Predetermined}}{\text{overhead rate}} = \frac{\text{Estimated total manufacturing overhead cost}}{\text{Estimated total amount of the allocation base}}$$

$$= \frac{\$800,000}{\$640,000 \text{ direct labour cost}} = 125\% \text{ of direct labour cost}$$

2.

	Overhead Applied
Milling Department: 90 MHs × $8.50 per MH ...	$765
Assembly Department: $160 × 125%	200
Total overhead cost applied	$965

3. Yes; if some jobs required a large amount of machine time and little labour cost, they would be charged substantially less overhead cost if a plantwide rate based on direct labour cost were being used. It appears, for example, that this would be true of job 407 which required considerable machine time to complete, but required only a small amount of labour cost.

Exercise 3-7 (15 minutes)
1. Item (a):   Actual manufacturing overhead costs for the year.
   Item (b):   Overhead cost applied to work in process for the year.
   Item (c):   Cost of goods manufactured for the year.
   Item (d):   Cost of goods sold for the year.

2. Manufacturing Overhead.............................   30,000
       Cost of Goods Sold..................................   30,000

3. The overapplied overhead will have to be allocated to the other accounts on the basis of the overhead applied during the year in the ending balance of each account:

Work in process.................................	$ 32,800	8 %
Finished goods....................................	41,000	10
Cost of goods sold.............................	336,200	82
Total cost	$410,000	100 %

   Using these percentages, the journal entry would be as follows:

Manufacturing Overhead	30,000	
Work in Process (8% × $30,000)...........		2,400
Finished Goods (10% × $30,000)		3,000
Cost of Goods Sold (82% × $30,000).....		24,600

Exercise 3-9 (20 minutes)

1. Since $320,000 of studio overhead cost was applied to Work in Process on the basis of $200,000 of direct staff costs, the apparent predetermined overhead rate is 160%:

$$\frac{\text{Studio overhead applied}}{\text{Total amount of the allocation base}} = \frac{\$320,000}{\$200,000 \text{ direct staff costs}}$$

$$= 160\% \text{ of direct staff costs}$$

2. The Krimmer Corporation Headquarters project is the only job remaining in Work in Process at the end of the month; therefore, the entire $40,000 balance in the Work in Process account at that point must apply to it. Recognizing that the predetermined overhead rate is 160% of direct staff costs, the following computation can be made:

Total cost added to the Krimmer Corporation Headquarters project		$40,000
Less: Direct staff costs	$13,500	
Studio overhead cost ($13,500 × 160%)................	21,600	35,100
Costs of subcontracted work		$ 4,900

With this information, we can now complete the job cost sheet for the Krimmer Corporation Headquarters project:

Costs of subcontracted work	$ 4,900
Direct staff costs	13,500
Studio overhead	21,600
Total cost to January 31..................	$40,000

Exercise 3-11 (30 minutes)

1.

	Williams	Chandler	Nguyen
Designer-hours.............................	200	80	120
Predetermined overhead rate.........	× $45	× $45	× $45
Overhead applied	$9,000	$3,600	$5,400

2.

	Williams	Chandler
Direct materials cost......................	$ 4,800	$1,800
Direct labour cost	2,400	1,000
Overhead applied	9,000	3,600
Total cost	$16,200	$6,400
Completed Projects*......................	22,600	
Work in Process		22,600

* $16,200 + $6,400

3. The balance in the Work in Process account consists entirely of the costs associated with the Nguyen project:

Direct materials cost.................................	$ 3,600
Direct labour cost	1,500
Overhead applied	5,400
Total cost in work in process.....................	$10,500

4. The balance in the Overhead account is determined as follows:

Overhead			
Actual overhead costs	16,000	18,000	Applied overhead costs
		2,000	Overapplied overhead

As indicated above, the credit balance in the Overhead account is called overapplied overhead.

Problem 3-13 (45 minutes)

1. and 2.

Cash					Accounts Receivable			
Bal.	15,000	225,000	(c)		Bal.	40,000	445,000	(l)
(l)	445,000	150,000	(m)		(k)	450,000		
Bal.	85,000				Bal.	45,000		

Raw Materials					Work in Process			
Bal.	25,000	90,000	(b)		Bal.	30,000	310,000	(j)
(a)	80,000				(b)	85,000		
					(c)	120,000		
					(i)	96,000		
Bal.	15,000				Bal.	21,000		

Finished Goods					Prepaid Insurance			
Bal.	45,000	300,000	(k)		Bal.	5,000	4,800	(f)
(j)	310,000							
Bal.	55,000				Bal.	200		

Buildings & Equipment				Accumulated Depreciation		
Bal.	500,000				210,000	Bal.
					30,000	(e)
					240,000	Bal.

Manufacturing Overhead					Accounts Payable			
(b)	5,000	96,000	* (i)		(m)	150,000	75,000	Bal.
(c)	30,000						80,000	(a)
(d)	12,000						12,000	(d)
(e)	25,000						40,000	(g)
(f)	4,000						17,000	(h)
(h)	17,000							
		3,000	Bal.				74,000	Bal.

$$* \frac{\$80,000}{\$100,000} = 80\% \text{ of direct labour cost; } \$120,000 \times 0.80 = \$96,000.$$

Retained Earnings			Capital Stock		
	125,000	Bal.		250,000	Bal.

Problem 3-13 (continued)

Salaries Expense	
(c) 75,000	

Depreciation Expense	
(e) 5,000	

Insurance Expense	
(f) 800	

Shipping Expense	
(g) 40,000	

Cost of Goods Sold	
(k) 300,000	

Sales	
	450,000 (k)

Problem 3-13 (continued)

3. Manufacturing overhead was overapplied by $3,000 for the year. This balance would be allocated between Work in Process, Finished Goods, and Cost of Goods Sold in proportion to the current period costs in these accounts. The allocation would be:

Work in Process, 12/31...............		$ 21,000	7.0 %
Finished Goods, 12/31.................		55,000	18.3
Cost of Goods Sold, 12/31	$300,000		
Less: Work in Process, 1/1	30,000		
Less: Finished Goods, 1/1	45,000	225,000	74.7
		$301,000	100.0 %

Manufacturing Overhead	3,000	
Work in Process (7.0% × $3,000)............		210
Finished Goods (18.3% × $3,000)		549
Cost of Goods Sold (74.7% × $3,000)......		2,241

4.

Fantastic Props, Inc.
Income Statement
For the Year Ended December 31

Sales..		$450,000
Less cost of goods sold ($300,000 − $2,241)...		297,759
Gross margin..		152,241
Less selling and administrative expenses:		
Salaries expense	$75,000	
Depreciation expense	5,000	
Insurance expense......................................	800	
Shipping expense..	40,000	120,800
Net operating income		$ 31,441

Problem 3-15 (45 minutes)

1. and 2.

Cash

Bal.	8,000	190,000	(l)
(k)	197,000		
Bal.	15,000		

Accounts Receivable

Bal.	13,000	197,000	(k)
(j)	200,000		
Bal.	16,000		

Raw Materials

Bal.	7,000	40,000	(b)
(a)	45,000		
Bal.	12,000		

Work in Process

Bal.	18,000	130,000	(i)
(b)	32,000		
(e)	40,000		
(h)	60,000		
Bal.	20,000		

Finished Goods

Bal.	20,000	120,000	(j)
(i)	130,000		
Bal.	30,000		

Prepaid Insurance

Bal.	4,000	3,000	(f)
Bal.	1,000		

Plant and Equipment

Bal.	230,000	

Accumulated Depreciation

		42,000	Bal.
		28,000	(d)
		70,000	Bal.

Manufacturing Overhead

(b)	8,000	60,000	*	(h)
(c)	14,600			
(d)	21,000			
(e)	18,000			
(f)	2,400			
Bal.	4,000	4,000		(m)

*$40,000 × 150\% = \$60,000$.

Accounts Payable

(l)	100,000	30,000	Bal.
		45,000	(a)
		14,600	(c)
		18,000	(g)
		7,600	Bal.

Salaries & Wages Payable

(l)	90,000	93,400	(e)
		3,400	Bal.

Retained Earnings

		78,000	Bal.

Problem 3-15 (continued)

Capital Stock			Sales Commissions Expense	
	150,000 Bal.	(e)	10,400	

Administrative Salaries Expense			Depreciation Expense	
(e)	25,000	(d)	7,000	

Insurance Expense			Miscellaneous Expense	
(f)	600	(g)	18,000	

Cost of Goods Sold			Sales	
(j)	120,000		200,000	(j)
(m)	4,000			

3. Overhead is underapplied. Entry (m) above records the closing of this underapplied overhead balance to Cost of Goods Sold.

4.

DURHAM COMPANY
Income Statement
For the Year Ended December 31

Sales..		$200,000
Less cost of goods sold ($120,000 + $4,000)...		124,000
Gross margin..		76,000
Less selling and administrative expenses:		
Depreciation expense......................................	$ 7,000	
Sales commissions expense	10,400	
Administrative salaries expense......................	25,000	
Insurance expense...	600	
Miscellaneous expense	18,000	61,000
Net operating income		$ 15,000

Problem 3-17 (60 minutes)

1.

Raw Materials			
Bal.	40,000	33,500	(a)

Work in Process			
Bal.	77,800*	60,700	(e)
(a)	29,500		
(b)	20,000		
(d)	32,000		
Bal.	98,600		

Finished Goods		
Bal.	85,000	
(e)	60,700	

Manufacturing Overhead			
(a)	4,000	32,000	(d)
(b)	8,000		
(c)	19,000		

Salaries & Wages Payable		
	28,000	(b)

Accounts Payable		
	19,000	(c)

```
*  Job 105 materials, labour, and overhead at November 30.      $50,300
   Job 106 materials, labour, and overhead at November 30.       27,500
   Total Work in Process inventory at November 30 .............   $77,800
```

2. a. Work in Process.. 29,500*
       Manufacturing Overhead 4,000
          Raw Materials......................................   33,500
       *$8,200 + $21,300 = $29,500.

   This entry is posted to the T-accounts as entry (a) above.

   b. Work in Process... 20,000 *
      Manufacturing Overhead........................... 8,000
         Salaries and Wages Payable................   28,000
      *$4,000 + $6,000 + $10,000 = $20,000.

   This entry is posted to the T-accounts as entry (b) above.

   c. Manufacturing Overhead 19,000
         Accounts Payable................................   19,000

   This entry is posted to the T-accounts as entry (c) above.

Problem 3-17 (continued)

3. Apparently, the company uses a predetermined overhead rate of 160% of direct labour cost. This figure can be determined by relating the November applied overhead cost on the job cost sheets to the November direct labour cost shown on these sheets. For example, in the case of job 105:

$$\frac{\text{November overhead cost}}{\text{November direct labour cost}} = \frac{\$20,800}{\$13,000} = 160\% \text{ of direct labour cost}$$

The overhead cost applied to each job during December would be:

Job 105: $4,000 × 160% .... $ 6,400
Job 106: $6,000 × 160% 9,600
Job 107: $10,000 × 160% 16,000
Total applied overhead $32,000

The entry to record the application of overhead cost to jobs would be as follows:

Work in Process............................... 32,000
    Manufacturing Overhead.............. 32,000

The entry is posted to the T-accounts as entry (d) above.

4. The total cost of job 105 would be:

Direct materials $16,500
Direct labour ($13,000 + $4,000) 17,000
Manufacturing overhead applied ($17,000 × 160%) 27,200
Total cost... $60,700

The entry to record the transfer of the completed job would be as follows:

Finished Goods... 60,700
    Work in Process 60,700

This entry is posted to the T-accounts as entry (e) above.

Problem 3-17 (continued)

5. As shown in the T-accounts above, the balance in Work in Process at December 31 was $98,600. The breakdown of this amount between jobs 106 and 107 would be as follows:

	Job 106	Job 107	Total
Direct materials	$17,500	$21,300	$38,800
Direct labour	13,000	10,000	23,000
Manufacturing overhead	20,800	16,000	36,800
Total cost	$51,300	$47,300	$98,600

Problem 3-19 (45 minutes)

1. a.

$$\text{Predetermined overhead rate} = \frac{\text{Estimated total manufacturing overhead cost}}{\text{Estimated total amount of the allocation base}}$$

$$= \frac{\$126,000}{\$84,000 \text{ direct labour cost}} = 150\% \text{ of direct labour cost}$$

b. Actual manufacturing overhead costs:

Insurance, factory	$ 7,000
Depreciation of equipment	18,000
Indirect labour	42,000
Property taxes	9,000
Maintenance	11,000
Rent, building	36,000
Total actual costs	123,000
Applied manufacturing overhead costs:	
$80,000 × 150%	120,000
Underapplied overhead	$ 3,000

Problem 3-19 (continued)

2.

PACIFIC MANUFACTURING COMPANY
Schedule of Cost of Goods Manufactured

Direct materials:

Raw materials inventory, beginning	$ 21,000	
Add purchases of raw materials	133,000	
Total raw materials available	154,000	
Deduct raw materials inventory, ending	16,000	
Raw materials used in production		$138,000
Direct labour		80,000
Manufacturing overhead applied to work in process		120,000
Total manufacturing cost		338,000
Add: Work in process, beginning		44,000
		382,000
Deduct: Work in process, ending		40,000
Cost of goods manufactured		$342,000

3. Cost of goods sold:

Finished good inventory, beginning	$ 68,000
Add: Cost of goods manufactured	342,000
Goods available for sale	410,000
Deduct: Finished goods inventory, ending	60,000
Cost of goods sold	$350,000

Under- or overapplied overhead may either be (1) closed directly to the Cost of Goods Sold account, or (2) allocated between Work in Process, Finished Goods, and Cost of Goods Sold in proportion to the overhead applied during the year in the ending balance of each of these accounts.

Problem 3-19 (continued)

4. Direct materials... $ 3,200
   Direct labour... 4,200
   Overhead applied (150% × 4,200)........................ 6,300
   Total manufacturing cost $13,700

   $13,700 × 140% = $19,180 price to customer.

5. The amount of overhead cost in Work in Process would be:

   $8,000 direct labour cost × 150% =$12,000

   The amount of direct materials cost in Work in Process would be:

   Total ending work in process...................... $40,000
   Deduct:
     Direct labour.................................... $ 8,000
     Manufacturing overhead...................... 12,000   20,000
   Direct materials $20,000

   The completed schedule of costs in Work in Process would be:

   Direct materials $20,000
   Direct labour 8,000
   Manufacturing overhead 12,000
   Work in process inventory......................... $40,000

Problem 3-21 (30 minutes)

1. Preparation Department predetermined overhead rate:

$$\text{Predetermined overhead rate} = \frac{\text{Estimated total manufacturing overhead cost}}{\text{Estimated total amount of the allocation base}}$$

$$= \frac{\$416,000}{80,000 \text{ machine-hours}} = \$5.20 \text{ per machine-hour}$$

Fabrication Department predetermined overhead rate:

$$\text{Predetermined overhead rate} = \frac{\text{Estimated total manufacturing overhead cost}}{\text{Estimated total amount of the allocation base}}$$

$$= \frac{\$720,000}{\$400,000 \text{ materials cost}} = 180\% \text{ of materials cost}$$

2. Preparation Department overhead applied:
   350 machine-hours × $5.20 per machine-hour $1,820
   Fabrication Department overhead applied:
   $1,200 direct materials cost × 180% 2,160
   Total overhead cost.. $3,980

3. Total cost of job 127:

	Preparation	Fabrication	Total
Direct materials................	$ 940	$1,200	$2,140
Direct labour....................	710	980	1,690
Manufacturing overhead ...	1,820	2,160	3,980
Total cost	$3,470	$4,340	$7,810

Unit product cost for job 127:

$$\text{Average cost per unit} = \frac{\$7,810}{25 \text{ units}} = \$312.40 \text{ per unit}$$

Problem 3-21 (continued)

4.

	Preparation	Fabrication
Manufacturing overhead cost incurred	$390,000	$740,000
Manufacturing overhead cost applied:		
73,000 machine-hours × $5.20 per machine-hour	379,600	
$420,000 direct materials cost × 180%...		756,000
Underapplied (or overapplied) overhead ...	$ 10,400	$(16,000)

Problem 3-23 (60 minutes)

1. The overhead applied to the Slug Fest job would be computed as follows:

	2002	2001
Estimated studio overhead cost (a)	$90,000	$90,000
Estimated hours of studio service (b)	750	1,000
Predetermined overhead rate (a) ÷ (b)	$120	$90
Slug Fest job's studio hours	× 30	× 30
Overhead applied to the Slug Fest job	$3,600	$2,700

Overhead is underapplied for both years as computed below:

	2002	2001
Predetermined overhead rate (see above) (a)...	$120	$90
Actual hours of studio service provided (b)	600	900
Overhead applied (a) × (b)..............................	$72,000	$81,000
Actual studio cost incurred.............................	90,000	90,000
Underapplied overhead...................................	$18,000	$ 9,000

2. If the predetermined overhead rate is based on the hours of studio service at capacity, the computations would be:

	2002	2001
Estimated studio overhead cost (a)	$90,000	$90,000
Hours of studio service at capacity (b)..............	1,800	1,800
Predetermined overhead rate (a) ÷ (b)	$50	$50
Slug Fest job's studio hours	× 30	× 30
Overhead applied to the Slug Fest job	$1,500	$1,500

Problem 3-23 (continued)

Overhead is underapplied for both years under this method as well:

	2002	*2001*
Predetermined overhead rate (see above) (a)......	$50	$50
Actual hours of studio service provided (b)..........	600	900
Overhead applied (a) × (b)................................	$30,000	$45,000
Actual studio cost incurred................................	90,000	90,000
Underapplied overhead....................................	$60,000	$45,000

3. When the predetermined overhead rate is based on capacity, the underapplied overhead is interpreted as the cost of idle capacity. Indeed, proponents of this method suggest that the underapplied overhead be treated as a period expense that would be separately disclosed on the income statement as Cost of Unused Capacity.

4. Skid Road Recording's fundamental problem is the competition that is drawing customers away. The competition is able to offer the latest equipment, excellent service, and attractive prices. The company must do something to counter this threat or it will ultimately face failure.

Under the conventional approach in which the predetermined overhead rate is based on the estimated studio hours, the apparent cost of the Slug Fest job has increased between 2001 and 2002. That happens because the company is losing business to competitors and therefore the company's fixed overhead costs are being spread over a smaller base. This results in costs that seem to increase as the volume declines. Under this method, Skid Road Recording's managers may be misled into thinking that the problem is rising costs and they may be tempted to raise prices to recover their apparently increasing costs. This would almost surely accelerate the company's decline.

Problem 3-23 (continued)

Under the alternative approach, the overhead cost of the Slug Fest job is stable at $1,500 and lower than the costs reported under the conventional method. Under the conventional method, managers may be misled into thinking that they are actually losing money on the Slug Fest job and they might refuse such jobs in the future—another sure road to disaster. This is much less likely to happen if the lower cost of $1,500 is reported. It is true that the underapplied overhead under the alternative approach is much larger than under the conventional approach and is growing. However, if it is properly labeled as the cost of idle capacity, management is much more likely to draw the appropriate conclusion that the real problem is the loss of business (and therefore more idle capacity) rather than an increase in costs.

While basing the predetermined rate on capacity rather than on estimated activity will not solve the company's basic problems, at least this method will be less likely to send managers misleading signals.

Managerial Accounting, 6th Canadian Edition

Problem 3-25 (60 minutes)

1. a.

$$\text{Predetermined overhead rate} = \frac{\text{Estimated total manufacturing overhead cost}}{\text{Estimated total amount of the allocation base}}$$

$$= \frac{\$1,440,000}{\$900,000 \text{ direct labour cost}} = 160\% \text{ of direct labour cost}$$

b. $21,200 × 160% = $33,920.

2. a.

	Cutting Department	Machining Department	Assembly Department
Estimated manufacturing overhead cost (a)	$540,000	$800,000	$100,000
Estimated direct labour cost (b)	$300,000	$200,000	$400,000
Predetermined overhead rate (a) ÷ (b)	180%	400%	25%

b.

Cutting Department:	
$6,500 × 180%	$11,700
Machining Department:	
$1,700 × 400%	6,800
Assembly Department:	
$13,000 × 25%	3,250
Total applied overhead	$21,750

3. The bulk of the labour cost on the Hastings job is in the Assembly Department, which incurs very little overhead cost. The department has an overhead rate of only 25% of direct labour cost as compared to much higher rates in the other two departments. Therefore, as shown above, use of departmental overhead rates results in a relatively small amount of overhead cost being charged to the job.

Problem 3-25 (continued)

Use of a plantwide overhead rate, however, in effect redistributes overhead costs proportionately between the three departments (at 160% of direct labour cost) and results in a large amount of overhead cost being charged to the Hastings job, as shown in Part 1. This may explain why the company bid too high and lost the job. Too much overhead cost was assigned to the job for the kind of work being done on the job in the plant.

On jobs that require a large amount of labour in the Cutting or Machining Departments the opposite will be true, and the company will tend to charge too little overhead cost to these jobs if a plantwide overhead rate is being used. The reason is that the plantwide overhead rate (160%) is much lower than the rates would be if these departments were considered separately.

4. The company's bid price was:

Direct materials	$ 18,500
Direct labour	21,200
Manufacturing overhead applied (above)	33,920
Total manufacturing cost	73,620
Bidding rate	× 1.5
Total bid price	$110,430

If departmental overhead rates had been used, the bid price would have been:

Direct materials	$ 18,500
Direct labour	21,200
Manufacturing overhead applied (above)	21,750
Total manufacturing cost	61,450
Bidding rate	× 1.5
Total bid price	$ 92,175

Problem 3-25 (continued)

Note that if departmental overhead rates had been used, Lenko Products would have been the low bidder on the Hastings job since the competitor underbid Lenko by only $10,000.

5. a.

Actual overhead cost	$1,482,000
Applied overhead cost ($870,000 × 160%)	1,392,000
Underapplied overhead cost	$ 90,000

b.

	Cutting	Machining	Assembly	Total Plant
Actual overhead cost	$560,000	$830,000	$92,000	$1,482,000
Applied overhead cost:				
$320,000 × 180%	576,000			
$210,000 × 400%		840,000		
$340,000 × 25%			85,000	1,501,000
Underapplied (overapplied) overhead cost	$(16,000)	$(10,000)	$ 7,000	$ (19,000)

Problem 3-27 (120 minutes)

1. a. Raw Materials.. 142,000
      Accounts Payable   142,000

   b. Work in Process................................... 150,000
      Raw Materials................................   150,000

   c. Manufacturing Overhead......................   21,000
      Accounts Payable   21,000

   d. Work in Process................................... 216,000
      Manufacturing Overhead.....................   90,000
      Salaries Expense.................................. 145,000
      Salaries and Wages Payable............   451,000

   e. Manufacturing Overhead......................   15,000
      Accounts Payable   15,000

   f. Advertising Expense............................ 130,000
      Accounts Payable   130,000

   g. Manufacturing Overhead......................   45,000
      Depreciation Expense..........................   5,000
      Accumulated Depreciation...............   50,000

   h. Manufacturing Overhead......................   72,000
      Rent Expense   18,000
      Accounts Payable   90,000

   i. Miscellaneous Expense.........................   17,000
      Accounts Payable   17,000

Problem 3-27 (continued)

j. Work in Process.................................... 240,000
        Manufacturing Overhead.................   240,000

$$\frac{\text{Estimated total manufacturing overhead cost}}{\text{Estimated direct materials cost}} = \frac{\$248,000}{\$155,000}$$

$$= 160\% \text{ of direct materials cost.}$$

$150,000 direct materials cost × 160% = $240,000 applied.

k. Finished Goods 590,000
        Work in Process.............................   590,000

l. Accounts Receivable............................ 1,000,000
        Sales...   1,000,000
   Cost of Goods Sold............................... 600,000
        Finished Goods   600,000

Problem 3-27 (continued)

2.

Accounts Receivable

(l)	1,000,000		

Raw Materials

Bal.	18,000	150,000	(b)
(a)	142,000		
Bal.	10,000		

Work in Process

Bal.	24,000	590,000	(k)
(b)	150,000		
(d)	216,000		
(j)	240,000		
Bal.	40,000		

Finished Goods

Bal.	35,000	600,000	(l)
(k)	590,000		
Bal.	25,000		

Manufacturing Overhead

(c)	21,000	240,000	(j)
(d)	90,000		
(e)	15,000		
(g)	45,000		
(h)	72,000		
Bal.	3,000		

Accounts Payable

		142,000	(a)
		21,000	(c)
		15,000	(e)
		130,000	(f)
		90,000	(h)
		17,000	(i)

Accumulated Depreciation

		50,000	(g)

Depreciation Expense

(g)	5,000	

Salaries & Wages Payable

		451,000	(d)

Salaries Expense

(d)	145,000	

Miscellaneous Expense

(i)	17,000	

Advertising Expense

(f)	130,000	

Rent Expense

(h)	18,000	

Cost of Goods Sold

(l)	600,000	

Sales

		1,000,000	(l)

Problem 3-27 (continued)

3.

SOUTHWORTH COMPANY
Schedule of Cost of Goods Manufactured

Direct materials:

Raw materials inventory, beginning	$ 18,000	
Purchases of raw materials	142,000	
Materials available for use	160,000	
Raw materials inventory, ending	10,000	
Materials used in production		$150,000
Direct labour		216,000
Manufacturing overhead applied to work in process		240,000
Total manufacturing cost		606,000
Add: Work in process, beginning		24,000
		630,000
Deduct: Work in process, ending		40,000
Cost of goods manufactured		$590,000

4.

Cost of Goods Sold	3,000	
Manufacturing Overhead		3,000

Schedule of cost of goods sold:

Finished goods inventory, beginning	$ 35,000
Add: Cost of goods manufactured	590,000
Goods available for sale	625,000
Finished goods inventory, ending	25,000
Unadjusted cost of goods sold	600,000
Add underapplied overhead	3,000
Adjusted cost of goods sold	$603,000

Problem 3-27 (continued)

5.

SOUTHWORTH COMPANY
Income Statement

Sales		$1,000,000
Less cost of goods sold................................		603,000
Gross margin		397,000
Less selling and administrative expenses:		
Salaries expense......................................	$145,000	
Advertising expense.................................	130,000	
Depreciation expense...............................	5,000	
Rent expense	18,000	
Miscellaneous expense.............................	17,000	315,000
Net operating income		$ 82,000

6.

Direct materials..	$ 3,600
Direct labour (400 hours × $11 per hour)	4,400
Manufacturing overhead cost applied (160% × $3,600)...	5,760
Total manufacturing cost	13,760
Add markup (75% × $13,760)	10,320
Total billed price of job 218...	$24,080

$24,080 ÷ 500 units = $48.16 per unit.

Case 3-29 (60 minutes)

This case is difficult; allow ample time for classroom discussion.

1. Work in process inventory, April 30 .... $5,300
2. Raw materials purchased during April $42,000
3. Overhead applied to work in process $15,600
4. Cost of goods sold for April $84,000
5. Overapplied overhead................................... $800
6. Raw materials usage during April $43,000
7. Raw materials inventory, April 30 .... $11,000

Entries given in the T-accounts are derived from the information given in the problem, and are keyed according to source (a, b, etc.).

a. Predetermined overhead rate: $180,000 ÷ 60,000 DLHs = $3 per DLH.

b. Work in process balance at April 30 consists of:

Materials	$2,600
Direct labour (300 hours × $6 per hour)	1,800
Overhead applied (300 hours × $3 per hour)	900
Total	$5,300

Case 3-29 (continued)

Raw Materials

(Given) Bal. 4/1		12,000	(g)	Direct materials	43,000
(c)		42,000			
(h)	Bal. 4/30	11,000			

Work in Process

(Given) Bal. 4/1		4,500	(f)	Cost of Goods Manufactured	89,000
(b,d)	Direct labour*	31,200			
(a,d)	Overhead applied**	15,600			
(g)	Direct materials	43,000			
(b)	Bal. 4/30	5,300			

Finished Goods

(e)	Bal. 4/1	11,000	(i)	Cost of Goods Sold	84,000
(f)	Cost of Goods Manufactured	89,000			
(Given) Bal. 4/30		16,000			

Manufacturing Overhead

(Given)		14,800	(a,d)	Overhead applied	15,600
				Overapplied overhead	800

Accounts Payable

(c)	Payments	40,000	(c)	Bal. 4/1	6,000
			(c)	Purchases must be	42,000
			(Given)	Bal. 4/30	8,000

Cost of Goods Sold

(i)	84,000	

* 5,200 DLHs * $6 = $31,200
** 5,200 DLHs * $3 = $15,600

Case 3-29 (continued)
Entries for which no information was provided:

g. The direct materials can be computed from what is already known about the Work in Process account.

h. The April 30 balance in Raw Materials can be determined after entry (g) is entered into the account.

i. The cost of goods sold can be computed from the amounts already determined in the Finished Goods Inventory account.

Case 3-31 (120 minutes)

1. Traditional approach:

Actual total manufacturing overhead cost incurred (assumed to equal the original estimate)....................	$2,000,000
Manufacturing overhead applied (80,000 units × $25 per unit)	2,000,000
Overhead under- or overapplied..................................	$ 0

TurboDrives, Inc.
Income Statement: Traditional Approach

Revenue (75,000 units × $70 per unit).........		$5,250,000
Cost of Goods Sold:		
Variable manufacturing (75,000 units × $18 per unit)	$1,350,000	
Manufacturing overhead applied (75,000 units × $25 per unit)	1,875,000	3,225,000
Gross margin		2,025,000
Administrative and selling expenses		1,950,000
Net operating income................................		$ 75,000

New approach:

TurboDrives, Inc.
Income Statement: New Approach

Revenue (75,000 units × $70 per unit)..........		$5,250,000
Cost of Goods Sold:		
Variable manufacturing (75,000 units × $18 per unit)	$1,350,000	
Manufacturing overhead applied (75,000 units × $20 per unit)	1,500,000	2,850,000
Gross margin		2,400,000
Cost of Unused Capacity [(100,000 units − 80,000 units) × $20 per unit]		400,000
Administrative and selling expenses..............		1,950,000
Net operating income		$ 50,000

Case 3-31 (continued)

2. Traditional approach:

Under the traditional approach, the reported net operating income can be increased by increasing the production level, which then results in overapplied overhead that is deducted from Cost of Goods Sold.

Additional net operating income required to attain target net operating income ($210,000 - $75,000) (a)	$135,000
Overhead applied per unit of output (b)	$25 per unit
Additional output required to attain target net operating income (a) ÷ (b)	5,400 units
Actual total manufacturing overhead cost incurred..........	$2,000,000
Manufacturing overhead applied [(80,000 units + 5,400 units) × $25 per unit]	2,135,000
Overhead overapplied	$ 135,000

TurboDrives, Inc.
Income Statement: Traditional Approach

Revenue (75,000 units × $70 per unit)		$5,250,000
Cost of Goods Sold:		
Variable manufacturing (75,000 units × $18 per unit)....................	$1,350,000	
Manufacturing overhead applied (75,000 units × $25 per unit)....................	1,875,000	
Less: Manufacturing overhead overapplied...	135,000	3,090,000
Gross margin		2,160,000
Administrative and selling expenses................		1,950,000
Net operating income		$ 210,000

Note: If the overapplied manufacturing overhead were prorated between ending inventories and Cost of Goods Sold, more units would have to be produced to attain the target net profit of $210,000.

Case 3-31 (continued)

New approach:

Under the new approach, the reported net operating income can be increased by increasing the production level which then results in less of a deduction on the income statement for the Cost of Unused Capacity.

Additional net operating income required to attain target net operating income ($210,000 - $50,000) (a)	$160,000
Overhead applied per unit of output (b)........................	$20 per unit
Additional output required to attain target net operating income (a) ÷ (b)..	8,000 units
Estimated number of units produced	80,000 units
Actual number of units to be produced	88,000 units

TurboDrives, Inc.
Income Statement: New Approach

Revenue (75,000 units × $70 per unit)		$5,250,000
Cost of Goods Sold:		
Variable manufacturing (75,000 units × $18 per unit).........................	$1,350,000	
Manufacturing overhead applied (75,000 units × $20 per unit).........................	1,500,000	2,850,000
Gross margin..		2,400,000
Cost of Unused Capacity [(100,000 units - 88,000 units) × $20 per unit]..		240,000
Administrative and selling expenses.....................		1,950,000
Net operating income..		$ 210,000

Case 3-31 (continued)

3. Net operating income is more volatile under the new method than under the old method. The reason for this is that the reported profit per unit sold is higher under the new method by $5, the difference in the predetermined overhead rates. As a consequence, swings in sales in either direction will have a more dramatic impact on reported profits under the new method.

4. As the computations in part (2) show, the "hat trick" is a bit harder to perform under the new method. Under the old method, the target net operating income can be attained by producing an additional 5,400 units. Under the new method, the production would have to be increased by 8,000 units. Again, this is a consequence of the difference in predetermined overhead rates. The drop in sales has had a more dramatic effect on net operating income under the new method as noted above in part (3). In addition, since the predetermined overhead rate is lower under the new method, producing excess inventories has less of an effect per unit on net operating income than under the traditional method and hence more excess production is required.

5. One can argue that whether the "hat trick" is unethical depends on the level of sophistication of the owners of the company and others who read the financial statements. If they understand the effects of excess production on net operating income and are not misled, it can be argued that the hat trick is ethical. However, if that were the case, there does not seem to be any reason to use the hat trick. Why would the owners want to tie up working capital in inventories just to artificially attain a target net operating income for the period? And increasing the rate of production toward the end of the year is likely to increase overhead costs due to overtime and other costs. Building up inventories all at once is very likely to be much more expensive than increasing the rate of production uniformly throughout the year. In the case, we assumed that there would not be an increase in overhead costs due to the additional production, but that is likely not to be true.

    In our opinion the hat trick is unethical unless there is a good reason for increasing production other than to artificially boost the current period's net operating income. It is certainly unethical if the purpose is to fool users of financial reports such as owners and creditors or if the purpose is to meet targets so that bonuses will be paid to top managers.

Case 3-33 (45 minutes)

1. (a) Inventory—raw materials 6,000
           Accounts Payable.. 6,000

   (b) Inventory—work in process 6,500
           Inventory 6,500

1201	$ 800
1202	700
1203	3,000
1204	2,000
	$6,500

   (c) Inventory—work in process 6,500
           Cash 6,500

1107	$ 300
1201	700
1202	2,000
1203	2,500
1204	1,000
	$6,500

   (d) Overhead—supervision................................. 2,000
           Cash 2,000

   (e) Overhead—depreciation—p & p 2,000
       Depreciation—vehicle....................................... 1,000
           Accumulated Depre—p & p.......................... 2,000
           Accumulated Depre—vehicle 1,000

   (f) Overhead—Insurance................................... 150
           Prepaid Insurance.. 150

   (g) Overhead—Maintenance............................... 500
           Cash 500

Case 3-33 (continued)

(h) Inventory—work in process	5,850	
Overhead—applied		5,850

1107	$ 270
1201	630
1202	1,800
1203	2,250
1204	900
	$5,850

(i) Bidding Expenses	800	
Cash		800
(j) Administrative Salary	2,500	
Cash		2,500
(k) Accounts Receivable	23,700	
Construction Revenue		23,700

1105	$ 2,000
1107	5,000
1201	2,500
1202	4,200
1203	10,000
	$23,700

Cost of Finished Jobs	18,750		
Inventory—finished jobs		800	(1105)
Inventory—work in process		17,950	

1107	$3,000 + $300 + $270 =	$ 3,570
1201	$800 + $700 + $630 =	$ 2,130
1202	$700 + $2,000 + $1,800 =	$ 4,500
1203	$3,000 + $2,500 + $2,250 =	$ 7,750
		$17,950

(l) Cash	23,000	
Accounts Receivable		23,000
(m) Accounts Payable	8,000	
Interest Expense	500	
Cash		8,500
(n) Overhead—Rework wind storm	290	
Inventory—raw materials		200
Cash		90

Case 3-33 (continued)

2.

Tibeau Construction Ltd.
Income—Jobs

	1107	1105	1203
Revenue.............................	$2,000	$5,000	$10,000
Cost of finished jobs			
Material.........................	800 *	3,000 *	3,000
Labour		300	2,500
Overhead		270	2,250
	800	3,570	7,750
Income per job....................	$1,200	$1,430	$ 2,250

*Prior period costs are not categorized.

3.

Inventory—work in process	Job 1204
Materials	$2,000
Labour	1,000
Overhead	900
Total....................	$3,900

Wind damage is a normal cost and thus spread over all jobs through being charged to overhead.

Chapter 4
Systems Design: Process Costing

Exercise 4-1 (10 minutes)

Work in Process—Mixing	330,000	
Raw Materials Inventory		330,000
Work in Process—Mixing	260,000	
Work in Process—Baking	120,000	
Wages Payable		380,000
Work in Process—Mixing	190,000	
Work in Process—Baking	90,000	
Manufacturing Overhead		280,000
Work in Process—Baking	760,000	
Work in Process—Mixing		760,000
Finished Goods	980,000	
Work in Process—Baking		980,000

Exercise 4-3 (10 minutes)

FIFO Method

	Equivalent Units	
	Materials	Conversion
Work in process, October 1:		
50,000 units × 10%*	5,000	
50,000 units × 40%*		20,000
Started and completed during October**	360,000	360,000
Work in process, October 31:		
30,000 units × 70%	21,000	
30,000 units × 50%		15,000
Equivalent units	386,000	395,000

* Work needed to complete these units.
** 390,000 units started into production – 30,000 units in ending work in process = 360,000 units started and completed

Exercise 4-5 (15 minutes)

FIFO Method

1. The number of kilograms completed and transferred out during the month would be the same regardless of the process costing method used. Thus, as in Exercise 4-4, 330,000 kilograms would have been completed and transferred out. However, under the FIFO method we must break this figure down between kilograms started and completed during the current period. The breakdown is shown in Part 2 below:

2. Kilograms to be accounted for:
   Work in process, May 1 (materials 80%
      complete; conversion 20% complete)................. 80,000
   Started into production during the month.............. <u>300,000</u>
   Total kilograms to be accounted for......................... <u>380,000</u>

   Kilograms accounted for as follows:
      Transferred out during the month:
         From beginning inventory 80,000
         Started and completed during the month............ 250,000 *
      Work in process, May 31 (materials 40%
         complete; conversion 10% complete)................. <u>50,000</u>
   Total kilograms accounted for .... <u>380,000</u>

   *   300,000 started – 50,000 ending work in process =
        250,000 started and completed

Exercise 4-7 (15 minutes)
FIFO Method

	Quantity Schedule
Kilograms to be accounted for:	
Work in process, May 1 (materials 100% complete, labour and overhead 55% complete)	30,000
Started into production during May	480,000
Total kilograms to be accounted for	510,000

		Equivalent Units	
		Materials	Labour & Overhead
Kilograms accounted for as follows:			
Transferred to Packing Department:			
From the beginning inventory	30,000	—	13,500 *
Started and completed this month**	460,000	460,000	460,000
Work in process, May 31 (materials 100% complete, labour and overhead 90% complete)	20,000	20,000	18,000
Total kilograms accounted for	510,000	480,000	491,500

*Work required to complete these units: 100% − 55% = 45%.
  45% × 30,000 kilograms = 13,500 kilograms
**480,000 kilograms started − 20,000 kilograms in ending work in process = 460,000 kilograms started and completed this month

Exercise 4-9 (20 minutes)
FIFO Method

1.

	Quantity Schedule
Litres to be accounted for:	
Work in process, May 1 (materials 80% complete, labour and overhead 75% complete)......................	80,000
Started into production	760,000
Total litres accounted for......	840,000

	Quantity Schedule	Equivalent Units		
		Materials	Labour	Overhead
Litres accounted for as follows:				
Transferred to the next department:				
From the beginning inventory	80,000	16,000*	20,000*	20,000*
Started and completed this month**...............	710,000	710,000	710,000	710,000
Work in process, May 31 (materials 60% complete, labour and overhead 20% complete)......................	50,000	30,000	10,000	10,000
Total litres accounted for......	840,000	756,000	740,000	740,000

   * Work required to complete the beginning inventory.
   ** 760,000 litres started − 50,000 litres in ending work in process = 710,000 litres started and completed.

Exercise 4-9 (continued)

2.

	Total Costs	Materials	Labour	Overhead	Whole Unit
Cost to be accounted for:					
Work in process, May 31 ...	$ 146,600				
Cost added during the month (a)	1,869,200	$907,200	$370,000	$592,000	
Total cost to be accounted for	$2,015,800				
Equivalent units (b)		756,000	740,000	740,000	
Cost per equivalent unit (a) ÷ (b)		$1.20 +	$0.50 +	$0.80 =	$2.50

Exercise 4-11 (15 minutes)

Weighted-Average Method

	Total Cost	Equivalent Units (EU)	
		Materials	Conversion
Cost accounted for as follows:			
Transferred to the next process:			
300,000 units at $2.12 each	$636,000	300,000	300,000
Work in process, June 30:			
Materials, at $1.38 per EU	27,600	20,000	
Conversion, at $0.74 per EU	7,400		10,000
Total work in process	35,000		
Total cost accounted for	$671,000		

Exercise 4-13 (20 minutes)

FIFO Method

	Total Cost	Equivalent Units (EU)	
		Materials	Conversion
Cost accounted for as follows:			
Transferred to the next process:			
From the beginning inventory:			
Cost in the beginning inventory.....	$ 71,500		
Cost to complete these units:			
Materials, at $1.40 per EU.........	21,000	15,000	
Conversion, at $0.75 per EU......	27,000		36,000
Total cost from beginning inventory..	119,500		
Units started and completed this month: 240,000 units × $2.15 per unit	516,000	240,000	240,000
Total cost transferred to the next process	635,500		
Work in process, June 30:			
Materials, at $1.40 per EU................	28,000	20,000	
Conversion, at $0.75 per EU.............	7,500		10,000
Total work in process, June 30............	35,500		
Total cost accounted for.......................	$671,000		

Problem 4-15 (45 minutes)

Weighted-Average Method

Quantity Schedule and Equivalent Units

	Quantity Schedule
Units to be accounted for:	
Work in process, June 1 (materials $5/7$ complete, conversion $3/7$ complete)	70,000
Started into production	460,000
Total units accounted for	530,000

	Quantity Schedule	Equivalent Units (EU) Materials	Conversion
Units accounted for as follows:			
Transferred to the next department	450,000	450,000	450,000
Work in process, June 30 (materials $3/4$ complete, conversion $5/8$ complete)	80,000	60,000	50,000
Total units accounted for	530,000	510,000	500,000

Problem 4-15 (continued)

Costs per Equivalent Unit

	Total	Materials	Conversion	Whole Unit
Costs to be accounted for:				
Work in process, June 1	$ 55,400	$ 37,400	$ 18,000	
Cost added during the month	673,000	391,000	282,000	
Total cost to be accounted for (a)	$728,400	$428,400	$300,000	
Equivalent units (b)		510,000	500,000	
Cost per equivalent unit (a) ÷ (b)		$0.84 +	$0.60 =	$1.44

Managerial Accounting, 6th Canadian Edition

Problem 4-15 (continued)

Cost Reconciliation

	Costs	Equivalent Units (EU)	
		Materials	Conversion
Cost accounted for as follows:			
Transferred to the next department: 450,000 units × $1.44 per unit	$648,000	450,000	450,000
Work in process, June 30:			
Materials, at $0.84 per EU	50,400	60,000	
Conversion, at $0.60 per EU	30,000		50,000
Total work in process, June 30	80,400		
Total cost accounted for	$728,400		

Problem 4-17 (45 minutes)

Weighted-Average Method

1., 2., and 3.

Quantity Schedule and Equivalent Units

	Quantity Schedule
Kilograms to be accounted for:	
Work in process, May 1 (materials 100% complete, conversion 90% complete)......	70,000
Started into production...............	350,000
Total kilograms to be accounted for..	420,000

		Equivalent Units (EU)	
		Materials	Conversion
Kilograms accounted for as follows:			
Transferred to Molding*	380,000	380,000	380,000
Work in process, May 31 (materials 75% complete, conversion 25% complete)...........	40,000	30,000	10,000
Total kilograms accounted for............	420,000	410,000	390,000

*70,000 + 350,000 − 40,000 = 380,000.

Costs per Equivalent Unit

	Total Cost	Materials	Conversion	Whole Unit
Costs to be accounted for:				
Work in process, May 1	$122,000	$ 86,000	$ 36,000	
Cost added during the month.............................	645,000	447,000	198,000	
Total cost to be accounted for (a)	$767,000	$533,000	$234,000	
Equivalent units (b).............		410,000	390,000	
Cost per equivalent unit (a) ÷ (b)...........................		$1.30 +	$0.60 =	$1.90

Cost Reconciliation

	Costs	Equivalent Units (EU)	
		Materials	*Conversion*
Cost accounted for as follows:			
Transferred to Molding:			
380,000 units × $1.90 per unit.........	$722,000	380,000	380,000
Work in process, May 31:			
Materials, at $1.30 per EU................	39,000	30,000	
Conversion, at $0.60 per EU.............	6,000		10,000
Total work in process	45,000		
Total cost accounted for......................	$767,000		

Problem 4-19 (45 minutes)

Weighted-Average Method

1. Total units transferred to the next department........ 30,000
   Less units in the May 1 inventory 5,000
   Units started and completed in May....................... 25,000

2. The equivalent units were:

	Quantity Schedule	Equivalent Units (EU) Materials	Conversion
Units accounted for as follows:			
Transferred to next department..	30,000	30,000	30,000
Work in process, May 31*	4,000	3,000	2,000
Total units accounted for	34,000	33,000	32,000

   * Materials: 4,000 units × 75% = 3,000 equivalent units;
       Conversion: 4,000 units × 50% = 2,000 equivalent units

Problem 4-19 (continued)

3. The unit costs were:

	Total Cost	Materials	Conversion	Whole Unit
Cost to be accounted for:				
Work in process, May 1	£ 13,400	£ 9,000	£ 4,400	
Cost added in the department......	87,800	57,000	30,800	
Total cost to be accounted for (a)...	£101,200	£66,000	£35,200	
Equivalent units (above) (b)		33,000	32,000	
Cost per equivalent unit (a) ÷ (b)...		£2.00 +	£1.10 =	£3.10

4. The ending work in process figure is verified as follows:

Materials, 3,000 equivalent units × £2.00 per unit.......	£6,000
Conversion, 2,000 equivalent units × £1.10 per unit.....	2,200
Total work in process................................	£8,200

5. Multiplying the unit cost figure of £3.10 per unit by 1,000 units does *not* provide a valid estimate of the incremental cost of processing an additional 1,000 units through the department. If there is sufficient idle capacity to process an additional 1,000 units, the incremental cost per unit is almost certainly less than £3.10 per unit since the conversion costs are likely to include fixed costs.

Problem 4-21 (45 minutes)

FIFO Method

Quantity Schedule and Equivalent Units

	Quantity Schedule
Kilograms to be accounted for:	
Work in process, July 1 (materials 100% complete, labour and overhead 30% complete)...............	10,000
Started into production.....................	170,000
Total kilograms to be accounted for.....	180,000

		Equivalent Units (EU)	
		Materials	Labour & Overhead
Kilograms accounted for as follows:			
Transferred to Forming:			
From the beginning inventory*.......	10,000	—	7,000
Started and completed this month**...................................	150,000	150,000	150,000
Work in process, July 31 (materials 100% complete, labour and overhead 40% complete)...............	20,000	20,000	8,000
Total kilograms accounted for.............	180,000	170,000	165,000

*(100% − 30%) × 10,000 kilograms = 7,000 kilograms

**170,000 kilograms started into production − 20,000 kilograms in ending work in process = 150,000 kilograms started and completed this month.

Problem 4-21 (continued)

Costs per Equivalent Unit

	Total Cost	Materials	Labour & Overhead	Whole Unit
Cost to be accounted for:				
Work in process, July 1	$ 13,400			
Cost added during the month (a)	383,600	$139,400	$244,200	
Total cost to be accounted for	$397,000			
Equivalent units (b)		170,000	165,000	
Cost per equivalent unit (a) ÷ (b)		$0.82 +	$1.48 =	$2.30

Problem 4-21 (continued)

Cost Reconciliation

	Total Cost	Equivalent Units (EU)	
		Materials	Conversion
Cost accounted for as follows:			
Transferred to Forming:			
From the beginning inventory:			
Cost in the beginning inventory.....	$ 13,400		
Cost to complete these units:			
Labour & overhead, at $1.48 per EU	10,360		7,000
Total cost from beginning inventory..	23,760		
Units started and completed this month: 150,000 kilograms × $2.30 per kilogram........................	345,000	150,000	150,000
Total cost transferred to Forming	368,760		
Work in process, July 31:			
Materials, at $0.82 per EU	16,400	20,000	
Labour and overhead, at $1.48 per EU..	11,840		8,000
Total work in process, July 31	28,240		
Total cost accounted for........................	$397,000		

Problem 4-23 (90 minutes)

Weighted-Average Method

1. a. Work in Process—Blending...................... 147,600
      Work in Process—Bottling 45,000
          Raw Materials   192,600

   b. Work in Process—Blending.................... 73,200
      Work in Process—Bottling 17,000
          Salaries and Wages Payable   90,200

   c. Manufacturing Overhead 596,000
          Accounts Payable............................   596,000

   d. Work in Process—Blending.................... 481,000
          Manufacturing Overhead   481,000
      Work in Process—Bottling..................... 108,000
          Manufacturing Overhead   108,000

   e. Work in Process—Bottling 722,000
          Work in Process—Blending   722,000

   f. Finished Goods 920,000
          Work in Process—Bottling...............   920,000

   g. Accounts Receivable............................. 1,400,000
          Sales..   1,400,000
      Cost of Goods Sold............................... 890,000
          Finished Goods   890,000

Problem 4-23 (continued)

2.

Work in Process—Bottling			
Bal.	49,000	920,000	(f)
(a)	45,000		
(b)	17,000		
(d)	108,000		
(e)	722,000		
Bal.	21,000		

Work in Process—Blending			
Bal.	32,800	722,000	(e)
(a)	147,600		
(b)	73,200		
(d)	481,000		
Bal.	12,600		

Manufacturing Overhead			
(c)	596,000	481,000	(d)
		108,000	(d)
Bal.	7,000		

Finished Goods			
Bal.	20,000	890,000	(g)
(f)	920,000		
Bal.	50,000		

Raw Materials			
Bal.	198,600	192,600	(a)
Bal.	6,000		

Accounts Payable		
	596,000	(c)

Salaries and Wages Payable		
	90,200	(b)

Sales		
	1,400,000	(g)

Accounts Receivable	
(g) 1,400,000	

Cost of Goods Sold	
(g) 890,000	

Managerial Accounting, 6th Canadian Edition

Problem 4-23 (continued)

3. The production report for the Blending Department follows:

Quantity Schedule and Equivalent Units

	Quantity Schedule
Units to be accounted for:	
Work in process, March 1.....	40,000
Started into production........	750,000 *
Total units to be accounted for......................................	790,000

		Equivalent Units (EU)		
		Materials	Labour	Overhead
Units accounted for as follows:				
Transferred to Bottling.........	760,000	760,000	760,000	760,000
Work in process, March 31...	30,000	18,000	12,000	12,000
Total units accounted for........	790,000	778,000	772,000	772,000

* 750,000 = 760,000 + 30,000 − 40,000

Problem 4-23 (continued)

Costs per Equivalent Unit

	Total Cost	Materials	Labour	Overhead	Whole Unit
Cost to be accounted for:					
Work in process, March 1	$ 32,800	$ 8,000	$ 4,000	$ 20,800	
Cost added during May	701,800	147,600	73,200	481,000	
Total cost to be accounted for (a)	$734,600	$155,600	$77,200	$501,800	
Equivalent units (above) (b)		778,000	772,000	772,000	
Cost per equivalent unit (a) ÷ (b)		$0.20 +	$0.10 +	$0.65 =	$0.95

Managerial Accounting, 6th Canadian Edition

Problem 4-23 (continued)

Cost Reconciliation

	Total Cost	Equivalent Units (EU)		
		Materials	Labour	Overhead
Cost accounted for as follows:				
Transferred to Bottling...........	$722,000	760,000	760,000	760,000
Work in process, March 31:				
Materials: 18,000 EU ×				
$0.20 per EU	3,600	18,000		
Labour: 12,000 EU ×				
$0.10 per EU	1,200		12,000	
Overhead: 12,000 EU ×				
$0.65 per EU	7,800			12,000
Total work in process,				
March 31...........................	12,600			
Total cost..............................	$734,600			

Problem 4-25 (35 minutes)

a.i) Weighted-average

	Direct Materials - Chemicals	Direct Materials - Cans	Conversion Costs
Units completed and sent to shipping	40,000	40,000	40,000
Work-in-process at May 30:			
Chemicals (100%)	10,000		
Cans (0%)		0	
Conversion costs (80%)			8,000
Equivalent units	50,000	40,000	48,000

ii) FIFO

	Direct Materials - Chemicals	Direct Materials - Cans	Conversion Costs
Transferred to shipping from May 1, work-in-process (8,000 @ 25%)			
Chemicals (0%)	0		
Cans (100%)		8,000	
Conversion costs (75%)			6,000
Current production transferred to shipping (100%)	32,000	32,000	32,000
May 30, work-in-process (10,000 @ 80%)			
Chemicals (100%)	10,000		
Cans (0%)		0	
Conversion costs (80%)			8,000
Equivalent units	42,000	40,000	46,000

b.i) Weighted-average

	Direct Materials - Chemicals	Direct Materials - Cans	Conversion Costs
Work-in-process at May 1	$ 68,400	$ 0	$ 23,750
May costs added	342,600	10,500	133,000
Total costs	411,000	10,500	156,750
Divided by weighted-average equivalent units	50,000	40,000	48,000
Cost per equivalent unit	$ 8.22	$ .2625	$ 3.266

Problem 4-25 (continued)

ii) FIFO

May costs incurred	$342,600	$10,500	$133,000
Divided by			
FIFO equivalent units	42,000	40,000	46,000
Cost per equivalent unit	$8.157	$.2625	$ 2.891

c. The main advantage of using the weighted average method is that it is usually easier to use, as the calculations are simpler. However, this method tends to obscure current period costs as the cost per equivalent unit includes both current costs as well as prior period costs that were in the beginning inventory. The weighted-average method would be most appropriate when conversion costs, inventory levels, and raw material prices do not fluctuate considerably from period to period.

CGA-Adapted

Case 4-27 (45 minutes)

Weighted-Average Method

1. The revised production report follows:

Quantity Schedule and Equivalent Units

	Quantity Schedule
Units to be accounted for:	
Work in process, October 1 (material 100% complete, conversion $7/8$ complete)	8,000
Received from the preceding department*	97,000
Total units to be accounted for	105,000

		Equivalent Units (EU)		
		Transferred In	Materials	Conversion
Units accounted for as follows:				
Transferred to Stamping..	100,000	100,000	100,000	100,000
Work in process, October 31 (material 0% complete, conversion $2/5$ complete)	5,000	5,000	—	2,000
Total units accounted for ...	105,000	105,000	100,000	102,000

*100,000 + 5,000 − 8,000 = 97,000.

Case 4-27 (continued)

Costs per Equivalent Unit

	Total Cost	Transferred In	Materials	Conversion	Whole Unit
Cost to be accounted for:					
Work in process, October 1	$ 22,420	$ 8,820	$ 3,400	$ 10,200	
Cost transferred in or added during the month	205,980	81,480	27,600	96,900	
Total cost to be accounted for (a)	$228,400	$ 90,300	$ 31,000	$107,100	
Equivalent units (b)		105,000	100,000	102,000	
Cost per equivalent unit (a) ÷ (b)		$0.86 +	$0.31 +	$1.05 =	$2.22

Cost Reconciliation

	Total Cost	Equivalent Units (EU)		
		Transferred In	Materials	Conversion
Cost accounted for as follows:				
Transferred to Stamping:				
100,000 units × $2.22 per unit	$222,000	100,000	100,000	100,000
Work in process, October 31:				
Transferred in cost, at $0.86 per EU	4,300	5,000		
Conversion, at $1.05 per EU	2,100			2,000
Total work in process	6,400			
Total cost accounted for	$228,400			

2. The unit cost figure on the report prepared by the accountant is high because none of the cost incurred during the month was assigned to the units in the ending work in process inventory.

Group Exercise 4-29

The answer to this exercise will depend on the industry that the students select to study.

Chapter 5
Cost Behaviour: Analysis and Use

Exercise 5-1 (45 minutes)

1.

	Units Shipped	Shipping Expense
High activity level	8	$3,600
Low activity level..............	2	1,500
Change	6	$2,100

Variable cost element:

$$\frac{\text{Change in cost}}{\text{Change in activity}} = \frac{\$2,100}{6 \text{ units}} = \$350 \text{ per unit}$$

Fixed cost element:

Shipping expense at the high activity level	$3,600
Less variable cost element ($350 per unit × 8 units)......	2,800
Total fixed cost...	$ 800

The cost formula is $800 per month plus $350 per unit shipped or

$$Y = \$800 + \$350X,$$

where X is the number of units shipped.

2. a. See the scattergraph on the following page.

   b. (Note: Students' answers will vary due to the imprecision and subjective nature of this method of estimating variable and fixed costs.)

Total cost at 5 units shipped per month [a point falling on the line in (a)]..	$2,600
Less fixed cost element (intersection of the Y axis)....	1,100
Variable cost element...	$1,500

   $1,500 ÷ 5 units = $300 per unit.

   The cost formula is $1,100 per month plus $300 per unit shipped or

   $$Y = \$1,100 + 300X,$$

where X is the number of units shipped.

Managerial Accounting, 6th Canadian Edition

Exercise 5-1 (continued)

2. a. The scattergraph appears below:

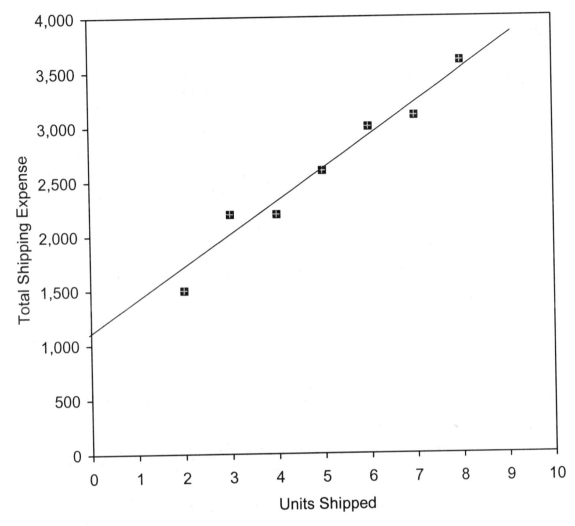

3. The cost of shipping units is likely to depend on the weight and volume of the units shipped and the distance traveled as well as on the number of units shipped. In addition, higher cost shipping might be necessary in to meet a deadline.

Exercise 5-3 (20 minutes)

1.

	X-rays Taken	X-ray Costs
High activity level (February)...........	7,000	$29,000
Low activity level (June)	3,000	17,000
Change......................................	4,000	$12,000

Variable cost per X-ray:

$$\frac{\text{Change in cost}}{\text{Change in activity}} = \frac{\$12,000}{4,000 \text{ X-rays}} = \$3.00 \text{ per X-ray}$$

Fixed cost per month:

X-ray cost at the high activity level	$29,000
Less variable cost element:	
7,000 X-rays × $3.00 per X-ray	21,000
Total fixed cost...	$ 8,000

The cost formula is $8,000 per month plus $3.00 per X-ray taken or, in terms of the equation for a straight line:

$$Y = \$8,000 + \$3.00X$$

where X is the number of X-rays taken.

2. Expected X-ray costs when 4,600 X-rays are taken:

Variable cost: 4,600 X-rays × $3.00 per X-ray..............	$13,800
Fixed cost	8,000
Total cost...	$21,800

Exercise 5-5 (20 minutes)

1. The company's variable cost per unit would be:

$$\frac{\$150,000}{60,000 \text{ units}} = \$2.50 \text{ per unit.}$$

Taking into account the difference in behaviour between variable and fixed costs, the completed schedule would be:

	Units produced and sold		
	60,000	80,000	100,000
Total costs:			
Variable costs	$150,000 *	$200,000	$250,000
Fixed costs	360,000 *	360,000	360,000
Total costs................................	$510,000 *	$560,000	$610,000
Cost per unit:			
Variable cost...........................	$2.50	$2.50	$2.50
Fixed cost................................	6.00	4.50	3.60
Total cost per unit.....................	$8.50	$7.00	$6.10

*Given.

2. The company's income statement in the contribution format would be:

Sales (90,000 units × $7.50 per unit)	$675,000
Less variable expenses (90,000 units × $2.50 per unit)..	225,000
Contribution margin...	450,000
Less fixed expenses...	360,000
Net operating income	$ 90,000

Exercise 5-7 (30 minutes)

1. Monthly operating costs at 70% occupancy:
   2,000 rooms × 70% = 1,400 rooms;

1,400 rooms × $21 per room per day × 30 days	$882,000
Monthly operating costs at 45% occupancy (given)...	792,000
Change in cost	$ 90,000

   Difference in rooms occupied:

70% occupancy (2,000 rooms × 70%)..................	1,400
45% occupancy (2,000 rooms × 45%)..................	900
Difference in rooms (change in activity)...................	500

   $$\text{Variable cost} = \frac{\text{Change in cost}}{\text{Change in activity}} = \frac{\$90,000}{500 \text{ rooms}} = \$180 \text{ per room.}$$

   $180 per room ÷ 30 days = $6 per room per day.

2.
Monthly operating costs at 70% occupancy (above)	$882,000
Less variable costs:	
1,400 rooms × $6 per room per day × 30 days	252,000
Fixed operating costs per month	$630,000

3. 2,000 rooms × 60% = 1,200 rooms occupied.

Fixed costs..	$630,000
Variable costs:	
1,200 rooms × $6 per room per day × 30 days	216,000
Total expected costs	$846,000

Exercise 5-9 (20 minutes)

1.

THE HAAKI SHOP, INC.
Income Statement—Surfboard Department
For the Quarter Ended May 31

Sales		$800,000
Less variable expenses:		
Cost of goods sold ($150 per surfboard × 2,000 surfboards*)...	$300,000	
Selling expenses ($50 per surfboard × 2,000 surfboards)...	100,000	
Administrative expenses (25% × $160,000)	40,000	440,000
Contribution margin...		360,000
Less fixed expenses:		
Selling expenses..	150,000	
Administrative expenses................................	120,000	270,000
Net operating income		$ 90,000

   *$800,000 sales ÷ $400 per surfboard = 2,000 surfboards.

2. Since 2,000 surfboards were sold and the contribution margin totaled $360,000 for the quarter, the contribution of each surfboard toward fixed expenses and profits was $180 ($360,000 ÷ 2,000 surfboards = $180 per surfboard). Another way to compute the $180 is:

Selling price per surfboard....................		$400
Less variable expenses:		
Cost per surfboard...........................	$150	
Selling expenses..............................	50	
Administrative expenses ($40,000 ÷ 2,000 surfboards)	20	220
Contribution margin per surfboard		$180

Problem 5-11 (45 minutes)

1. Cost of goods sold...................... Variable
   Shipping expense .... Mixed
   Advertising expense .... Fixed
   Salaries and commissions .... Mixed
   Insurance expense .... Fixed
   Depreciation expense .... Fixed

2. Analysis of the mixed expenses:

	Units	Shipping Expense	Salaries and Comm. Expense
High level of activity	4,500	£56,000	£143,000
Low level of activity	3,000	44,000	107,000
Change	1,500	£12,000	£ 36,000

Variable cost element:

$$\text{Variable cost per unit} = \frac{\text{Change in cost}}{\text{Change in activity}}$$

Shipping expense: $\dfrac{£12,000}{1,500 \text{ units}} = £8 \text{ per unit}$

Salaries and comm. expense: $\dfrac{£36,000}{1,500 \text{ units}} = £24 \text{ per unit}$

Fixed cost element:

	Shipping Expense	Salaries and Comm. Expense
Cost at high level of activity	£56,000	£143,000
Less variable cost element:		
4,500 units × £8 per unit........	36,000	
4,500 units × £24 per unit......		108,000
Fixed cost element...................	£20,000	£ 35,000

Problem 5-11 (continued)

The cost formulas are:

Shipping expense: £20,000 per month plus £8 per unit or
$$Y = £20,000 + £8X.$$

Salaries and Comm. expense: £35,000 per month plus £24 per unit or
$$Y = £35,000 + £24X.$$

3.

FRANKEL LTD.
Income Statement
For the Month Ended June 30

Sales revenue		£630,000
Less variable expenses:		
Cost of goods sold		
(4,500 units × £56 per unit)	£252,000	
Shipping expense		
(4,500 units × £8 per unit)	36,000	
Salaries and commissions expense		
(4,500 units × £24 per unit)	108,000	396,000
Contribution margin...		234,000
Less fixed expenses:		
Shipping expense..	20,000	
Advertising	70,000	
Salaries and commissions............................	35,000	
Insurance..	9,000	
Depreciation..	42,000	176,000
Net operating income		£ 58,000

Problem 5-13 (45 minutes)

1.

Number of Leagues (X)	Total Cost (Y)
5	$13,000
2	7,000
4	10,500
6	14,000
3	10,000

A spreadsheet application such as Excel or a statistical software package can be used to compute the slope and intercept of the least-squares regression line for the above data. The results are:

Intercept (fixed cost)	$4,100
Slope (variable cost per unit)......	$1,700
R^2	0.96

Therefore, the variable cost per league is $1,700 and the fixed cost is $4,100 per year.

Note that the R^2 is 0.96, which means that 96% of the variation in cost is explained by the number of leagues. This is a very high R^2 and indicates a very good fit.

2. Y = $4,100 + $1,700X

3. The expected total cost for 7 leagues would be:

Fixed cost	$ 4,100
Variable cost (7 leagues × $1,700 per league)........	11,900
Total cost	$16,000

The problem with using the cost formula from (2) to estimate total cost in this particular case is that an activity level of 7 leagues may be outside the relevant range—the range of activity within which the fixed cost is approximately $4,100 per year and the variable cost is approximately $1,700 per league. These approximations appear to be reasonably accurate within the range of 2 to 6 leagues, but they may be invalid outside this range.

4.

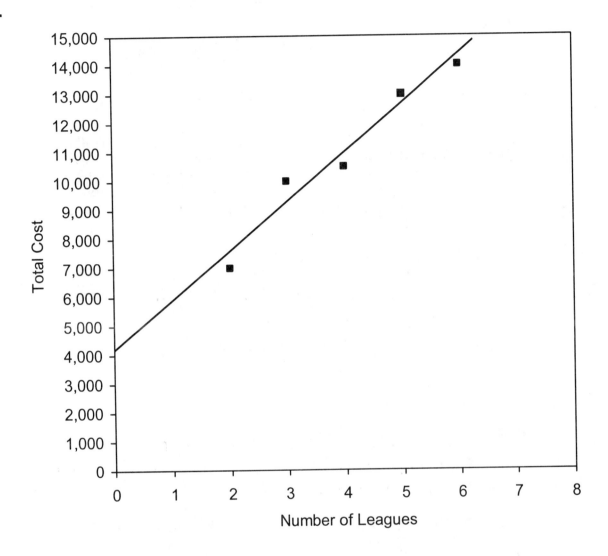

Problem 5-15 (45 minutes)

1. Maintenance cost at the 70,000 machine-hour level of activity can be isolated as follows:

	Level of Activity	
	40,000 MH	70,000 MH
Total factory overhead cost	$170,200	$241,600
Deduct:		
Utilities cost @ $1.30 per MH*	52,000	91,000
Supervisory salaries	60,000	60,000
Maintenance cost.............................	$ 58,200	$ 90,600

*$52,000 ÷ 40,000 MHs = $1.30 per MH

2. High-low analysis of maintenance cost:

	Maintenance Cost	Machine-Hours
High activity level	$90,600	70,000
Low activity level	58,200	40,000
Change	$32,400	30,000

Variable cost per unit of activity:

$$\frac{\text{Change in cost}}{\text{Change in activity}} = \frac{\$32,400}{30,000 \text{ MHs}} = \$1.08 \text{ per MH}$$

Total fixed cost:

Total maintenance cost at the low activity level	$58,200
Less the variable cost element	
(40,000 MHs × $1.08 per MH)	43,200
Fixed cost element...	$15,000

Therefore, the cost formula is $15,000 per month plus $1.08 per machine-hour or Y = $15,000 + $1.08X, where X represents machine-hours.

Problem 5-15 (continued)

3.

	Variable Rate per Machine-Hour	Fixed Cost
Maintenance cost	$1.08	$15,000
Utilities cost	1.30	
Supervisory salaries cost......		60,000
Totals	$2.38	$75,000

Therefore, the cost formula would be $75,000 plus $2.38 per machine-hour, or $Y = \$75,000 + \$2.38X$.

4.

Fixed costs..	$ 75,000
Variable costs: $2.38 per MH × 45,000 MHs............	107,100
Total overhead costs..	$182,100

Problem 5-17 (45 minutes)

1.

	July—Low 9,000 Units	October—High 12,000 Units
Direct materials cost @ $15 per unit..	$135,000	$180,000
Direct labour cost @ $6 per unit........	54,000	72,000
Manufacturing overhead cost	107,000 *	131,000 *
Total manufacturing costs	296,000	383,000
Add: Work in process, beginning	14,000	22,000
	310,000	405,000
Deduct: Work in process, ending	25,000	15,000
Cost of goods manufactured	$285,000	$390,000

*Computed by working upwards through the statements.

2.

	Units Produced	Cost Observed
October—High level of activity.............	12,000	$131,000
July—Low level of activity	9,000	107,000
Change..	3,000	$ 24,000

$$\text{Variable cost} = \frac{\text{Change in cost}}{\text{Change in activity}}$$

$$= \frac{\$24,000}{3,000 \text{ units}} = \$8 \text{ per unit}$$

Total cost at the high level of activity	$131,000
Less variable cost element	
($8 per unit × 12,000 units)	96,000
Fixed cost element...	$ 35,000

Therefore, the cost formula is: $35,000 per month plus $8 per unit produced, or Y = $35,000 + $8X, where X represents the number of units produced.

Problem 5-17 (continued)

3. The cost of goods manufactured if 9,500 units are produced:

Direct materials cost (9,500 units × $15 per unit)...		$142,500
Direct labour cost (9,500 units × $6 per unit).........		57,000
Manufacturing overhead cost:		
Fixed portion	$35,000	
Variable portion (9,500 units × $8 per unit).........	76,000	111,000
Total manufacturing costs		310,500
Add: Work in process, beginning		16,000
		326,500
Deduct: Work in process, ending		19,000
Cost of goods manufactured.................................		$307,500

© McGraw-Hill Ryerson, 2004

Problem 5-19 (30 minutes)

1. The least squares regression method:

Number of Ingots (X)	Power Cost (Y)
110	$5,500
90	4,500
80	4,400
100	5,000
130	6,000
120	5,600
70	4,000
60	3,200
50	3,400
40	2,400

A spreadsheet application such as Excel or a statistical software package can be used to compute the slope and intercept of the least-squares regression line for the above data. The results are:

Intercept (fixed cost) $1,185
Slope (variable cost per unit)...... $37.82
R^2 .... 0.97

Therefore, the variable cost of power per ingot is $37.82 and the fixed cost of power is $1,185 per month and the cost formula is:

$$Y = \$1,185 + \$37.82X.$$

Note that the R^2 is 0.97, which means that 97% of the variation in power cost is explained by the number of ingots. This is a very high R^2 and indicates a very good fit.

Problem 5-19 (continued)

2.

Method	Total Fixed Cost	Variable Cost per Ingot
High-low	$ 800	$40.00
Quick scattergraph	1,200	38.00
Least squares	1,185	37.82

The high-low method is accurate only in those situations where the variable cost is truly constant, or where the high and the low points *happen* to fall on the correct regression line. Due to the high degree of potential inaccuracy, this method is less useful than the least-squares regression method.

The quick scattergraph method is imprecise and the results will depend on where the analyst chooses to place the line. However, the scattergraph plot can provide invaluable clues about nonlinearities and other problems with the data.

The least squares regression method is generally considered to be the most accurate method of cost analysis. However, it should always be used in conjunction with a scattergraph plot to ensure that the underlying relation really is linear.

Problem 5-21 (30 minutes)

1. Least squares regression analysis:

Meals Served (000s) (X)	Total Cost (Y)
4	$18,000
5	21,000
6	24,000
10	33,000
12	35,000
11	33,000
9	30,000
8	27,000
7	26,000

A spreadsheet application such as Excel or a statistical software package can be used to compute the slope and intercept of the least-squares regression line for the above data. The results are:

Intercept (fixed cost) $10,644
Slope (variable cost per unit)...... $2,100
R^2 .... 0.98

Therefore, the variable cost of food per thousand meals is $2,100 and the fixed cost of food is $10,644 per month.

Note that the R^2 is 0.98, which means that 98% of the variation in food cost is explained by the number of meals served. This is a very high R^2 and indicates a very good fit.

2. The cost formula for food is: Y = $10,644 + $2.10X, where X = meals served.

Case 5-23 (90 minutes)

Note to the instructor: This case requires the ability to build on concepts that are introduced only briefly in the text. To some degree, this case anticipates issues that will be covered in more depth in later chapters.

1. In order to estimate the contribution to profit of the charity event, it is first necessary to estimate the variable costs of catering the event. The costs of food and beverages and labour are all apparently variable with respect to the number of guests. However, the situation with respect overhead expenses is less clear. A good first step is to plot the labour hour and overhead expense data in a scattergraph as shown below.

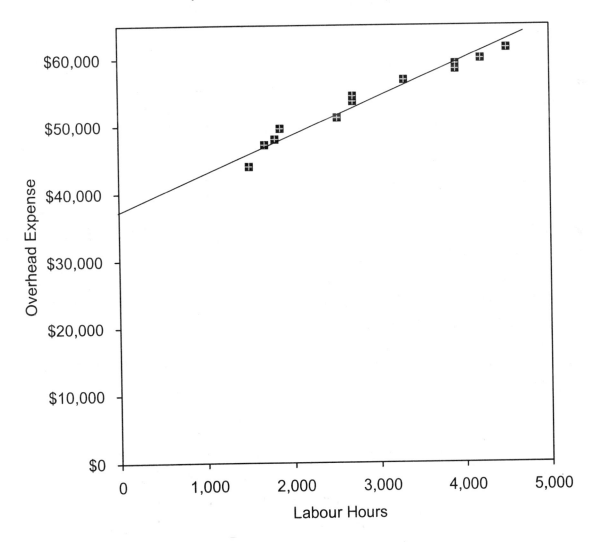

Case 5-23 (continued)

This scattergraph reveals several interesting points about the behaviour of overhead costs:

- The relation between overhead expense and labour hours is approximated reasonably well by a straight line. (However, there appears to be a slight downward bend in the plot as the labour hours increase—evidence of increasing returns to scale. This is a common occurrence in practice. See Noreen & Soderstrom, "Are overhead costs strictly proportional to activity?" *Journal of Accounting and Economics*, vol. 17, 1994, pp. 255-278.)

- The data points are all fairly close to the straight line. This indicates that most of the variation in overhead expenses is explained by labour hours. As a consequence, there probably wouldn't be much benefit to investigating other possible cost drivers for the overhead expenses.

- Most of the overhead expense appears to be fixed. Jasmine should ask herself if this is reasonable. Does the company have large fixed expenses such as rent, depreciation, and salaries?

The overhead expenses can be decomposed into fixed and variable elements using the high-low method, least-squares regression method, or even the quick method based on the scattergraph.

- The high-low method throws away most of the data and bases the estimates of variable and fixed costs on data for only two months. For that reason, it is a decidedly inferior method in this situation. Nevertheless, if the high-low method were used, the estimates would be computed as follows:

	Labour Hours	Overhead Expense
High level of activity	4,500	$61,600
Low level of activity	1,500	44,000
Change	3,000	$17,600

Case 5-23 (continued)

$$\text{Variable cost} = \frac{\text{Change in cost}}{\text{Change in activity}}$$

$$= \frac{\$17,600}{3,000 \text{ labour hours}} = \$5.87 \text{ per labour hour}$$

$$\text{Fixed cost element} = \text{Total cost} - \text{Variable cost element}$$

$$= \$61,600 - (\$5.87 \times 4,500)$$

$$= \$35,185$$

- In contrast, the least-squares regression method yields estimates of $5.27 per labour hour for the variable cost and $38,501 per month for the fixed cost using statistical software. (The adjusted R^2 is 96%.) To obtain these estimates, use a statistical software package or a spreadsheet application such as Excel.

Using the least-squares regression estimates of the variable overhead cost, the total variable cost per guest is computed as follows:

Food and beverages............................	$17.00
Labour (0.5 hour @ $10 per hour).........	5.00
Overhead (0.5 hour @ $5.27 per hour)..	2.64
Total variable cost per guest..................	$24.64

The total contribution from 120 guests paying $45 each is computed as follows:

Revenue (120 guests @ $45.00 per guest)...........	$5,400.00
Variable cost (120 guests @ $24.64 per guest).....	2,956.80
Contribution to profit	$2,443.20

Fixed costs are not included in the above computation because there is no indication that any additional fixed costs would be incurred as a consequence of catering the cocktail party. If additional fixed costs were incurred, they should also be subtracted from revenue.

Case 5-23 (continued)

2. Assuming that no additional fixed costs are incurred as a result of catering the charity event, any price greater than the variable cost per guest of $24.64 would contribute to profits.

3. We would favour bidding slightly less than $42 to get the contract. Any bid above $24.64 would contribute to profits and a bid at the normal price of $45 is unlikely to land the contract. And apart from the contribution to profit, catering the event would show off the company's capabilities to potential clients. The danger is that a price that is lower than the normal bid of $45 might set a precedent for the future or it might initiate a price war among caterers. However, the price need not be publicized and the lower price could be justified to future clients because this is a charity event. Another possibility would be for Jasmine to maintain her normal price but throw in additional services at no cost to the customer. Whether to compete on price or service is a delicate issue that Jasmine will have to decide after getting to know the personality and preferences of the customer.

Case 5-25 (30 minutes)

1. The completed scattergraph for the number of units produced as the activity base is presented below:

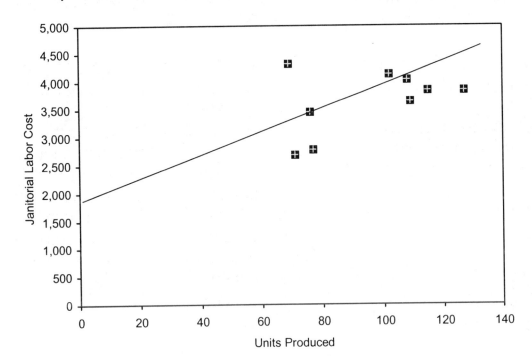

Case 5-25 (continued)

2. The completed scattergraph for the number of workdays as the activity base is presented below:

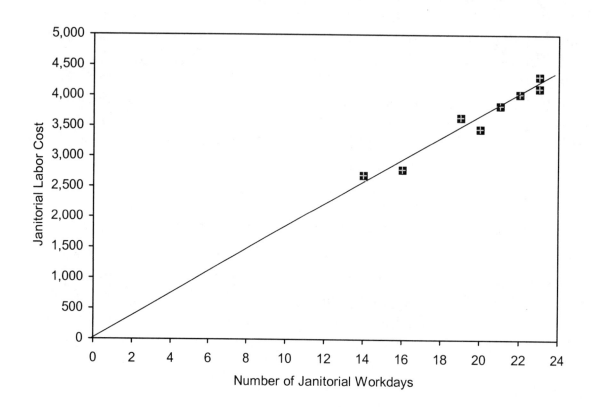

Case 5-25 (continued)

3. The number of workdays should be used as the activity base rather than the number of units produced. There are several reasons for this. First, the scattergraphs reveal that there is a much stronger relationship (i.e., higher correlation) between janitorial costs and number of workdays than between janitorial costs and number of units produced. Second, from the description of the janitorial costs, one would expect that variations in those costs have little to do with the number of units produced. Two janitors each work an eight-hour shift—apparently irrespective of the number of units produced or how busy the company is. Variations in the janitorial labour costs apparently occur because of the number of workdays in the month and the number of days the janitors call in sick. Third, for planning purposes, the company is likely to be able to predict the number of working days in the month with much greater accuracy than the number of units that will be produced.

Note that the scattergraph in part (1) seems to suggest that the janitorial labour costs are variable with respect to the number of units produced. This is false. Janitorial labour costs do vary, but the number of units produced isn't the cause of the variation. However, since the number of units produced tends to go up and down with the number of workdays and since the janitorial labour costs are driven by the number of workdays, it *appears* on the scattergraph that the number of units drives the janitorial labour costs to some extent. Analysts must be careful not to fall into this trap of using the wrong measure of activity as the activity base just because it appears there is some relationship between cost and the measure of activity. Careful thought and analysis should go into the selection of the activity base.

Group Exercise 5-27

Student answers will depend on who they contact. Perhaps surprisingly, many organizations make no attempt to formally distinguish between variable and fixed costs in their planning and in controlling operations.

Managerial Accounting, 6th Canadian Edition

Chapter 6
Cost-Volume-Profit Relationships

Exercise 6-1 (20 minutes)

	Total	Per Unit
1. Sales (30,000 units × 1.15 = 34,500 units)....	$172,500	$5.00
Less variable expenses	103,500	3.00
Contribution margin.....................................	69,000	$2.00
Less fixed expenses.....................................	50,000	
Net operating income	$ 19,000	
2. Sales (30,000 units × 1.20 = 36,000 units)....	$162,000	$4.50
Less variable expenses	108,000	3.00
Contribution margin.....................................	54,000	$1.50
Less fixed expenses.....................................	50,000	
Net operating income	$ 4,000	
3. Sales (30,000 units × 0.95 = 28,500 units)....	$156,750	$5.50
Less variable expenses	85,500	3.00
Contribution margin.....................................	71,250	$2.50
Less fixed expenses ($50,000 + $10,000)......	60,000	
Net operating income	$ 11,250	
4. Sales (30,000 units × 0.90 = 27,000 units)....	$151,200	$5.60
Less variable expenses	86,400	3.20
Contribution margin.....................................	64,800	$2.40
Less fixed expenses.....................................	50,000	
Net operating income	$ 14,800	

Exercise 6-3 (30 minutes)

1. Sales = Variable expenses + Fixed expenses + Profits
   $90Q = $63Q + $135,000 + $0
   $27Q = $135,000
      Q = $135,000 ÷ $27 per lantern
      Q = 5,000 lanterns, or at $90 per lantern, $450,000 in sales

   Alternative solution:

   $$\text{Break-even point in unit sales} = \frac{\text{Fixed expenses}}{\text{Unit contribution margin}}$$

   $$= \frac{\$135,000}{\$27 \text{ per lantern}} = 5,000 \text{ lanterns,}$$

   or at $90 per lantern, $450,000 in sales

2. An increase in the variable expenses as a percentage of the selling price would result in a higher break-even point. The reason is that if variable expenses increase as a percentage of sales, then the contribution margin will decrease as a percentage of sales. A lower CM ratio would mean that more lanterns would have to be sold to generate enough contribution margin to cover the fixed costs.

Managerial Accounting, 6th Canadian Edition

Exercise 6-3 (continued)

3.

	Present: 8,000 Lanterns		Proposed: 10,000 Lanterns*	
	Total	Per Unit	Total	Per Unit
Sales	$720,000	$90	$810,000	$81 **
Less variable expenses	504,000	63	630,000	63
Contribution margin...........	216,000	$27	180,000	$18
Less fixed expenses...........	135,000		135,000	
Net operating income	$ 81,000		$ 45,000	

　* 8,000 lanterns × 1.25 = 10,000 lanterns
　** $90 per lantern × 0.9 = $81 per lantern

As shown above, a 25% increase in volume is not enough to offset a 10% reduction in the selling price; thus, net operating income decreases.

4. Sales = Variable expenses + Fixed expenses + Profits
$81Q = $63Q + $135,000 + $72,000
$18Q = $207,000
　Q = $207,000 ÷ $18 per lantern
　Q = 11,500 lanterns

Alternative solution:

$$\text{Unit sales to attain target profit} = \frac{\text{Fixed expenses + Target profit}}{\text{Unit contribution margin}}$$

$$= \frac{\$135,000 + \$72,000}{\$18 \text{ per lantern}} = 11,500 \text{ lanterns}$$

Exercise 6-5 (30 minutes)

1.

	Model A100		Model B900		Total Company	
	Amount	%	Amount	%	Amount	%
Sales	$700,000	100	$300,000	100	$1,000,000	100
Less variable expenses........	280,000	40	90,000	30	370,000	37
Contribution margin	$420,000	60	$210,000	70	630,000	63 *
Less fixed expenses........					598,500	
Net operating income...........					$ 31,500	

*630,000 ÷ $1,000,000 = 63%.

2. The break-even point for the company as a whole would be:

$$\text{Break-even point in total dollar sales} = \frac{\text{Fixed expenses}}{\text{Overall CM ratio}}$$

$$= \frac{\$598,500}{0.63} = \$950,000 \text{ in sales}$$

3. The additional contribution margin from the additional sales can be computed as follows:

$$\$50,000 \times 63\% \text{ CM ratio} = \$31,500$$

Assuming no change in fixed expenses, all of this additional contribution margin should drop to the bottom line as increased net operating income.

This answer assumes no change in selling prices, variable costs per unit, fixed expenses, or sales mix.

Exercise 6-7 (30 minutes)

1. Variable expenses: $60 \times (100\% - 40\%) = \$36$.

2. a.

Selling price	$60	100%
Less variable expenses	36	60
Contribution margin	$24	40%

Let Q = Break-even point in units.

$$\text{Sales} = \text{Variable expenses} + \text{Fixed expenses} + \text{Profits}$$
$$\$60Q = \$36Q + \$360{,}000 + \$0$$
$$\$24Q = \$360{,}000$$
$$Q = \$360{,}000 \div \$24 \text{ per unit}$$
$$Q = 15{,}000 \text{ units}$$

In sales dollars: 15,000 units $\times$ $60 per unit = $900,000

Alternative solution:

Let X = Break-even point in sales dollars.
$$X = 0.60X + \$360{,}000 + \$0$$
$$0.40X = \$360{,}000$$
$$X = \$360{,}000 \div 0.40$$
$$X = \$900{,}000$$

In units: $900,000 $\div$ $60 per unit = 15,000 units

b.
$$\$60Q = \$36Q + \$360{,}000 + \$90{,}000$$
$$\$24Q = \$450{,}000$$
$$Q = \$450{,}000 \div \$24 \text{ per unit}$$
$$Q = 18{,}750 \text{ units}$$

In sales dollars: 18,750 units $\times$ $60 per unit = $1,125,000

Exercise 6–7 (continued)

Alternative solution:

$$X = 0.60X + \$360{,}000 + \$90{,}000$$
$$0.40X = \$450{,}000$$
$$X = \$450{,}000 \div 0.40$$
$$X = \$1{,}125{,}000$$

In units: $\$1{,}125{,}000 \div \$60$ per unit = 18,750 units

c. The company's new cost/revenue relationships will be:

Selling price..	$60	100%
Less variable expenses ($36 − $3).........	33	55
Contribution margin	$27	45%

$$\$60Q = \$33Q + \$360{,}000 + \$0$$
$$\$27Q = \$360{,}000$$
$$Q = \$360{,}000 \div \$27 \text{ per unit}$$
$$Q = 13{,}333 \text{ units (rounded).}$$

In sales dollars: 13,333 units × $60 per unit = $800,000 (rounded)

Alternative solution:

$$X = 0.55X + \$360{,}000 + \$0$$
$$0.45X = \$360{,}000$$
$$X = \$360{,}000 \div 0.45$$
$$X = \$800{,}000$$

In units: $\$800{,}000 \div \$60$ per unit = 13,333 units (rounded)

Exercise 6–7 (continued)

3. a. $\dfrac{\text{Break-even point}}{\text{in unit sales}} = \dfrac{\text{Fixed expenses}}{\text{Unit contribution margin}}$

$$= \$360{,}000 \div \$24 \text{ per unit} = 15{,}000 \text{ units}$$

In sales dollars: 15,000 units × $60 per unit = $900,000

Alternative solution:

$\dfrac{\text{Break-even point}}{\text{in sales dollars}} = \dfrac{\text{Fixed expenses}}{\text{CM ratio}}$

$$= \$360{,}000 \div 0.40 = \$900{,}000$$

In units: $900,000 ÷ $60 per unit = 15,000 units

b. $\dfrac{\text{Unit sales to attain}}{\text{target profit}} = \dfrac{\text{Fixed expenses} + \text{Target profit}}{\text{Unit contribution margin}}$

$$= (\$360{,}000 + \$90{,}000) \div \$24 \text{ per unit}$$

$$= 18{,}750 \text{ units}$$

In sales dollars: 18,750 units × $60 per unit = $1,125,000

Alternative solution:

$\dfrac{\text{Dollar sales to attain}}{\text{target profit}} = \dfrac{\text{Fixed expenses} + \text{Target profit}}{\text{CM ratio}}$

$$= (\$360{,}000 + \$90{,}000) \div 0.40$$

$$= \$1{,}125{,}000$$

In units: $1,125,000 ÷ $60 per unit = 18,750 units

Exercise 6-7 (continued)

c. $\dfrac{\text{Break-even point}}{\text{in unit sales}} = \dfrac{\text{Fixed expenses}}{\text{Unit contribution margin}}$

$\qquad\qquad = \$360,000 \div \$27 \text{ per unit}$

$\qquad\qquad = 13,333 \text{ units (rounded)}$

In sales dollars: 13,333 units × $60 per unit = $800,000 (rounded)

Alternative solution:

$\dfrac{\text{Break-even point}}{\text{in sales dollars}} = \dfrac{\text{Fixed expenses}}{\text{CM ratio}}$

$\qquad\qquad = \$360,000 \div 0.45 = \$800,000$

In units: $800,000 ÷ $60 per unit = 13,333 (rounded)

Problem 6-9 (60 minutes)

1. The CM ratio is 30%.

	Total	Per Unit	Percentage
Sales (13,500 units)..........	$270,000	$20	100%
Less variable expenses......	189,000	14	70
Contribution margin..........	$ 81,000	$ 6	30%

The break-even point is:

$$\text{Sales} = \text{Variable expenses} + \text{Fixed expenses} + \text{Profits}$$
$$\$20Q = \$14Q + \$90,000 + \$0$$
$$\$6Q = \$90,000$$
$$Q = \$90,000 \div \$6 \text{ per unit}$$
$$Q = 15,000 \text{ units}$$

15,000 units × $20 per unit = $300,000 in sales

Alternative solution:

$$\frac{\text{Break-even point}}{\text{in unit sales}} = \frac{\text{Fixed expenses}}{\text{Unit contribution margin}}$$

$$= \frac{\$90,000}{\$6 \text{ per unit}} = 15,000 \text{ units}$$

$$\frac{\text{Break-even point}}{\text{in sales dollars}} = \frac{\text{Fixed expenses}}{\text{CM ratio}}$$

$$= \frac{\$90,000}{0.30} = \$300,000 \text{ in sales}$$

2. Incremental contribution margin:

$70,000 increased sales × 30% CM ratio	$21,000
Less increased fixed costs:	
Increased advertising cost....................................	8,000
Increase in monthly net operating income	$13,000

Since the company presently has a loss of $9,000 per month, if the changes are adopted, the loss will turn into a profit of $4,000 per month.

Problem 6-9 (continued)

3. Sales (27,000 units × $18 per unit*) $486,000
    Less variable expenses
        (27,000 units × $14 per unit) 378,000
    Contribution margin 108,000
    Less fixed expenses ($90,000 + $35,000) 125,000
    Net operating loss .... $(17,000)

   *$20 − ($20 × 0.10) = $18

4.   Sales = Variable expenses + Fixed expenses + Profits
    $ 20Q = $14.60Q* + $90,000 + $4,500
    $5.40Q = $94,500
          Q = $94,500 ÷ $5.40 per unit
          Q = 17,500 units

   *$14.00 + $0.60 = $14.60.

   Alternative solution:

   $$\text{Unit sales to attain target profit} = \frac{\text{Fixed expenses + Target profit}}{\text{CM per unit}}$$

   $$= \frac{\$90,000 + \$4,500}{\$5.40 \text{ per unit**}}$$

   $$= 17,500 \text{ units}$$

      **$6.00 − $0.60 = $5.40.

5. a. The new CM ratio would be:

	Per Unit	Percentage
Sales	$20	100%
Less variable expenses	7	35
Contribution margin	$13	65%

Problem 6-9 (continued)

The new break-even point would be:

$$\frac{\text{Break-even point}}{\text{in unit sales}} = \frac{\text{Fixed expenses}}{\text{Unit contribution margin}}$$

$$= \frac{\$208,000}{\$13 \text{ per unit}} = 16,000 \text{ units}$$

$$\frac{\text{Break-even point}}{\text{in sales dollars}} = \frac{\text{Fixed expenses}}{\text{CM ratio}}$$

$$= \frac{\$208,000}{0.65} = \$320,000 \text{ in sales}$$

b. Comparative income statements follow:

	Not Automated			Automated		
	Total	Per Unit	%	Total	Per Unit	%
Sales (20,000 units).......	$400,000	$20	100	$400,000	$20	100
Less variable expenses...	280,000	14	70	140,000	7	35
Contribution margin	120,000	$ 6	30	260,000	$13	65
Less fixed expenses	90,000			208,000		
Net operating income.....	$ 30,000			$ 52,000		

Problem 6-9 (continued)

c. Whether or not one would recommend that the company automate its operations depends on how much risk he or she is willing to take, and depends heavily on prospects for future sales. The proposed changes would increase the company's fixed costs and its break-even point. However, the changes would also increase the company's CM ratio (from 30% to 65%). The higher CM ratio means that once the break-even point is reached, profits will increase more rapidly than at present. If 20,000 units are sold next month, for example, the higher CM ratio will generate $22,000 more in profits than if no changes are made.

The greatest risk of automating is that future sales may drop back down to present levels (only 13,500 units per month), and as a result, losses will be even larger than at present due to the company's greater fixed costs. (Note the problem states that sales are erratic from month to month.) In summary, the proposed changes will help the company if sales continue to trend upward in future months; the changes will hurt the company if sales drop back down to or near present levels.

Note to the Instructor: Although it is not asked for in the problem, if time permits you may want to compute the point of indifference between the two alternatives in terms of units sold; i.e., the point where profits will be the same under either alternative. At this point, total revenue will be the same; hence, we include only costs in our equation:

$$\text{Let } Q = \text{Point of indifference in units sold}$$
$$\$14Q + \$90,000 = \$7Q + \$208,000$$
$$\$7Q = \$118,000$$
$$Q = \$118,000 \div \$7 \text{ per unit}$$
$$Q = 16,857 \text{ units (rounded)}$$

If more than 16,857 units are sold, the proposed plan will yield the greatest profit; if less than 16,857 units are sold, the present plan will yield the greatest profit (or the least loss).

Managerial Accounting, 6th Canadian Edition

Problem 6-11 (30 minutes)

1.

	Product							
	Sinks		Mirrors		Vanities		Total	
Percentage of total sales	32%		40%		28%		100%	
Sales	$160,000	100%	$200,000	100%	$140,000	100%	$500,000	100%
Less variable expenses	48,000	30	160,000	80	77,000	55	285,000	57
Contribution margin	$112,000	70%	$40,000	20%	$63,000	45%	215,000	43%*
Less fixed expenses							223,600	
Net operating income (loss)							$(8,600)	

*$215,000 ÷ $500,000 = 43%.

Problem 6-11 (continued)

2. Break-even sales:

$$\frac{\text{Break-even point}}{\text{in total dollar sales}} = \frac{\text{Fixed expenses}}{\text{CM ratio}}$$

$$= \frac{\$223,600}{0.43} = \$520,000 \text{ in sales}$$

3. Memo to the president:

Although the company met its sales budget of $500,000 for the month, the mix of products sold changed substantially from that budgeted. This is the reason the budgeted net operating income was not met, and the reason the break-even sales were greater than budgeted. The company's sales mix was planned at 48% Sinks, 20% Mirrors, and 32% Vanities. The actual sales mix was 32% Sinks, 40% Mirrors, and 28% Vanities.

As shown by these data, sales shifted away from Sinks, which provides our greatest contribution per dollar of sales, and shifted strongly toward Mirrors, which provides our least contribution per dollar of sales. Consequently, although the company met its budgeted level of sales, these sales provided considerably less contribution margin than we had planned, with a resulting decrease in net operating income. Notice from the attached statements that the company's overall CM ratio was only 43%, as compared to a planned CM ratio of 52%. This also explains why the break-even point was higher than planned. With less average contribution margin per dollar of sales, a greater level of sales had to be achieved to provide sufficient contribution margin to cover fixed costs.

Managerial Accounting, 6th Canadian Edition

Problem 6-13 (45 minutes)

1. Sales (25,000 units × SFr 90 per unit)............... SFr 2,250,000

   Less variable expenses

   (25,000 units × SFr 60 per unit)............... 1,500,000

   Contribution margin.. 750,000

   Less fixed expenses... 840,000

   Net operating loss.. SFr (90,000)

2. Break-even point   =   Fixed expenses
   in unit sales   Unit contribution margin

                        =   SFr 840,000   = 28,000 units
                             SFr 30 per unit

   28,000 units × SFr 90 per unit = SFr 2,520,000 to break even.

3.

Unit Sales Price	Unit Variable Expense	Unit Contribution Margin	Volume (Units)	Total Contribution Margin	Fixed Expenses	Net Operating Income
SFr 90	SFr 60	SFr 30	25,000	SFr 750,000	SFr 840,000	SFr (90,000)
88	60	28	30,000	840,000	840,000	0
86	60	26	35,000	910,000	840,000	70,000
84	60	24	40,000	960,000	840,000	120,000
82	60	22	45,000	990,000	840,000	150,000
80	60	20	50,000	1,000,000	840,000	160,000
78	60	18	55,000	990,000	840,000	150,000

Problem 6-13 (continued)

Thus, the maximum profit is SFr 160,000. This level of profit can be earned by selling 50,000 units at a selling price of SFr 80 per unit.

4. At a selling price of SFr 80 per unit, the contribution margin is SFr 20 per unit. Therefore:

$$\text{Break-even point in unit sales} = \frac{\text{Fixed expenses}}{\text{Unit contribution margin}}$$

$$= \frac{\text{SFr } 840,000}{\text{SFr } 20 \text{ per unit}}$$

$$= 42,000 \text{ units}$$

42,000 units × SFr 80 per unit = SFr 3,360,000 to break even.

This break-even point is different from the break-even point in (2) because of the change in selling price. With the change in selling price, the unit contribution margin drops from SFr 30 to SFr 20, thereby driving up the break-even point.

Problem 6-15 (30 minutes)

1. The numbered components are as follows:

(1)   Dollars of revenue and costs.

(2)   Volume of output, expressed in units,% of capacity, sales, or some other measure of activity.

(3)   Total expense line.

(4)   Variable expense area.

(5)   Fixed expense area.

(6)   Break-even point.

(7)   Loss area.

(8)   Profit area.

(9)   Revenue line.

Problem 6-15 (continued)

2. a. Line 3:   Remain unchanged.
     Line 9:   Have a flatter slope.
     Break-even point: Increase.

   b. Line 3:   Have a steeper slope.
     Line 9:   Remain unchanged.
     Break-even point: Increase.

   c. Line 3:   Shift downward.
     Line 9:   Remain unchanged.
     Break-even point: Decrease.

   d. Line 3:   Remain unchanged.
     Line 9:   Remain unchanged.
     Break-even point: Remain unchanged.

   e. Line 3:   Shift upward and have a flatter slope.
     Line 9:   Remain unchanged.
     Break-even point: Probably change, but the direction is
                              uncertain.

   f. Line 3:   Have a flatter slope.
     Line 9:   Have a flatter slope.
     Break-even point: Remain unchanged in terms of units;
                              decrease in terms of total dollars of sales.

   g. Line 3:   Shift upward.
     Line 9:   Remain unchanged.
     Break-even point: Increase.

   h. Line 3:   Shift downward and have a steeper slope.
     Line 9:   Remain unchanged.
     Break-even point: Probably change, but the direction is
                              uncertain.

Managerial Accounting, 6th Canadian Edition

Problem 6-17 (25 minutes)

1. The break-even point in units:

   SP - $25 ($625,000/25,000)
   VC-   _15_ ($375,000/25,000)
   CM $10

   $$BEP = \frac{FC}{CM} = \frac{\$150,000}{\$10} = 15,000 \text{ UNITS}$$

   Break-even ($) = 15,000 units x $25 = $375,000 sales

2. Margin of safety   = Sales – break-even sales
                        = $625,000 - $375,000 = $250,000.

3. Targeted net income before taxes is equal to the net income after taxes divided by (1– tax rate). The pre-tax income is then added to fixed costs and divided by the UCM to find the necessary number of units.

   $66,000/.55 = $120,000 net income before taxes.

   $$\frac{\$150,000 + \$120,000}{\$10 \text{ UCM}} = 27,000 \text{ UNITS}$$

4. The break-even point is 19,250 units given increases FC and VC.

   The UCM would decrease to $8 ($25 sales price - $17), and FC would increase by $4,000, next year's portion of depreciation ($20,000/5 years). New FC would be $154,000.

   $$BEP = \frac{\$154,000}{\$8 \text{ UCM}} = 19,250 \text{ units}$$

5. To earn the same net income, after taxes as last year would require earning the same net income before taxes (i.e.) $100,000.

   $$BEP = \frac{\$154,000 \text{ (FC)} + \$100,000 \text{ (NI)}}{\$8 \text{ (UCM)}} = 31,750 \text{ units}$$

Problem 6-17 (continued)

6. This year's contribution margin ratio was 40% ($10 CM/$25 SP), which gives a variable cost ratio of 60% ($15 VC/$25 SP). Variable costs are increased to $17 per unit. So, to hold the CM ratio steady, a selling price of $28.33 is necessary ($17/.60).

Problem 6-19 (75 minutes)

1. a.

Selling price	$37.50	100%
Less variable expenses	22.50	60
Contribution margin............	$15.00	40%

$$\text{Sales} = \text{Variable expenses} + \text{Fixed expenses} + \text{Profits}$$
$$\$37.50Q = \$22.50Q + \$480,000 + \$0$$
$$\$15.00Q = \$480,000$$
$$Q = \$480,000 \div \$15.00 \text{ per skateboard}$$
$$Q = 32,000 \text{ skateboards}$$

Alternative solution:

$$\frac{\text{Break-even point}}{\text{in unit sales}} = \frac{\text{Fixed expenses}}{\text{CM per unit}}$$

$$= \frac{\$480,000}{\$15 \text{ per skateboard}}$$

$$= 32,000 \text{ skateboards}$$

b. The degree of operating leverage would be:

$$\text{Degree of operating leverage} = \frac{\text{Contribution margin}}{\text{Net opearating income}}$$

$$= \frac{\$600,000}{\$120,000} = 5.0$$

2. The new CM ratio will be:

Selling price	$37.50	100%
Less variable expenses..............	25.50	68
Contribution margin..................	$12.00	32%

Problem 6-19 (continued)

The new break-even point will be:

Sales = Variable expenses + Fixed expenses + Profits
$37.50Q = $25.50Q + $480,000 + $0
$12.00Q = $480,000
Q = $480,000 ÷ $12.00 per skateboard
Q = 40,000 skateboards

Alternative solution:

$$\text{Break-even point in unit sales} = \frac{\text{Fixed expenses}}{\text{CM per unit}}$$

$$= \frac{\$480,000}{\$12 \text{ per skateboard}}$$

$$= 40,000 \text{ skateboards}$$

3. Sales = Variable expenses + Fixed expenses + Profits
$37.50Q = $25.50Q + $480,000 + $120,000
$12.00Q = $600,000
Q = $600,000 ÷ $12.00 per skateboard
Q = 50,000 skateboards

Alternative solution:

$$\text{Unit sales to attain target profit} = \frac{\text{Fixed expenses + Target profit}}{\text{CM per unit}}$$

$$= \frac{\$480,000 + \$120,000}{\$12 \text{ per skateboard}}$$

$$= 50,000 \text{ skateboards}$$

Problem 6-19 (continued)

Thus, sales will have to increase by 10,000 skateboards (50,000 skateboards, less 40,000 skateboards currently being sold) to earn the same amount of net operating income as earned last year. The computations above and in part (2) show quite clearly the dramatic effect that increases in variable costs can have on an organization. These effects from a $3 per unit increase in labour costs for Tyrene Company are summarized below:

	Present	Expected
Break-even point (in skateboards)	32,000	40,000
Sales (in skateboards) needed to earn net operating income of $120,000	40,000	50,000

Note particularly that if variable costs do increase next year, then the company will just break even if it sells the same number of skateboards (40,000) as it did last year.

4. The contribution margin ratio last year was 40%. If we let P equal the new selling price, then:

$$P = \$25.50 + 0.40P$$
$$0.60P = \$25.50$$
$$P = \$25.50 \div 0.60$$
$$P = \$42.50$$

To verify:	Selling price	$42.50	100%
	Less variable expenses	25.50	60
	Contribution margin	$17.00	40%

Therefore, to maintain a 40% CM ratio, a $3 increase in variable costs would require a $5 increase in the selling price.

Problem 6-19 (continued)

5. The new CM ratio would be:

Selling price	$37.50	100%
Less variable expenses...........	13.50 *	36
Contribution margin...............	$24.00	64%

*$22.50 − ($22.50 × 40%) = $13.50

The new break-even point would be:

$$\text{Sales} = \text{Variable expenses} + \text{Fixed expenses} + \text{Profits}$$
$$\$37.50Q = \$13.50Q + \$912,000^* + \$0$$
$$\$24.00Q = \$912,000$$
$$Q = \$912,000 \div \$24.00 \text{ per skateboard}$$
$$Q = 38,000 \text{ skateboards}$$

*$480,000 × 1.9 = $912,000

Alternative solution:

$$\frac{\text{Break-even point}}{\text{in unit sales}} = \frac{\text{Fixed expenses}}{\text{CM per unit}}$$

$$= \frac{\$912,000}{\$24 \text{ per skateboard}}$$

$$= 38,000 \text{ skateboards}$$

Although this break-even figure is greater than the company's present break-even figure of 32,000 skateboards [see part (1) above], it is less than the break-even point will be if the company does not automate and variable labour costs rise next year [see part (2) above].

Problem 6-19 (continued)

6. a.

Sales = Variable expenses + Fixed expenses + Profits

$37.50Q = $13.50Q + $912,000* + $120,000

$24.00Q = $1,032,000

Q = $1,032,000 ÷ $24.00 per skateboard

Q = 43,000 skateboards

*480,000 × 1.9 = $912,000

Alternative solution:

$$\frac{\text{Unit sales to attain}}{\text{target profit}} = \frac{\text{Fixed expenses + Target profit}}{\text{CM per unit}}$$

$$= \frac{\$912,000 + \$120,000}{\$24 \text{ per skateboard}}$$

$$= 43,000 \text{ skateboards}$$

Thus, the company will have to sell 3,000 more skateboards (43,000 − 40,000 = 3,000) than now being sold to earn a profit of $120,000 each year. However, this is still far less than the 50,000 skateboards that would have to be sold to earn a $120,000 profit if the plant is not automated and variable labour costs rise next year [see part (3) above].

Problem 6-19 (continued)

b. The contribution income statement would be:

Sales	
(40,000 skateboards × $37.50 per skateboard).....	$1,500,000
Less variable expenses	
(40,000 skateboards × $13.50 per skateboard).....	540,000
Contribution margin...	960,000
Less fixed expenses...	912,000
Net operating income...	$ 48,000

$$\text{Degree of operating leverage} = \frac{\text{Contribution margin}}{\text{Net operating income}}$$

$$= \frac{\$960,000}{\$48,000} = 20$$

c. This problem shows the difficulty faced by many firms today. Variable costs for labour are rising, yet because of competitive pressures it is often difficult to pass these cost increases along in the form of a higher price for products. Thus, firms are forced to automate (to some degree) resulting in higher operating leverage, often a higher break-even point, and greater risk for the company.

There is no clear answer as to whether one should have been in favour of constructing the new plant. However, this question provides an opportunity to bring out points such as in the preceding paragraph and it forces students to think about the issues.

Problem 6-21 (60 minutes)

1. The income statements would be:

	Present			Proposed		
	Amount	Per Unit	%	Amount	Per Unit	%
Sales....................	$800,000	$20	100	$800,000	$20	100
Less variable expenses..............	560,000	14	70	320,000	8 *	40
Contribution margin....	240,000	$6	30	480,000	$12	60
Less fixed expenses....	192,000			432,000		
Net operating income.................	$ 48,000			$ 48,000		

*$14 − $6 = $8

2. a.

	Present	Proposed
Degree of operating leverage.................	$\frac{\$240,000}{\$48,000}=5$	$\frac{\$480,000}{\$48,000}=10$

b.

Break-even point in dollars....................	$\frac{\$192,000}{0.30}=\$640,000$	$\frac{\$432,000}{0.60}=\$720,000$

c.
Margin of safety =
  Total sales less
  Break-even sales:

$800,000 − $640,000 ...	$160,000	
$800,000 − $720,000 ...		$80,000

Margin of safety
  percentage =
  Margin of safety divided
  by Total sales:

$160,000 ÷ $800,000...	20%	
$80,000 ÷ $800,000.....		10%

Problem 6-21 (continued)

3. The major factor would be the sensitivity of the company's operations to cyclical movements in the economy. In years of strong economic activity, the company will be better off with the new equipment. The new equipment will increase the CM ratio and, as a consequence, profits would rise more rapidly in years with strong sales. However, the company will be worse off with the new equipment in years in which sales drop. The greater fixed costs of the new equipment will result in losses being incurred more quickly and they will be deeper. Thus, management must decide whether the potential greater profits in good years is worth the risk of deeper losses in bad years.

4. Notice that no information is given on either the new variable expenses or the new contribution margin ratio. Both of these items must be determined before the new break-even point can be computed. The computations are:

   New variable expenses:

$$\text{Sales} = \text{Variable expenses} + \text{Fixed expenses} + \text{Profits}$$
$$\$1,200,000* = \text{Variable expenses} + \$160,000 + \$80,000**$$
$$\$960,000 = \text{Variable expenses}$$

   * New level of sales: $\$800,000 \times 1.5 = \$1,200,000$
   ** New level of net operating income: $\$48,000 \times 1^2/_3 = \$80,000$

   New CM ratio:

Sales...................................	$1,200,000	100%
Less variable expenses.............	960,000	80
Contribution margin.................	$ 240,000	20%

   With the above data, the new break-even point can be computed:

$$\frac{\text{Break-even point}}{\text{in dollar sales}} = \frac{\text{Fixed expenses}}{\text{CM ratio}} = \frac{\$160,000}{0.20} = \$800,000$$

Problem 6-21 (continued)

The greatest risk with the new method is that the president's estimates of increases in sales and net operating income will not materialize and that sales will remain at their present level. Note that the present level of sales is $800,000, which is just equal to the break-even level of sales under the new marketing method. Thus, if the new method is adopted and sales remain unchanged, profits will drop from the current level of $48,000 per month to zero.

Although not required in the problem, you may wish to work out the level of sales needed under the new method to generate at least $48,000 in profits each month. The computations are:

$$\text{Dollar sales to attain target profit} = \frac{\text{Fixed expenses} + \text{Target profit}}{\text{CM ratio}}$$

$$= \frac{\$160,000 + \$48,000}{0.20}$$

$$= \$1,040,000 \text{ in sales each month}$$

Problem 6-23 (40 minutes)

a. Target net income for this year:

Contribution margin per unit: $23 – ($12 + $5) = $6

Fixed costs: $600,000 + $300,000 = $900,000
Target net income: (185,000 × $6) – ($900,000) = $210,000

This year:

Fixed costs ($900,000 – $59,000)	$ 841,000
Plus: target net income	210,000
Total contribution margin needed	1,051,000
Less: earned so far on units sold (30,000 × $6)	(180,000)
Remaining contribution margin	$ 871,000

Contribution margin per unit required on remaining (160,000 – 30,000) = 130,000 units

$871,000/130,000 = $6.70 per unit

b)

	Current Cost Structure	New Cost Structure
Sales (185,000 × $23)	$ 4,255,000	$ 4,255,000
Variable costs		
(185,000 × $17)	3,145,000	
(185,000 × ($3.35 + $5))		1,544,750
Contribution margin	1,110,000	2,710,250
Fixed costs	900,000	2,500,000
Net operating income	$ 210,000	$ 210,250

Problem 6-23 (continued)

Degree of operating leverage (DOL)

$1,110,000 ÷ $210,000 $2,710,250 ÷ 210,250

= 5.28   = 12.89

If sales increase by 19%

Sales	$ 5,063,450
Variable costs	3,742,550
Contribution margin	1,320,900
Fixed costs	900,000
Net operating income	$ 420,990[1]

	$ 5,063,450
	1,838,252
	3,225,198
	2,500,000
	$ 725,198[2]

If sales decrease by 19%

Sales	$ 3,446,550
Variable costs	2,547,450
Contribution margin	899,100
Fixed costs	900,000
Net operating income (loss)	$ (900)[1]

	$ 3,446,550
	1,251,247
	2,195,303
	2,500,000
	$ (304,697)[2]

1 Using DOL: NI = 210,000 ± (210,000 x 0.19 x 5.28) = $210,000 ± $210,672

2 Using DOL: NI = 210,250 ± (210,250 x 0.19 x 12.89) = $210,250 ± $514,923

Problem 6-23 (continued)

MEMO

To: President
From: Cost analyst
Subject: **Proposed Cost Structure**

As you can see from the above analysis, a move to the new cost structure has potential benefits, but it is also considerably more risky. Should sales volume increase by approximately 20% over this year, the new cost structure will generate an increase in net operating income of over 3 times the present net operating income, compared to approximately 2 times the present net income under the current cost structure. However, should sales volume decrease by about 20% from this year's, under the old structure we will be in essentially a break-even position, while under the proposed structure we will incur a significant loss. In general, a move to a structure with high fixed costs and low variable costs is much more sensitive to upswings and downswings in sales volume. If there is a high probability of sales volume increases in the future, the changes are probably a good idea; if there is some uncertainty about future sales volumes, the changes may not be such a good idea.

CGA-Adapted

Problem 6-25 (20 minutes)
1. Decision tree:

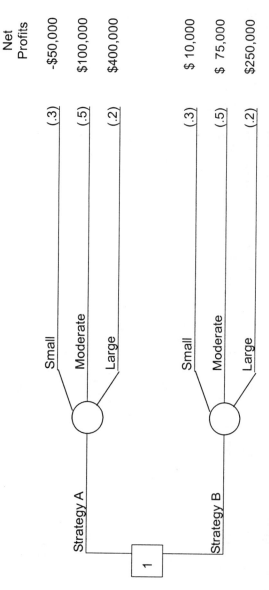

		Net Profits
Small	(.3)	-$50,000
Moderate	(.5)	$100,000
Large	(.2)	$400,000
Small	(.3)	$ 10,000
Moderate	(.5)	$ 75,000
Large	(.2)	$250,000

2. Strategy A
Expected net profits:
= -$50,000 (.3) + $100,000 (.5)
+$400,000 (.2)
= -$15,000 + $50,000 + $80,000
= $115,000

Strategy B:
Expected net profits:
= $10,000 (.3) + $75,000 (.5)
+$250,000 (.2)
= $3,000 + $37,500 + $50,000
= $90,500

The manager should choose strategy A.

(CGA-Canada Solution Adapted)

Managerial Accounting, 6th Canadian Edition

Problem 6-27 (20 minutes)

IF win

Proposals	Costs	Revenue	Net	Tax 40%	After Tax
A	$60,000	$200,000	$140,000	$56,000	$84,000
B	20,000	200,000	180,000	72,000	108,000

IF Lose

A	60,000	0	(60,000)	24,000	(36,000)
B	20,000	0	(20,000)	8,000	(12,000)

Decision Tree

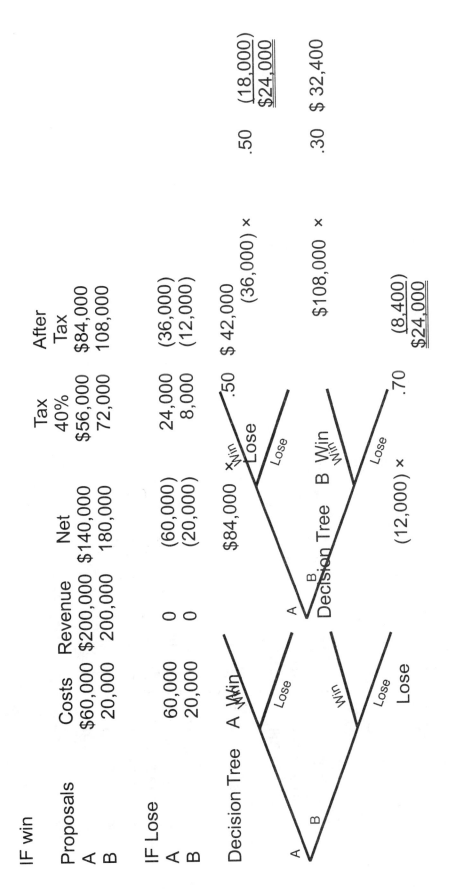

Decision analysis:

The firm may be indifferent between either alternative. However proposal B may have more risk than proposal A. The actual recommendation will depend on the risk preferences of the decision maker.

(SMAC Adapted)

Case 6-29 (60 minutes)

1 and 2.

	Part 1		Part 2a		Part 2b	
	Total	Per Unit	Total	Per Unit	Total	Per Unit
Sales	$480,000	$12.00	$630,000 [3]	$9.00	$900,000 [4]	$15.00
Less variable expenses:						
Direct materials	120,000	3.00	210,000	3.00	180,000	3.00
Direct labour	65,600	1.64	114,800	1.64	98,400	1.64
Variable overhead	20,000	0.50	35,000	0.50	30,000	0.50
Variable selling:						
Commissions	38,400	0.96 [1]	50,400	0.72 [1]	108,000	1.80 [1]
Shipping	14,000	0.35	24,500	0.35	21,000	0.35
Variable administrative	3,200	0.08	5,600	0.08	4,800	0.08
Total variable exp.	261,200	6.53	440,300	6.29	442,200	7.37
Contribution margin	218,800	$ 5.47	189,700	$2.71	457,800	$ 7.63
Less fixed expenses:						
Manufacturing overhead	70,000 [2]		70,000		70,000	
Selling	110,000		110,000		200,000 [5]	
Administrative	85,000		85,000		85,000	
Total fixed expenses	265,000		265,000		355,000	
Net operating income (loss)	$(46,200)		$(75,300)		$102,800	

[1]8% of sales dollars for parts 1 and 2a; 12% for part 2b.

© McGraw-Hill Ryerson, 2004

[2] $90,000 − (40,000 units × $0.50 per unit) = $70,000.

[3] $12 − ($12 × 25%) = $9; $9 per unit × 70,000 units = $630,000.

[4] $12 + ($12 × 25%) = $15; 40,000 units × 1.5 = 60,000 units; 60,000 units × $15 per unit = $900,000.

[5] $110,000 + $90,000 = $200,000.

Case 6-29 (continued)

3. Selling price per unit.. $12.00
   Original unit variable expense (from part 1)........ $6.53
   Less reduction in materials cost.......................... 1.73
   New contribution margin per unit............................ 4.80
                                                                              $ 7.20

   Unit sales to attain = $\dfrac{\text{Fixed expenses + Target profit}}{\text{CM per unit}}$
   target profit

   $= \dfrac{\$265,000 + \$59,000}{\$7.20 \text{ per unit}}$

   $= 45,000$ units

4. Contribution margin generated
   (60,000 units × $5.47 per unit) $328,200
   Less:
   Fixed costs to be covered (from part 1)............ $265,000
   Target profit (60,000 units × $12 per unit =
   $720,000; $720,000 × 4.5% = $32,400) 32,400 297,400
   Contribution margin available for increased
   advertising .... $ 30,800

Case 6-29 (continued)

5. The quoted price per unit would be computed as follows:

Variable production expense	
($3.00 + $1.64 + $0.50)	$ 5.14
Shipping expense ($0.35 × 1.8)	0.63
Variable administrative expense ($0.08 × 0.5)	0.04
Foreign import duty ($3,150 ÷ 15,000 units)	0.21
Present net loss ($46,200 ÷ 15,000 units)	3.08
Desired profit ($18,000 ÷ 15,000 units)	1.20
Quoted price per unit	$10.30

It should be pointed out, however, that the price charged to the overseas distributor should be determined by how much the overseas distributor is willing to pay and competitive conditions rather than by Alpine's desired profit. Any price greater than the cost of $6.02 per unit (=$10.30 - $1.20 - $3.08) would reduce Alpine's loss. On the other hand, if the distributor is willing to pay more than $10.30 per unit, it would be foolish to leave the additional profit on the table.

Case 6-31 (60 minutes)

1. The total annual fixed cost of the Cardiac Care Department can be computed as follows:

Annual Patient-Days	Aides @ $18,000	Nurses @ $29,000	Supervising Nurses @ $38,000	Total Personnel	Other Fixed Cost	Total Fixed Cost
10,000–12,000	$126,000	$435,000	$114,000	$675,000	$1,370,000	$2,045,000
12,001–13,750	144,000	435,000	114,000	693,000	1,370,000	2,063,000
13,751–16,500	162,000	464,000	152,000	778,000	1,370,000	2,148,000
16,501–18,250	180,000	464,000	152,000	796,000	1,370,000	2,166,000
18,251–20,750	180,000	493,000	190,000	863,000	1,370,000	2,233,000
20,751–23,000	198,000	522,000	190,000	910,000	1,370,000	2,280,000

2. The "break-even" can be computed for each range of activity by dividing the total fixed cost for that range of activity by the contribution margin per patient-day, which is $150 (=$240 revenue − $90 variable cost).

Annual Patient-Days	(a) Total Fixed Cost	(b) Contribution Margin	"Break-Even" (a) ÷ (b)	Within Relevant Range?
10,000–12,000	$2,045,000	$150	13,633	No
12,001–13,750	2,063,000	150	13,753	No
13,751–16,500	2,148,000	150	14,320	Yes
16,501–18,250	2,166,000	150	14,440	No
18,251–20,750	2,233,000	150	14,887	No
20,751–23,000	2,280,000	150	15,200	No

Case 6-31 (continued)

While a "break-even" can be computed for each range of activity (i.e., relevant range), all but one of these break-evens is bogus. For example, within the range of 10,000 to 12,000 patient-days, the computed break-even is 13,633 (rounded) patient-days. However, this level of activity is outside this relevant range. To serve 13,633 patient-days, the fixed costs would have to be increased from $2,045,000 to $2,063,000 by adding one more aide. The only "break-even" that occurs within its own relevant range is 14,320. This is the only legitimate break-even.

3. The level of activity required to earn a profit of $360,000 can be computed as follows:

Annual Patient-Days	Total Fixed Cost	Target Profit	(a) Total Fixed Cost + Target Profit	(b) Contribution Margin	Activity to Attain Target Profit (a) ÷ (b)	Within Relevant Range?
10,000-12,000	$2,045,000	$360,000	$2,405,000	$150	16,033	No
12,001-13,750	2,063,000	360,000	2,423,000	150	16,153	No
13,751-16,500	2,148,000	360,000	2,508,000	150	16,720	No
16,501-18,250	2,166,000	360,000	2,526,000	150	16,840	Yes
18,251-20,750	2,233,000	360,000	2,593,000	150	17,287	No
20,751-23,000	2,280,000	360,000	2,640,000	150	17,600	No

In this case, the only solution that is within the appropriate relevant range is 16,840 patient-days.

Case 6-33 (90 minutes)

1. a. Before the income statement can be completed, we need to estimate the company's revenues and expenses for the month.

   The first step is to compute the sales for the month in both units and dollars. Sales in units would be:

   90,000 units (August sales) ÷ 1.20 = 75,000 units sold in July.

   To determine the sales in dollars, we must integrate the break-even point, the margin of safety in dollars, and the margin of safety percentage. The computations are:

   Margin of safety in dollars = Total sales - Break-even sales

   $$= \text{Total sales} - \$1,012,500$$

   $$\text{Margin of safety percentage (25\%)} = \frac{\text{Margin of safety in dollars}}{\text{Total sales}}$$

   If the margin of safety in dollars is 25% of total sales, then the break-even point in dollars must be 75% of total sales. Therefore, total sales would be:

   $$\frac{\$1,012,500}{\text{Total sales}} = 75\%$$

   Total sales = $1,012,500÷75%

   Total sales = $1,350,000

   The selling price per unit would be:

   $1,350,000 total sales ÷ 75,000 units = $18 per unit.

   The second step is to determine the total contribution margin for the month of July. This can be done by using the operating leverage concept. Note that a 20% increase in sales has resulted in an 80% increase in net operating income between July and August:

   $$\frac{\text{August increased net income}}{\text{July net income}} = \frac{\$243,000 - \$135,000}{\$135,000} = \frac{\$108,000}{\$135,000} = 80\%$$

Case 6-33 (continued)

Since the net operating income for August increased by 80% when sales increased by 20%, the degree of operating leverage for July must be 4. Therefore, total contribution margin for July must have been:

$$4 \times \$135,000 = \$540,000.$$

With this figure, July's income statement can be completed by inserting known data and computing unknown data:

PUTREX COMPANY
Actual Income Statement
For the Month Ended July 31

	Total	Per Unit	Percent
Sales (75,000 units)...........	$1,350,000	$18.00	100
Less variable expenses.......	810,000 *	10.80 *	60 *
Contribution margin..........	540,000	$ 7.20	40 *
Less fixed expenses..........	405,000 *		
Net operating income........	$ 135,000		

*Computed by working from known data.

b. The break-even point:

$$\text{Break-even point in unit sales} = \frac{\text{Fixed expenses}}{\text{CM per unit}} = \frac{\$405,000}{\$7.20 \text{ per unit}} = 56,250 \text{ units}$$

In dollars: 56,250 units × $18 per unit = $1,012,500

Case 6-33 (continued)

c. The margin of safety:

$$\text{Margin of safety in dollars} = \text{Total sales - Break-even sales}$$

$$= \$1,350,000 - \$1,012,500 = \$337,500$$

$$\text{Margin of safety percentage} = \frac{\text{Margin of safety in dollars}}{\text{Total sales}}$$

$$= \frac{\$337,500}{\$1,350,000} = 25\%$$

d. The degree of operating leverage:

$$\frac{\text{Contribution margin}}{\text{Net operating income}} = \frac{\$540,000}{\$135,000} = 4$$

2. a. August's income statement can be completed using data given in the problem and data derived for July's income statement above:

PUTREX COMPANY
Projected Income Statement
For the Month Ended August 31

	Total	Per Unit	Percent
Sales (90,000 units)................	$1,620,000	$18.00	100
Less variable expenses............	972,000	10.80	60
Contribution margin................	648,000	$ 7.20	40
Less fixed expenses................	405,000		
Net operating income.............	$ 243,000		

Case 6-33 (continued)

b. The margin of safety:

Margin of safety in dollars = Total sales - Break-even sales

$$= \$1,620,000 - \$1,012,500$$

$$= \$607,500$$

$$\text{Margin of safety percentage} = \frac{\text{Margin of safety in dollars}}{\text{Total sales}}$$

$$= \frac{\$607,500}{\$1,620,000} = 37.5\%$$

The degree of operating leverage:

$$\frac{\text{Contribution margin}}{\text{Net operating income}} = \frac{\$648,000}{\$243,000} = 2.7 \text{ (rounded)}$$

The margin of safety has gone up since the company's sales will be greater in August than they were in July, thus moving the company farther away from its break-even point.

The degree of operating leverage operates in the opposite manner from the margin of safety. As a company moves farther away from its break-even point, the degree of operating leverage decreases. The reason it decreases is that both contribution margin and net operating income are increasing at the same *dollar* rate as additional units are sold, and, mathematically, dividing one by the other will yield a progressively smaller figure. As sales increase, the sale of an additional unit will have a progressively smaller percentage impact on total net operating income.

Case 6-33 (continued)

3. The new variable expense will total $11.70 per unit ($10.80 + $0.90), and the new contribution margin ratio will be:

Sales..	$18.00	100%
Less variable expenses..................	11.70	65
Contribution margin......................	$ 6.30	35%

The target profit per unit will be:

$15\% \times \$18 = \$2.70$.

Therefore,

$$\text{Sales} = \text{Variable expenses} + \text{Fixed expenses} + \text{Profits}$$
$$\$18.00Q = \$11.70Q + \$405,000 + \$2.70Q$$
$$\$3.60Q = \$405,000$$
$$Q = \$405,000 \div \$3.60 \text{ per unit}$$
$$Q = 112,500 \text{ units}$$

Alternative solution:

$$\text{Sales} = \text{Variable expenses} + \text{Fixed expenses} + \text{Profits}$$
$$X = 0.65X + \$405,000 + 0.15X$$
$$0.20X = \$405,000$$
$$X = \$405,000 \div 0.20$$
$$X = \$2,025,000; \text{ or, at \$18 per unit, } 112,500 \text{ units}$$

Group Exercise 6-35

1. The answer to this question will vary from school to school.

2. Managers will hire more support staff, such as security and vending personnel, for big games that predictably draw more people. These costs are variable with respect to the number of *expected* attendees, but are fixed with respect to the number of people who actually buy tickets. Most other costs are fixed with respect to both the number of expected and actual tickets sold—including the costs of the coaching staff, athletic scholarships, uniforms and equipment, facilities, and so on.

3. The answer to this question will vary from school to school, but a clear distinction should be drawn between the costs that are variable with respect to the number of tickets sold (i.e., actual attendees) versus the costs that are variable with respect to the number of tickets that are expected to be sold. The costs that are variable with respect to the number of tickets actually sold, given the number of expected tickets sold, are probably inconsequential since, as discussed above, staffing is largely decided based on expectations.

4. The answer to this question will vary from school to school. The lost profit is the difference between the ticket price and the variable cost of filling a seat multiplied by the number of unsold seats.

5. The answer to this question will vary from school to school.

6. The answer to this question will vary from school to school, but should be based on the answers to parts (4) and (5) above.

Group Exercise 6-37

1. If 9% increases continue for ten years, then the cost of tuition and room and board at a private college will cost 2.37 times as much as today ($1.09^{10}=2.37$). Thus, the annual costs of a university education that costs $16,800 today would cost $39,816 in ten years. This appears to be quite unaffordable for many people—particularly if family incomes increase at much less than the 9% rate.

2. The cost of adding an additional student to a class is virtually zero. Basically, all of a university's costs are fixed with respect to how many students are enrolled in a particular scheduled class.

3. Increasing enrollment will lead to more efficient use of the currently underutilized capacity of higher education. If more students are enrolled in a college whose enrollments are below capacity, then the cost per student should decrease. Consequently, tuition should decrease as well, unless capacity is expanded to accommodate the additional students.

Chapter 7
Variable Costing: A Tool for Management

Exercise 7-1 (30 minutes)

1. a. The unit product cost under absorption costing would be:

Direct materials	$18
Direct labour	7
Variable manufacturing overhead...	2
Total variable manufacturing costs.......................................	27
Fixed manufacturing overhead ($160,000 ÷ 20,000 units)	8
Unit product cost...	$35

b. The absorption costing income statement:

Sales (16,000 units × $50 per unit) $800,000
Less cost of goods sold:
  Beginning inventory .... $ 0
  Add cost of goods manufactured
    (20,000 units × $35 per unit).................. 700,000
  Goods available for sale............................ 700,000
  Less ending inventory
    (4,000 units × $35 per unit).................... 140,000   560,000
Gross margin...   240,000
Less selling and administrative expenses.......   190,000 *
Net operating income.................................. $ 50,000
*(16,000 units × $5 per unit) + $110,000 = $190,000.

Exercise 7-1 (continued)

2. a. The unit product cost under variable costing would be:

Direct materials	$18
Direct labour	7
Variable manufacturing overhead.........................	2
Unit product cost..	$27

b. The variable costing income statement:

Sales (16,000 units × $50 per unit)		$800,000
Less variable expenses:		
Variable cost of goods sold:		
Beginning inventory.................................	$ 0	
Add variable manufacturing costs		
(20,000 units × $27 per unit)	540,000	
Goods available for sale	540,000	
Less ending inventory		
(4,000 units × $27 per unit)	108,000	
Variable cost of goods sold	432,000 *	
Variable selling expense		
(16,000 units × $5 per unit).....................	80,000	512,000
Contribution margin...		288,000
Less fixed expenses:		
Fixed manufacturing overhead.....................	160,000	
Fixed selling and administrative	110,000	270,000
Net operating income......................................		$ 18,000

   * The variable cost of goods sold could be computed more simply
      as: 16,000 units × $27 per unit = $432,000.

Exercise 7-3 (15 minutes)

1. Under absorption costing, all manufacturing costs (variable and fixed) are included in product costs.

Direct materials	R120
Direct labour	140
Variable manufacturing overhead	50
Fixed manufacturing overhead (R600,000 ÷ 10,000 units)	60
Unit product cost	R370

2. Under variable costing, only the variable manufacturing costs are included in product costs.

Direct materials	R120
Direct labour	140
Variable manufacturing overhead	50
Unit product cost	R310

Note that selling and administrative expenses are not treated as product costs under either absorption or variable costing; that is, they are not included in the costs that are inventoried. These expenses are always treated as period costs and are charged against the current period's revenue.

Exercise 7-5 (30 minutes)

1. Under variable costing, only the variable manufacturing costs are included in product costs.

Direct materials	$ 60
Direct labour	30
Variable manufacturing overhead.........................	10
Unit product cost...	$100

Note that selling and administrative expenses are not treated as product costs; that is, they are not included in the costs that are inventoried. These expenses are always treated as period costs and are charged against the current period's revenue.

2. The variable costing income statement appears below:

Sales..		$1,800,000
Less variable expenses:		
Variable cost of goods sold:		
Beginning inventory..........................$	0	
Add variable manufacturing costs		
(10,000 units × $100 per unit)	1,000,000	
Goods available for sale	1,000,000	
Less ending inventory (1,000 units		
× $100 per unit)............................	100,000	
Variable cost of goods sold*	900,000	
Variable selling and administrative		
(9,000 units × $20 per unit)..............	180,000	1,080,000
Contribution margin...............................		720,000
Less fixed expenses:		
Fixed manufacturing overhead.............	300,000	
Fixed selling and administrative	450,000	750,000
Net operating loss.................................		$ (30,000)

  * The variable cost of goods sold could be computed more simply as:
    9,000 units sold × $100 per unit = $900,000.

Exercise 7-5 (continued)

3. The break-even point in units sold can be computed using the contribution margin per unit as follows:

Selling price per unit.. $200
Variable cost per unit... 120
Contribution margin per unit .... $ 80

$$\text{Break-even unit sales} = \frac{\text{Fixed expenses}}{\text{Unit contribution margin}}$$

$$= \frac{\$750{,}000}{\$80 \text{ per unit}}$$

$$= 9{,}375 \text{ units}$$

Exercise 7-7 (20 minutes)

1. The company is using variable costing. The computations are:

	Variable Costing	Absorption Costing
Direct materials	$10	$10
Direct labour	5	5
Variable manufacturing overhead.......	2	2
Fixed manufacturing overhead ($90,000 ÷ 30,000 units)	—	3
Unit product cost...........................	$17	$20
Total cost, 5,000 units....................	$85,000	$100,000

2. a. No, the $85,000 figure is not the correct figure to use, since variable costing is not generally accepted for external reporting purposes or for tax purposes.

   b. The finished goods inventory account should be stated at $100,000, which represents the absorption cost to manufacture the 5,000 unsold units. Thus, the account should be increased by $15,000 for external reporting purposes. This $15,000 consists of the amount of fixed manufacturing overhead cost that is allocated to the 5,000 unsold units under absorption costing:

   5,000 units × $3 per unit fixed manufacturing overhead cost = $15,000

Problem 7-9 (45 minutes)

1. a. The unit product cost under absorption costing:

Direct materials	$15
Direct labour	7
Variable manufacturing overhead........................	2
Fixed manufacturing overhead	
(640,000 ÷ 40,000 units)	16
Unit product cost...	$40

b. The absorption costing income statement follows:

Sales (35,000 units × $60 per unit)...........		$2,100,000
Less cost of goods sold:		
Beginning inventory	$ 0	
Add cost of goods manufactured		
(40,000 units × $40 per unit)	1,600,000	
Goods available for sale	1,600,000	
Less ending inventory		
(5,000 units × $40 per unit)	200,000	1,400,000
Gross margin		700,000
Less selling and administrative expenses ...		630,000 *
Net operating income		$ 70,000

*(35,000 units × $2 per unit) + $560,000 = $630,000.

2. a. The unit product cost under variable costing:

Direct materials	$15
Direct labour	7
Variable manufacturing overhead........................	2
Unit product cost...	$24

Problem 7-9 (continued)

b. The variable costing income statement follows:

Sales (35,000 units × $60 per unit)		$2,100,000
Less variable expenses:		
Variable cost of goods sold:		
Beginning inventory..................................	$ 0	
Add variable manufacturing costs		
(40,000 units × $24 per unit)	960,000	
Goods available for sale	960,000	
Less ending inventory		
(5,000 units × $24 per unit)...................	120,000	
Variable cost of goods sold	840,000	
Variable selling expense		
(35,000 units × $2 per unit).....................	70,000	910,000
Contribution margin.......................................		1,190,000
Less fixed expenses:		
Fixed manufacturing overhead.....................	640,000	
Fixed selling and administrative expense	560,000	1,200,000
Net operating loss...		$ (10,000)

3. The difference in the ending inventory relates to a difference in the handling of fixed manufacturing overhead costs. Under variable costing, these costs have been expensed in full as period costs. Under absorption costing, these costs have been added to units of product at the rate of $16 per unit ($640,000 ÷ 40,000 units produced = $16 per unit). Thus, under absorption costing a portion of the $640,000 fixed manufacturing overhead cost of the month has been added to the inventory account rather than expensed on the income statement:

Added to the ending inventory	
(5,000 units × $16 per unit)	$ 80,000
Expensed as part of cost of goods sold	
(35,000 units × $16 per unit)	560,000
Total fixed manufacturing overhead cost for the month.....	$640,000

Since $80,000 of fixed manufacturing overhead cost has been deferred in inventory under absorption costing, the net operating income reported under that costing method is $80,000 higher than the net operating income under variable costing, as shown in parts (1) and (2) above.

Problem 7-11 (45 minutes)

1. a. and b.

	Absorption Costing	Variable Costing
Direct materials....................................	$ 6	$ 6
Direct labour	12	12
Variable manufacturing overhead	4	4
Fixed manufacturing overhead ($240,000 ÷ 30,000 units)	8	—
Unit product cost..................................	$30	$22

2.

	May	June
Sales	$1,040,000	$1,360,000
Less variable expenses:		
Variable production costs @ $22 per unit	572,000	748,000
Variable selling and administrative @ $3 per unit	78,000	102,000
Total variable expenses................................	650,000	850,000
Contribution margin.....................................	390,000	510,000
Less fixed expenses:		
Fixed manufacturing overhead.....................	240,000	240,000
Fixed selling and administrative	180,000	180,000
Total fixed expenses....................................	420,000	420,000
Net operating income (loss)	$ (30,000)	$ 90,000

3.

	May	June
Variable costing net operating income (loss) ...	$ (30,000)	$ 90,000
Add: Fixed manufacturing overhead cost deferred in inventory under absorption costing (4,000 units × $8 per unit)	32,000	
Deduct: Fixed manufacturing overhead cost released from inventory under absorption costing (4,000 units × $8 per unit)		(32,000)
Absorption costing net operating income	$ 2,000	$ 58,000

Problem 7-11 (continued)

4. As shown in the reconciliation in part (3) above, $32,000 of fixed manufacturing overhead cost was deferred in inventory under

absorption costing at the end of May, since $8 of fixed manufacturing overhead cost "attached" to each of the 4,000 unsold units that went into inventory at the end of that month. This $32,000 was part of the $420,000 total fixed cost that has to be covered each month in order for the company to break even. Since the $32,000 was added to the inventory account, and thus did not appear on the income statement for May as an expense, the company was able to report a small profit for the month even though it sold less than the break-even volume of sales. In short, only $388,000 of fixed cost ($420,000 − $32,000) was expensed for May, rather than the full $420,000 as contemplated in the break-even analysis. As stated in the text, this is a major problem with the use of absorption costing internally for management purposes. The method does not harmonize well with the principles of cost-volume-profit analysis, and can result in data that are unclear or confusing to management.

Problem 7-13 (75 minutes)

1.

	Year 1	Year 2	Year 3
Sales	$1,000,000	$ 800,000	$1,000,000
Less variable expenses:			
Variable cost of goods sold @ $4 per unit.............................	200,000	160,000	200,000
Variable selling and administrative @ $2 per unit....	100,000	80,000	100,000
Total variable expenses.................	300,000	240,000	300,000
Contribution margin......................	700,000	560,000	700,000
Less fixed expenses:			
Fixed manufacturing overhead....	600,000	600,000	600,000
Fixed selling and administrative ..	70,000	70,000	70,000
Total fixed expenses....................	670,000	670,000	670,000
Net operating income (loss)	$ 30,000	$(110,000)	$ 30,000

Problem 7-13 (continued)

2. a.

	Year 1	Year 2	Year 3
Variable manufacturing cost..............	$ 4	$ 4	$ 4
Fixed manufacturing cost:			
$600,000 ÷ 50,000 units................	12		
$600,000 ÷ 60,000 units................		10	
$600,000 ÷ 40,000 units................			15
Unit product cost.............................	$16	$14	$19

	Year 1	Year 2	Year 3
b. Variable costing net operating income (loss)	$30,000	$(110,000)	$ 30,000
Add (Deduct): Fixed manufacturing overhead cost deferred in inventory from Year 2 to Year 3 under absorption costing (20,000 units × $10 per unit)		200,000	(200,000)
Add: Fixed manufacturing overhead cost deferred in inventory from Year 3 to the future under absorption costing (10,000 units × $15 per unit).................................			150,000
Absorption costing net operating income (loss)	$30,000	$ 90,000	$(20,000)

3. Production went up sharply in Year 2 thereby reducing the unit product cost, as shown in (2a). This reduction in cost, combined with the large amount of fixed manufacturing overhead cost deferred in inventory for the year, more than offset the loss of revenue. The net result is that the company's net operating income rose even though sales were down.

4. The fixed manufacturing overhead cost deferred in inventory from Year 2 was charged against Year 3 operations, as shown in the reconciliation in (2b). This added charge against Year 3 operations was offset somewhat by the fact that part of Year 3's fixed manufacturing overhead costs was deferred in inventory to future years [again see (2b)]. Overall, the added costs charged against Year 3 were greater than the costs deferred to future years, so the company reported less income for the year even though the same number of units was sold as in Year 1.

Problem 7-13 (continued)

5. a. Several things would have been different if the company had been using JIT inventory methods. First, in each year production would have been geared to sales so that little or no inventory of finished goods would have been built up in either Year 2 or Year 3. Second, unit product costs probably would have been the same in all three years, since these costs would have been established on the basis of *expected* sales (50,000 units) for each year. Third, since only 40,000 units were sold in Year 2, the company would have produced only that number of units and therefore would have had some underapplied overhead cost for the year. (See the discussion on underapplied overhead in the following paragraph.)

   b. If JIT had been in use, the net operating income under absorption costing would have been the same as under variable costing in all three years. The reason is that with production geared to sales, there would have been no ending inventory on hand, and therefore there would have been no fixed manufacturing overhead costs deferred in inventory to other years. Assuming that the company *expected* to sell 50,000 units in each year and that unit product costs were set on the basis of that level of expected activity, the income statements under absorption costing would have appeared as follows:

	Year 1	Year 2	Year 3
Sales	$1,000,000	$ 800,000	$1,000,000
Less cost of goods sold:			
Cost of goods manufactured @ $16 per unit	800,000	640,000 *	800,000
Add underapplied overhead		120,000 **	
Cost of goods sold	800,000	760,000	800,000
Gross margin	200,000	40,000	200,000
Selling and administrative expenses	170,000	150,000	170,000
Net operating income (loss)	$ 30,000	$(110,000)	$ 30,000

   * 40,000 units × $16 per unit = $640,000.
   ** 10,000 units *not* produced × $12 per unit fixed manufacturing overhead cost = $120,000 fixed manufacturing overhead cost not applied to products.

Problem 7-15 (45 minutes)

1. a. and b.

	Absorption Costing		Variable Costing	
	Year 1	Year 2	Year 1	Year 2
Variable production costs	$ 6	$ 6	$6	$6
Fixed manufacturing overhead costs:				
$600,000 ÷ 40,000 units....................	15		—	
$600,000 ÷ 50,000 units....................	—	12		—
Unit product cost.................................	$21	$18	$6	$6

2.

	Year 1		
Sales		$1,250,000	
Less variable expenses:			
Variable cost of goods sold:			
Beginning inventory......................................	$ 0		$
Add variable manufacturing costs................	240,000		300
Goods available for sale.............................	240,000		300
Less ending inventory.................................	0		60
Variable cost of goods sold...........................	240,000		240
Variable selling and administrative expenses			
(40,000 units × $2 per unit)	80,000	320,000	80
Contribution margin...		930,000	
Less fixed expenses:			
Fixed manufacturing overhead.......................	600,000		600
Fixed selling and administrative expenses........	270,000	870,000	270
Net operating income		$ 60,000	

Managerial Accounting, 6th Canadian Edition

Problem 7-15 (continued)

3.

	Year 1	Year 2
Variable costing net operating income	$ 60,000	$ 60,000
Add: Fixed manufacturing overhead cost deferred in inventory under absorption costing (10,000 units × $12 per unit).....	—	120,000
Absorption costing net operating income ..	$ 60,000	$180,000

4. The increase in production in Year 2, in the face of level sales, caused a buildup of inventory and a deferral of a portion of Year 2's fixed manufacturing overhead costs to the next year. This deferral of cost relieved Year 2 of $120,000 (10,000 units × $12 per unit) of fixed manufacturing overhead cost that it otherwise would have borne. Thus, net operating income was $120,000 higher in Year 2 than in Year 1, even though the same number of units was sold each year. In sum, by increasing production and building up inventory, profits increased without any increase sales or reduction in costs. This is a major criticism of the absorption costing approach.

5. a. Two things would have been different under JIT. First, production would have been geared to sales, rather than production exceeding sales in order to have a stock of goods on hand. Second, the unit costs under absorption costing would have been the same as in Year 1, since the same number of units would have been produced in each year.

   b. Under JIT, the net operating income for Year 2 using absorption costing would have been $60,000—the same as in Year 1. The reason is that with production geared to sales and no ending inventory, no fixed manufacturing overhead costs would have been deferred in inventory. The entire $600,000 in fixed manufacturing overhead costs would have been charged against Year 2 operations, rather than having $120,000 of it deferred to future periods through the inventory account. Thus, net operating income would have been the same in each year under *both* variable and absorption costing.

Problem 7-17 (30 minutes)

1.

ALTA PRODUCTS LTD.
Absorption Costing Income Statement
For month ended August 31, 2003

Sales		$ 180,000
Cost of goods sold:		
Finished goods, beginning inventory	$ —	
Cost of goods manufactured		
[1,500 x ($25 + 30 + $5 + $40[1])]	150,000	
Less: Finished goods, ending inventory		
(300 x $100[2])	30,000	120,000
Gross profit		60,000
Selling and administrative costs:		
Variable (6% of sales)	$ 10,800	
Fixed	45,000	55,800
Net operating income		$ 4,200

1 $40 = $60,000 ÷ 1,500
2 $100 = $25 + $30 + $5 + $40

2.

ALTA PRODUCTS LTD.
Variable Costing Income Statement
For month ended August 31, 2003

Sales		$ 180,000
Less: Variable costs:		
Cost of sales		
[1200 x ($25 + $5 + $30)]	72,000	
Selling and administrative (6% of sales)	10,800	(82,800)
Contribution margin		$ 97,200
Less: Fixed costs:		
Overhead	$ 60,000	
Selling and administrative	45,000	(105,000)
Net operating income (loss)		$ (7,800)

Problem 7-17 (continued)

3. Reconciliation of absorption costing operating income and direct costing operating income:

Fixed overhead cost per unit = $60,000/1,500 = $40 per unit
Reconciliation:

Operating income under absorption costing	$ 4,200
Less: Fixed costs deferred in inventory (300 x$40)	12,000
Operating income under variable costing	$ (7,800)

4. Proponents of variable costing appeal to the cost avoidance criterion as a necessary condition for asset recognition. The incurrence of fixed manufacturing costs this period will not allow the firm to avoid or eliminate them next period, so fixed manufacturing costs should not be recognized as assets. It is also pointed out that use of absorption costing can lead to manipulation of the net income figure by managing levels of production and inventory.

Proponents of absorption costing argue that the finished goods should bear a fair share of all the costs that were incurred to bring the goods to saleable condition, and that all costs should be properly included in inventory. Under Canadian generally accepted accounting principles, either absorption costing or variable costing is acceptable, provided the selected method is used consistently. However, it is argued that in the long run, variable costing can be misleading for purposes of long-run costing and pricing.

CGA-Adapted

Case 7-19 (50 minutes)

1. Break-even point under variable costing

Per unit: Revenue		$25
Variable costs:		
Manufacturing	$9	
Selling and administrative	6	15
Contribution margin		$10

Fixed costs:

$560,000 + [$650,000-($6 × 75,000)] = $760,000

Break-even point $760,000/$10 = 76,000 units or

76,000 × $25 = $1,900,000

Note:

This calculation of monthly fixed costs uses August figures. Use of either July or September figures will give the same results.

2. i) Calculation of variable costing net income

	July	August	September
Sales	$1,750,000	$1,875,000	$2,000,000
Less variable expenses:			
Variable manufacturing costs @ $15 per unit	1,050,000	1,125,000	1,200,000
Contribution margin	700,000	750,000	800,000
Less fixed expenses:			
Fixed manufacturing overhead	560,000 *	560,000	560,000
Fixed selling and administrative	200,000 **	200,000	200,000
Total fixed expenses	760,000	760,000	760,000
Net operating income (loss)	$ (60,000)	$ (10,000)	$ 40,000

Reconciliation of absorption costing (AC) and variable costing b.i)

Calculation of variable costing net income

	July	August	September
Net income (AC)	$45,000	$ 25,000	$(100,000)
Net income (VC)	(60,000)	(10,000)	40,000
AC>VC(VC>AC)	$105,000	$ 35,000	$(140,000)

Managerial Accounting, 6th Canadian Edition

Case 7-19 (continued)

3. Explanation of difference between absorption costing and variable costing net incomes:

> July increase in inventory:
> $(\$32,000 - \$80,000) \div \$16^1 = 15,000$ units
> $15,000 \times \$7^1 = \$105,000$

> August increase in inventory:
> $(\$400,000 - \$320,000) \div \$16^1 = 5,000$ units
> $5,000 \times \$7^1 = \$35,000$

> September decrease in inventory:
> $(\$80,000 - \$400,000) \div \$16^1 = 20,000$ units
> $20,000 \times \$7^1 = \$140,000$

> [1] Fixed manufacturing costs per unit = $\$1,680,000 \div (3 \times 80,000) =$ $\$\ 7$
> Plus: variable manufacturing costs per unit $\underline{\ \ \ 9}$
> $\underline{\$\ 16}$

ii) In July, production exceeded sales by 15,000 units and, as a result. $105 (\$7 \times 15,000$ units) of fixed manufacturing overhead costs were converted to inventory assets on the balance sheet under absorption costing.

In August, production exceeded sales by 5,000 units and, as a result, $35,000 (\$7 \times 5,000$ units) of fixed manufacturing overhead costs were converted to inventory assets on the balance sheet under absorption costing.

In September, sales exceeded production by 20,000 units and, as a result. $140,000 (\$7 \times 20,000$ units) of inventory assets were converted to expenses on the income statement under absorption costing.

CGA - Adapted

Case 7-21 (90 minutes)

1. Under absorption costing, the net operating income of a particular period is dependent on both production and sales. For this reason, the controller's explanation was accurate. He should have pointed out, however, that the curtailment in production resulted in a large amount of underapplied overhead, which was added to cost of goods sold in the Second Quarter. By producing fewer units than planned, the company was not able to absorb all the fixed manufacturing overhead incurred during the quarter into units of product. The result was that this unabsorbed overhead ended up on the income statement as a charge against the period, thereby slashing income sharply.

2.

	First Quarter	Second Quarter
Sales	$1,600,000	$2,000,000
Less variable expenses:		
Variable manufacturing @ $30 per unit.....................................	480,000	600,000
Variable selling and administrative @ $5 per unit..	80,000	100,000
Total variable expenses...........................	560,000	700,000
Contribution margin..............................	1,040,000	1,300,000
Less fixed expenses:		
Fixed manufacturing overhead..............	800,000	800,000
Fixed selling and administrative	230,000*	230,000*
Total fixed expenses..............................	1,030,000	1,030,000
Net operating income	$ 10,000	$ 270,000

* Selling and administrative expenses,	
First Quarter	$310,000
Less variable portion (16,000 units × $5 per unit).................	80,000
Fixed selling and administrative expenses	$230,000

Managerial Accounting, 6th Canadian Edition

Case 7-21 (continued)

3. To answer this part, it is helpful to prepare a schedule of inventories, production, and sales in units:

	Beginning Inventory	Units Produced	Units Sold	Ending Inventory
First Quarter...............	3,000	20,000	16,000	7,000
Second Quarter	7,000	14,000	20,000	1,000

Using these inventory data, the reconciliation would be as follows:

	First Quarter	Second Quarter
Variable costing net operating income............	$ 10,000	$270,000
Deduct: Fixed manufacturing overhead cost released from inventory during the First Quarter (3,000 units × $40 per unit)...........	(120,000)	
Add (deduct): Fixed manufacturing overhead cost deferred in inventory from the First Quarter to the Second Quarter (7,000 units × $40 per unit)	280,000	(280,000)
Add: Fixed overhead manufacturing cost deferred in inventory from the Second Quarter to the future (1,000 units × $40 per unit)...		40,000
Absorption costing net operating income........	$170,000	$ 30,000

Alternative solution:

Variable costing net operating income............	$ 10,000	$270,000
Add: Fixed manufacturing overhead cost deferred in inventory to the Second Quarter (4,000 unit increase × $40 per unit)..	160,000	
Deduct: Fixed manufacturing overhead cost released from inventory due to a decrease in inventory during the Second Quarter (6,000 unit decrease × $40 per unit)		(240,000)
Absorption costing net operating income........	$170,000	$ 30,000

4. The advantages of using the variable costing method for internal reporting purposes include the following:

- Variable costing aids in forecasting and reporting income for decision-making purposes.

- Fixed costs are reported in total amount, thereby increasing the opportunity for more effective control of these costs.

- Profits vary directly with sales volume and are not affected by changes in inventory levels.

- Analysis of cost-volume-profit relationships is facilitated and management is able to determine the break-even point and total profit for a given volume of production and sales.

The disadvantages of using the variable costing method for internal reporting purposes include the following:

- Variable costing is rarely used for external financial reporting. As a result, additional record keeping costs may be required.

- It may be difficult to determine what costs are fixed and what costs are variable.

5. a. Under JIT, production is geared strictly to sales. Therefore, the company would have produced only enough units during the quarter to meet sales needs above the inventory of units on hand at the start of the quarter. The computations are:

Units sold	20,000
Less units in inventory at the beginning of the quarter	7,000
Units produced during the quarter under JIT	13,000

Case 7-21 (continued)

Although not asked for in the problem, a move to JIT during the Second Quarter would have reduced the company's reported net operating income even further. The loss for the quarter would have been:

Sales..		$2,000,000
Less cost of goods sold:		
Beginning inventory	$ 490,000	
Add cost of goods manufactured (13,000 units × $70 per unit)..............	910,000	
Goods available for sale.......................	1,400,000	
Ending inventory.................................	0	
Cost of goods sold	1,400,000	
Add underapplied overhead.....................	280,000*	1,680,000
Gross margin......................................		320,000
Less selling and administrative expenses...		330,000
Net operating loss................................		$ (10,000)

* Overhead rates are based on 20,000 units produced each quarter. If only 13,000 units are produced, then the underapplied fixed manufacturing overhead will be: 7,000 units × $40 per unit = $280,000.

b. Starting with the Third Quarter, there will be little or no difference between the income reported under variable costing and under absorption costing. The reason is that there will be few inventories on hand and therefore no way to shift fixed manufacturing overhead cost between periods under absorption costing.

Group Exercise 7-23

1. Absorption costing, which includes both fixed and variable manufacturing costs in the product cost, is widely considered to be required on external financial reports in the Canada.

2 A firm with sales below the break-even point may still report a profit if its inventories increase. Break-even points are computed assuming that fixed costs are expensed in the year in which they are incurred. However, if production exceeds sales and the company uses absorption costing, a portion of the fixed manufacturing costs will be included as part of ending inventories on the balance sheet rather being expensed on the income statement.

3. Under absorption costing, whenever inventories increase, profits will increase. Inventories could increase because management intentionally manipulates profits, but they could also increase for other reasons. For example, inventories may increase if the company is expecting an increase in demand for the company's products early in the next accounting period.

4. Under absorption costing, accounting profits are reduced when inventories decrease. Fixed manufacturing overhead costs that are deferred in inventories are released to the income statement whenever inventories are reduced. Inventories may be reduced for a number of good reasons including a switch to JIT operations or an anticipated fall in demand early in the next accounting period.

Chapter 8
Activity-Based Costing: A Tool to Aid Decision-Making

Exercise 8-1 (10 minutes)

	Activity	*Level*
a.	The purchasing department orders the specific colour of paint specified by the customer from the company's supplier	Batch-level
b.	A steering wheel is installed in a golf cart	Unit-level
c.	An outside attorney draws up a new generic sales contract for the company limiting Green Glider's liability in the case of accidents that involve its golf carts	Organization-sustaining
d.	The company's paint shop makes a stencil for a customer's logo	Batch-level
e.	A sales representative visits an old customer to check on how the company's golf carts are working out and to try to make a new sale	Customer-level
f.	The accounts receivable department prepares the bill for a completed order	Batch-level
g.	Electricity is used to heat and light the factory and the administrative offices........	Organization-sustaining
h.	A golf cart is painted	Unit-level
i.	The company's engineer modifies the design of a model to eliminate a potential safety problem..........................	Product-level
j.	The marketing department has a catalogue printed and then mails them to golf course managers..........................	Customer-level
k.	Completed golf carts are each tested on the company's test track	Unit-level
l.	A new model golf cart is shipped to the leading golfing trade magazine to be	Product-level

© McGraw-Hill Ryerson, 2004

evaluated for the magazine's annual
rating of golf carts ....

Exercise 8-3 (15 minutes)

1. & 2.

	Activity	Activity Classification	Examples of Activity Measures
a.	Preventive maintenance is performed on general-purpose production equipment.	Organization-sustaining	Not applicable; these costs probably should not be assigned to products or customers.
b.	Products are assembled by hand.	Unit-level	Time spent assembling products.
c.	Reminder notices are sent to customers who are late in making payments.	Customer-level	Number of reminders; time spent preparing reminders.
d.	Purchase orders are issued for materials to be used in production.	Batch-level	Number of purchase orders; time spent preparing purchase orders
e.	Modifications are made to product designs.	Product-level	Number of modifications made; time spent making modifications
f.	New employees are hired by the personnel office.	Organization-sustaining	Not applicable; these costs probably should not be assigned to products or customers.
g.	Machine settings are changed between batches of different products.	Batch-level	Number of batch setups; time spent making setups
h.	Parts inventories are maintained in the storeroom. (Each product requires its own unique parts.)	Product-level	Number of products; number of parts; time spent maintaining inventories of parts
i.	Insurance costs are incurred on the company's facilities.	Organization-sustaining	Not applicable; these costs probably should not be assigned to products or customers.

Exercise 8-5 (20 minutes)

1. Computation of activity rates:

Activity Cost Pools	(a) Total Cost	(b) Total Activity	
Opening accounts...........................	$7,000	200 accounts opened	$35.00
Processing deposits and withdrawals	$123,000	50,000 deposits and withdrawals	$2.46
Processing other customer transactions .	$57,000	1,000 other customer transactions	$57.00

Exercise 8-5 (continued)

2. The cost of opening an account at the Avon branch is apparently much higher than at the lowest cost branch ($35.00 versus $24.35). On the other hand, the cost of processing deposits and withdrawals is lower than at the lowest cost branch ($2.46 versus $2.72). The cost of processing other customer transactions is somewhat higher at the Avon branch ($57.00 versus $48.90). This suggests that the other branches may have something to learn from Avon concerning processing deposits and withdrawals and Avon may benefit from learning about how some of the other branches open accounts and process other transactions. It may be particularly instructive to compare the details of the activity rates. For example, is the cost of opening accounts at Avon apparently high because of the involvement of the assistant branch manager in this activity? Perhaps tellers open new accounts at other branches.

It should be mentioned that the apparent differences in the costs of the activities at the various branches could be due to inaccuracies in employees' reports of the amount of time they devote to the activities. The differences in costs may also reflect different strategies. For example, the Avon branch may purposely spend more time with new customers to win their loyalty. The higher cost of opening new accounts at the Avon branch may be justified by future benefits of having more satisfied customers. Nevertheless, comparative studies of the costs of activities may provide a useful starting point for identifying best practices within a company and where improvements can be made.

Exercise 8-7 (30 minutes)

1.

	Order Size 150 direct labour-hours	Customer Orders 1 customer order	Product Testing 18 product testing hours	Selling 3 sales calls	Total
Total activity for the order					
Manufacturing:					
Indirect labour	R 1,440	R 231	R 648	R 0	R 2,319
Factory depreciation	1,050	0	324	0	1,374
Factory utilities	30	0	18	0	48
Factory administration	0	46	432	36	514
General selling & administrative:					
Wages and salaries	120	72	0	2,895	3,087
Depreciation	0	11	0	108	119
Taxes and insurance	0	0	0	147	147
Selling expenses	0	0	0	1,296	1,296
Total overhead cost	R 2,640	R 360	R 1,422	R 4,482	R 8,904

Example: R 9.60 per direct labour-hour × 150 direct labour-hours = R 1,440

According to these calculations, the overhead cost of the order was R 8,904. This agrees with the computations in Exercise 8-6.

Exercise 8-7 (continued)

2. The table prepared in part (1) above allows two different perspectives on the overhead cost of the order. The column totals that appear in the last row of the table tell us the cost of the order in terms of the activities it required. The row totals that appear in the last column of the table tell us how much the order cost in terms of the overhead accounts in the underlying accounting system. Another way of saying this is that the column totals tell us what the costs were incurred *for*. The row totals tell us what the costs were incurred *on*. For example, you may spend money *on* a chocolate bar to satisfy your craving *for* chocolate. Both perspectives are important. To control costs, it is necessary both to know what the costs were incurred for and what actual costs would have to be adjusted (i.e., what the costs were incurred on).

The two different perspectives can be explicitly shown as follows:

What the overhead costs were incurred *on*:

Manufacturing:

Indirect labour	R 2,319
Factory depreciation	1,374
Factory utilities	48
Factory administration	514

General selling & administrative:

Wages and salaries	3,087
Depreciation	119
Taxes and insurance	147
Selling expenses	1,296
Total overhead cost	R 8,904

What the overhead costs were incurred *for*:

Order size	R 2,640
Customer orders	360
Product testing	1,422
Selling	4,482
Total overhead cost	R 8,904

Exercise 8-9 (45 minutes)

1. The overhead costs for the order from CineMax Entertainment are computed below:

	Volume	Batch Processing	Order Processing	Total
Total activity for the order	1,920 direct labour-hours	4 batches	1 order	
Production overhead:				
Indirect labour	$ 3,456	$288	$ 18	$ 3,762
Factory equipment depreciation......	14,112	13	0	14,125
Factory administration	4,032	28	28	4,088
General selling & administrative overhead:				
Wages and salaries..................	960	52	153	1,165
Depreciation.......................	0	3	6	9
Marketing expenses.................	480	0	79	559
Total overhead cost.................	$23,040	$384	$284	$23,708

Example: $1.80 per direct labour-hour × 1,920 direct labour-hours = $3,456

Exercise 8-9 (continued)

The action analysis report for the order can be constructed using the row totals from the activity rate table, organized according to the ease of adjustment codes.

Sales (2,400 seats × $137.95 per seat)...................		$331,080
Green costs:		
Direct materials (2,400 seats × $112 per seat)........		268,800
Green margin		62,280
Yellow costs:		
Direct labour (2,400 seats × 0.8 DLH per seat ×		
$18 per DLH)......................................	$ 34,560	
Indirect labour...	3,762	
Marketing expenses	559	38,881
Yellow margin..		23,399
Red costs:		
Factory equipment depreciation............................	14,125	
Factory administration..	4,088	
Selling and administrative wages and salaries..........	1,165	
Selling and administrative depreciation...................	9	19,387
Red margin		$ 4,012

Exercise 8-9 (continued)

2. An action analysis report for the customer can be prepared by including the customer service costs in the overhead analysis.

	Volume 1,920 direct labour-hours	Batch Processing 4 batches	Order Processing 1 order	Customer Service 1 customer	Total
Total activity for the order					
Production overhead:					
Indirect labour	$ 3,456	$288	$ 18	$ 0	$ 3,762
Factory equipment depreciation	14,112	13	0	0	14,125
Factory administration	4,032	28	28	268	4,356
General selling & administrative overhead:					
Wages and salaries	960	52	153	1,864	3,029
Depreciation	0	3	6	26	35
Marketing expenses	480	0	79	462	1,021
Total overhead cost	$23,040	$384	$284	$2,620	$26,328

Managerial Accounting, 6th Canadian Edition

Exercise 8-9 (continued)

The action analysis report for the customer can be constructed using the row totals from the activity rate table, organized according to the ease of adjustment codes.

Sales (2,400 seats × $137.95 per seat)...................		$331,080
Green costs:		
Direct materials (2,400 seats × $112 per seat)........		268,800
Green margin		62,280
Yellow costs:		
Direct labour (2,400 seats × 0.8 DLH per seat ×		
$18 per DLH)...	$34,560	
Indirect labour...	3,762	
Marketing expenses*	1,021	39,343
Yellow margin..		22,937
Red costs:		
Factory equipment depreciation............................	14,125	
Factory administration*..	4,356	
Selling and administrative wages and salaries*........	3,029	
Selling and administrative depreciation*.................	35	21,545
Red margin		$ 1,392

*From total column of action analysis report.

Exercise 8-11 (60 minutes)

1. First-stage allocations of overhead costs to the activity cost pools:

Distribution of Resource Consumption Across Activity Cost Pools

	Volume	Order Processing	Customer Support	Other	Totals
Wages and salaries.........	30%	35%	25%	10%	100%
Other overhead costs	25%	15%	20%	40%	100%

	Volume	Order Processing	Customer Support	Other	Totals
Wages and salaries.........	$105,000	$122,500	$ 87,500	$ 35,000	$350,000
Other overhead costs	50,000	30,000	40,000	80,000	200,000
Total cost	$155,000	$152,500	$127,500	$115,000	$550,000

Example: 30% of $350,000 is $105,000.

Other entries in the table are determined in a similar manner.

Exercise 8-11 (continued)

2. The activity rates are computed by dividing the costs in the cells of the first-stage allocation above by the total activity from the top of the column.

	Volume	Order Processing	Customer Support
Total activity	10,000 DLHs	500 orders	100 customers
Wages and salaries	$10.50	$245.00	$ 875.00
Other overhead costs ..	5.00	60.00	400.00
Total cost	$15.50	$305.00	$1,275.00

Example: $105,000 ÷ 10,000 DLHs = $10.50 per DLH

Volume-related wages and salaries from the first-stage allocation above.

3. The overhead cost for the order is computed as follows:

	Volume	Order Processing	Total
Activity	50 DLHs	1 order	
Wages and salaries	$525	$245	$ 770
Other overhead costs	250	60	310
Total cost	$775	$305	$1,080

Example: 50 DLHs × $10.50 per DLH = $525

Activity rate for volume-related wages and salaries from part (2) above.

Exercise 8-11 (continued)

4. The activity view report can be constructed using the column totals at the bottom of the overhead cost analysis in part (3) above.

Product Profitability Analysis

Sales (100 units × $295 per unit).....................		$29,500
Costs:		
Direct materials (100 units × $264 per unit)	$26,400	
Direct labour (100 units × 0.5 DLH per unit × $25 per DLH)	1,250	
Volume overhead	775	
Customer support overhead............................	305	28,730
Product margin...		$ 770

Customer Profitability Analysis

Product margin of order	$ 770	
Less: Customer support overhead	1,275	
Customer margin	$ (505)	

5. The action analysis report can be constructed using the row totals from the activity rate table, organized according to the ease of adjustment codes:

Sales (100 units × $295 per unit)......................		$29,500
Green costs:		
Direct materials (100 units × $264 per unit).....		26,400
Green margin..		3,100
Yellow costs:		
Direct labour (100 units × 0.5 DLH per unit × $25 per DLH)...	$1,250	
Wages and salaries (see part (3) above)..........	770	2,020
Yellow margin...		1,080
Red costs:		
Other overhead costs (see part (3) above).......	310	310
Red margin...		$ 770

Exercise 8-11 (continued)

6. The first step is to include the customer support costs in the overhead cost analysis as follows:

	Volume	Order Processing	Customer Support	Total
Activity	50 DLHs	1 order	1 customer	
Wages and salaries	$525	$245	$ 875	$1,645
Other overhead costs ...	250	60	400	710
Total cost	$775	$305	$1,275	$2,355

The action analysis report can then be easily constructed as follows:

Sales (100 units × $295 per unit).......................		$29,500
Green costs:		
Direct materials (100 units × $264 per unit).....		26,400
Green margin..		3,100
Yellow costs:		
Direct labour (100 units × 0.5 DLH per unit × $25 per DLH)..	$1,250	
Wages and salaries (see above)	1,645	2,895
Yellow margin..		205
Red costs:		
Other overhead costs (see above)		710
Red margin..		$ (505)

Exercise 8-11 (continued)

7. While the company apparently incurred a loss on its business with Indus Telecom, caution must be exercised. The green margin on the business was $3,100. Silicon Optics really incurred a loss on this business only if at least $3,100 of the yellow and red costs would have been avoided if the Indus Telecom order had been rejected. For example, we don't know what specific costs are included in the "Other overhead" category. If these costs are committed fixed costs that cannot be avoided in the short-run, then the company would been worse off if the Indus Telecom order had not been accepted.

   Suppose that Indus Telecom will be submitting a similar order every year. As a general policy, the company might consider turning down this business in the future. Costs that cannot be avoided in the short-run, may be avoided in the long-run through the budgeting process or in some other manner. However, if the Indus Telecom business is turned down, management must make sure that at least $3,100 of the yellow and red costs are really eliminated or the resources represented by those costs are really redeployed to the constraint. If these costs remain unchanged, then the company would be better off accepting the Indus Telecom business in the future.

Problem 8-13 (45 minutes)

1. a. When direct labour-hours are used to apply overhead cost to products, the company's predetermined overhead rate would be:

$$\text{Predetermined overhead rate} = \frac{\text{Manufacturing overhead cost}}{\text{Direct labour hours}}$$

$$= \frac{\$1,480,000}{20,000 \text{ DLHs}} = \$74 \text{ per DLH}$$

b.

	Model	
	XR7	ZD5
Direct materials	$35.00	$25.00
Direct labour:		
$20 per hour × 0.2 DLH, 0.4 DLH	4.00	8.00
Manufacturing overhead:		
$74 per hour × 0.2 DLH, 0.4 DLH	14.80	29.60
Total unit product cost	$53.80	$62.60

2. a. Predetermined overhead rates for the activity cost pools:

Activity Cost Pool	(a) Total Cost	(b) Total Activity	(a) ÷ (b) Activity Rate
Machine setups	$180,000	250 setups	$720 per setup
Special milling	$300,000	1,000 MHs	$300 per MH
General factory	$1,000,000	20,000 DLHs	$50 per DLH

The manufacturing overhead cost that would be applied to each model can be computed as follows:

	Model	
	XR7	ZD5
Machine setups:		
$720 per setup × 150 setups, 100 setups	$108,000	$ 72,000
Special milling:		
$300 per MH × 1,000 MHs, 0 MHs	300,000	0
General factory:		
$50 per DLH × 4,000 DLHs, 16,000 DLHs	200,000	800,000
Total manufacturing overhead cost applied	$608,000	$872,000

Problem 8-13 (continued)

b. Before we can determine the unit product cost under activity-based costing, we must first take the overhead costs applied to each model in part 2(a) above and express them on a per-unit basis:

	Model	
	XR7	ZD5
Total overhead cost applied (a).........................	$608,000	$872,000
Number of units produced (b)...........................	20,000	40,000
Manufacturing overhead cost per unit (a) ÷ (b).	$30.40	$21.80

With this information, the unit product cost of each model under activity-based costing would be computed as follows:

	Model	
	XR7	ZD5
Direct materials	$35.00	$25.00
Direct labour:		
$20 per hour × 0.2 DLH, 04.DLH....................	4.00	8.00
Manufacturing overhead (above)	30.40	21.80
Total unit product cost	$69.40	$54.80

Comparing these unit cost figures with the unit costs in Part 1(b), we find that the unit product cost for Model XR7 has increased from $53.80 to $69.40, and the unit product cost for Model ZD5 has decreased from $62.60 to $54.80.

3. It is especially important to note that, even under activity-based costing, 68% of the company's overhead costs continue to be applied to products on the basis of direct labour-hours:

Machine setups (number of setups)....	$ 180,000	12%
Special milling (machine-hours)..........	300,000	20
General factory (direct labour-hours)..	1,000,000	68
Total overhead cost..........................	$1,480,000	100%

Thus, the shift in overhead cost from the high-volume product (Model ZD5) to the low-volume product (Model XR7) occurred as a result of reassigning only 32% of the company's overhead costs.

Problem 8-13 (continued)

The increase in unit product cost for Model XR7 can be explained as follows: First, where possible, overhead costs have been traced to the products rather than being lumped together and spread uniformly over production. Therefore, the special milling costs, which are traceable to Model XR7, have all been assigned to Model XR7 and none assigned to Model ZD5 under the activity-based costing approach. It is common in industry to have some products that require special handling or special milling of some type. This is especially true in modern factories that produce a variety of products. Activity-based costing provides a vehicle for assigning these costs to the appropriate products.

Second, the costs associated with the batch-level activity (machine setups) have also been assigned to the specific products to which they relate. These costs have been assigned according to the number of setups completed for each product. However, since a batch-level activity is involved, another factor affecting unit costs comes into play. That factor is batch size. Some products are produced in large batches and some are produced in small batches. *The smaller the batch, the higher the per unit cost of the batch activity.* In the case at hand, the data can be analyzed as shown below.

Model XR7:

Cost to complete one setup [see 2(a)]	$720	(a)
Number of units processed per setup (20,000 units ÷ 150 setups)	133.33	(b)
Setup cost per unit (a) ÷ (b)	$5.40	

Model ZD5:

Cost to complete one setup (above)...............	$720	(a)
Number of units processed per setup (40,000 units ÷ 100 setups)	400	(b)
Setup cost per unit (a) ÷ (b)	$1.80	

Problem 8-13 (continued)

Thus, the cost per unit for setups is three times as great for Model XR7, the low-volume product, as it is for Model ZD5, the high-volume product. Such differences in cost are obscured when direct labour-hours (or any other volume measure) is used as a basis for applying overhead cost to products.

In summary, overhead cost has shifted from the high-volume product to the low-volume product as a result of more appropriately assigning some costs to the products on the basis of the activities involved, rather than on the basis of direct labour-hours.

Managerial Accounting, 6th Canadian Edition

Problem 8-15 (20 minutes)

1. The cost of serving the local commercial market according to the ABC model can be determined as follows:

Activity Cost Pool	(a) Activity Rate	(b) Activity
Animation concept...........	$6,000 per proposal	20 proposals
Animation production	$7,700 per minute of animation	12 minutes
Contract administration....	$6,600 per contract	8 contracts

2. The product margin of the local commercial market is negative, as shown below:

Product Profitability Analysis

Sales		$240,000
Costs:		
Animation concept...................................	$120,000	
Animation production	92,400	
Contract administration...........................	52,800	265,200
Product margin.......................................		($25,200)

3. It appears that the local commercial market is losing money and the company would be better off dropping this market segment. However, as discussed in Problem 8-16, not all of the costs included above may be avoidable. If more than $25,200 of the total costs of $265,200 is not avoidable, then the company really isn't losing money on the local commercial market and the segment should not be dropped. These issues will be discussed in more depth in Chapters 12 and 13.

Problem 8-17 (45 minutes)

1. The company's estimated direct labour-hours (DLHs) can be computed as follows:

   Deluxe model: 15,000 units × 1.6 DLH per unit.......   24,000
   Regular model: 120,000 units × 0.8 DLH per unit....   96,000
   Total direct labour-hours......................................   120,000

   Using direct labour-hours as the base, the predetermined overhead rate would be:

   $$\frac{\text{Estimated overhead cost}}{\text{Estimated direct labour-hours}} = \frac{\$6,000,000}{120,000 \text{ DLHs}} = \$50 \text{ per DLH}$$

   The unit product cost of each model using the company's traditional costing system would be:

	Deluxe	Regular
Direct materials	$154	$112
Direct labour	16	8
Manufacturing overhead:		
$50 per DLH × 1.6 DLHs ...	80	
$50 per DLH × 0.8 DLHs ...		40
Total unit product cost.........	$250	$160

2. Overhead rates are computed below:

Activity Cost Pool	(a) Estimated Overhead Cost	(b) Expected Activity	(a) ÷ (b) Predetermined Overhead Rate
Purchase orders	$252,000	1,200 purchase orders	$210 per purchase order
Scrap/rework orders...	$648,000	900 scrap/ rework orders	$720 per scrap/ rework order
Product testing...........	$1,350,000	15,000 tests	$90 per test
Machine related	$3,750,000	50,000 MHs	$75 per MH

Problem 8-17 (continued)

3. a. The overhead applied to each product can be determined as follows:

The Deluxe Model

Activity Cost Pool	(a) Predetermined Overhead Rate	(b) Activity	(a) × (b) Overhead Applied
Purchase orders	$210 per PO	400 POs	$ 84,000
Scrap/rework orders	$720 per order	500 orders	360,000
Product testing	$90 per test	6,000 tests	540,000
Machine related	$75 per MH	20,000 MHs	1,500,000
Total overhead cost (a)			$2,484,000
Number of units produced (b)			15,000
Overhead cost per unit (a) ÷ (b)			$165.60

The Regular Model

Activity Cost Pool	(a) Predetermined Overhead Rate	(b) Activity	(a) × (b) Overhead Applied
Purchase orders	$210 per PO	800 POs	$ 168,000
Scrap/rework orders	$720 per order	400 orders	288,000
Product testing	$90 per test	9,000 tests	810,000
Machine related	$75 per MH	30,000 MHs	2,250,000
Total overhead cost (a)			$3,516,000
Number of units produced (b)			120,000
Overhead cost per unit (a) ÷ (b)			$29.30

Problem 8-17 (continued)

b. Using activity-based costing, the unit product cost of each model would be:

	Deluxe	Regular
Direct materials............................	$154.00	$112.00
Direct labour	16.00	8.00
Manufacturing overhead (above).....	165.60	29.30
Total unit product cost...................	$335.60	$149.30

4. It is risky to draw any definite conclusions based on the above analysis. The activity-based costing system used in this company is not completely suitable for making decisions. Product costs probably include the costs of idle capacity and organization-sustaining costs. They also exclude nonmanufacturing costs that may be caused by the products. Nevertheless, the above analysis is suggestive. Unit costs appear to be distorted as a result of using direct labour-hours as the base for assigning overhead cost to products. Although the deluxe model requires twice as much labour time as the regular model, it still is not being assigned enough overhead cost, as shown in the analysis in part 3(a).

When the company's overhead costs are analyzed on an activities basis, it appears that the deluxe model is more expensive to manufacture than the company realizes. Note that the deluxe model accounts for 40% of the machine-hours, although it represents a small part of the company's total production. Also, it consumes a disproportionately large amount of the activities.

When activity-based costing is used in place of direct labour as the basis for assigning overhead cost to products, the unit product cost of the deluxe model jumps from $250 to $335.60. If the $250 cost figure is being used as the basis for pricing, then the selling price for the deluxe model may be too low. This may be one reason why profits have been declining over the last several years. It may also be the reason why sales of the deluxe model have been increasing rapidly.

Problem 8-19 (45 minutes)

1. The first-stage allocation of costs to activity cost pools appears below:

Distribution of Resource Consumption Across Activity Cost Pools

	Cleaning Carpets	Travel to Jobs	Job Support	Other	Total
Wages	75%	15%	0%	10%	100%
Cleaning supplies	100%	0%	0%	0%	100%
Cleaning equipment depreciation	70%	0%	0%	30%	100%
Vehicle expenses	0%	80%	0%	20%	100%
Office expenses	0%	0%	60%	40%	100%
President's compensation	0%	0%	30%	70%	100%

	Cleaning Carpets	Travel to Jobs	Job Support	Other	Total
Wages	$105,000	$21,000	$ 0	$14,000	$140,000
Cleaning supplies	25,000	0	0	0	25,000
Cleaning equipment depreciation	7,000	0	0	3,000	10,000
Vehicle expenses	0	24,000	0	6,000	30,000
Office expenses	0	0	36,000	24,000	60,000
President's compensation	0	0	22,500	52,500	75,000
Total cost	$137,000	$45,000	$58,500	$99,500	$340,000

75% of $140,000 = $105,000
Other entries in the table are determined in a similar manner.

Problem 8-19 (continued)

2. The activity rates are computed as follows:

Activity Cost Pool	(a) Total Cost	(b) Total Activity	(a) ÷ (b) Activity Rate
Cleaning carpets...	$137,000	10,000 hundred square feet	$13.70 per hundred square feet
Travel to jobs.......	$45,000	80,000 kilometres	$0.5625 per kilometre
Job support..........	$58,500	1,800 jobs	$32.50 per job

3. The cost for the Lazy Bee Ranch job is computed as follows:

Activity Cost Pool	(a) Activity Rate	(b) Activity	(a) × (b) ABC Cost
Cleaning carpets...	$13.70 per hundred square feet	6 hundred square feet	$ 82.20
Travel to jobs.......	$0.5625 per kilometre	80 kilometres	45.00
Job support..........	$32.50 per job	1 job	32.50
Total			$159.70

4. The product margin can be easily computed below from an activity view by using the costs calculated in part (3) above.

Sales.........................		$137.70
Costs:		
Cleaning carpets	$82.20	
Travel to jobs	45.00	
Job support	32.50	159.70
Product margin..........		$(22.00)

Problem 8-19 (continued)

5. Gore Range Carpet Cleaning appears to be losing money on the Lazy Bee Ranch job. However, caution is advised. Some of the costs may not be avoidable and hence would have been incurred even if the Lazy Bee Ranch job had not been accepted. An action analysis (discussed in Appendix 8A) is a more appropriate starting point for analysis than the simple report in part (4) above.

   Nevertheless, there is a point at which travel costs eat up all of the profit from a job. With the company's current policy of charging a flat fee for carpet cleaning irrespective of how far away the client is from the office, there clearly is some point at which jobs should be turned down. (What if a potential customer is located in PEI?)

6. The company should consider charging a fee for travel to outlying customers based on the distance traveled and a flat fee per job. At present, close-in customers are in essence subsidizing service to outlying customers and large-volume customers are subsidizing service to low-volume customers. With fees for travel and for job support, the fee per hundred square feet can be dropped substantially. This may result in losing some low-volume jobs in outlying areas, but the lower fee per hundred square feet may result in substantially more business close to Eagle-Vail. (If the fee is low enough, the added business may not even have to come at the expense of competitors. Some customers may choose to clean their carpets more frequently if the price were more attractive.)

Problem 8-21 (45 minutes)

1. The company expects to work 60,000 direct labour-hours during the year, computed as follows:

Mono-circuit: 40,000 units × 1 DLH per unit............ 40,000
Bi-circuit: 10,000 units × 2 DLH per unit............... 20,000
Total direct labour-hours....................................... 60,000

Using direct labour-hours as the base, the predetermined manufacturing overhead rate would be:

$$\frac{\text{Estimated overhead cost}}{\text{Estimated direct labour-hours}} = \frac{\$3,000,000}{60,000 \text{ DLHs}} = \$50 \text{ per DLH}$$

The unit product cost of each product would be:

	Mono-circuit	Bi-circuit
Direct materials (given)......................	$ 40	$ 80
Direct labour (given)..........................	18	36
Manufacturing overhead:		
$50 per DLH × 1 DLH and 2 DLHs	50	100
Total unit product cost.......................	$108	$216

2. The predetermined overhead rates would be computed as follows:

Activity Centre	(a) Estimated Overhead Costs	(b) Expected Activity	(a) ÷ (b) Predetermined Overhead Rate
Maintaining parts inventory..............	$360,000	900 part types	$400 per part type
Processing purchase orders.....	$540,000	3,000 orders	$180 per order
Quality control	$600,000	8,000 tests	$75 per test
Machine-related	$1,500,000	50,000 MHs	$30 per MH

Managerial Accounting, 6th Canadian Edition

Problem 8-21 (continued)

3. a.

	Mono-circuit		Bi-circuit	
	Expected Activity	Amount	Expected Activity	Amount
Maintaining parts inventory, at $400 per part type..........	300	$ 120,000	600	$ 240,000
Processing purchase orders, at $180 per order...	2,000	360,000	1,000	180,000
Quality control, at $75 per test...........	2,000	150,000	6,000	450,000
Machine-related, at $30 per machine-hour	20,000	600,000	30,000	900,000
Total manufacturing overhead cost (a)........................		$1,230,000		$1,770,000
Number of units (b) ..		40,000		10,000
Manufacturing overhead cost per unit (a) ÷ (b).........		$30.75		$177.00

b. Using activity-based costing, the unit product cost of each product would be:

	Mono-circuit	Bi-circuit
Direct materials.............................	$40.00	$ 80.00
Direct labour	18.00	36.00
Manufacturing overhead (above)...	30.75	177.00
Total unit product cost..................	$88.75	$293.00

4. Although the bi-circuit accounts for only 20% of the company's total production, it is responsible for two-thirds of the part types carried in inventory and 60% of the machine-hours. It is also responsible for one-third of the purchase orders and three-fourths of the quality control tests. These factors have been concealed as a result of using direct labour-hours as the base for assigning overhead cost to products. Since the bi-circuit is responsible for a majority of the activity in the company, under activity-based costing it is assigned a larger amount of overhead cost.

Managers should be cautious about drawing firm conclusions about the profitability of products from the above activity-based cost analysis. The ABC system used in this company is not completely suitable for making decisions. Product costs probably include costs of idle capacity and organization-sustaining costs. They also exclude nonmanufacturing costs that may be caused by the products. Nevertheless, the above analysis is suggestive. The bi-circuit may not be as profitable as management believes, and this may be the reason for the company's declining profits. Note that from part (1), the unit product cost of the bi-circuit is $216. In part (3), however, the activity-based costing system sets the unit product cost of the bi-circuit at $293. This is a difference of $77 per unit. If the unit product cost of $216 is being used to set the selling price for the bi-circuit, the selling price may not be high enough to cover the company's costs.

Case 8-23 (120 minutes)

1. a. The predetermined overhead rate is computed as follows:

$$\text{Predetermined overhead rate} = \frac{\text{Estimated manufacturing overhead cost}}{\text{Estimated direct labour-hours}}$$

$$= \frac{\$600,000}{80,000\text{DLHs}} = \$7.50 \text{ per DLH}$$

b. The margins for the windows ordered by the two customers are computed as follows under the traditional costing system:

	Avon Construction	Lynx Builders
Sales	$9,995	$54,995
Costs:		
Direct materials	$3,400	$17,200
Direct labour	4,500	27,000
Manufacturing overhead (@ $7.50 per DLH)	1,875	11,250
	9,775	55,450
Margin	$ 220	$(455)

Case 8-23 (continued)

2. a. The first-stage allocation of costs to activity cost pools appears below:

	Making Windows	Processing Orders	Customer Relations	Other	Totals
Indirect factory wages	$ 60,000	$120,000	$ 24,000	$ 36,000	$ 240,000
Production equipment depreciation	200,000	0	0	50,000	250,000
Other factory costs	44,000	0	0	66,000	110,000
Administrative wages and salaries	0	60,000	84,000	96,000	240,000
Office expenses	0	12,000	18,000	30,000	60,000
Marketing expenses	0	0	210,000	70,000	280,000
Total cost	$304,000	$192,000	$336,000	$348,000	$1,180,000

According to the data in the problem, 25% of the indirect factory wages are attributable to the activity of making windows.

25% of $240,000 = $60,000

The other entries in the table are determined in a similar manner.

Case 8-23 (continued)

2. b. The activity rates are computed as follows:

	Making Windows 80,000 DLHs	Processing Orders 1,000 orders	Customer Relations 200 customers
Total activity			
Indirect factory wages	$0.75	$120	$ 120
Production equipment depreciation	2.50	0	0
Other factory costs	0.55	0	0
Administrative wages and salaries	0.00	60	420
Office expenses	0.00	12	90
Marketing expenses	0.00	0	1,050
Total cost	$3.80	$192	$1,680

Example: $60,000 ÷ 80,000 DLHs = $0.75 per DLH

Indirect factory wages attributable to the activity of making windows from the first-stage allocation above.

Case 8-23 (continued)

2. c. The overhead cost of serving Avon Construction is computed as follows:

Activity for Avon Construction	Making Windows 250 DLHs	Processing Orders 2 orders	Customer Relations 1 customer	Total
Indirect factory wages	$187.50	$240.00	$ 120.00	$ 547.50
Production equipment depreciation	625.00	0.00	0.00	625.00
Other factory costs	137.50	0.00	0.00	137.50
Administrative wages and salaries	0.00	120.00	420.00	540.00
Office expenses	0.00	24.00	90.00	114.00
Marketing expenses	0.00	0.00	1,050.00	1,050.00
Total cost	$950.00	$384.00	$1,680.00	$3,014.00

Example: $0.75 per DLH × 250 DLHs = $187.50

Activity rate for indirect wages for the activity making windows.

Managerial Accounting, 6th Canadian Edition

Case 8-23 (continued)

The overhead cost of serving Lynx Builders is computed as follows:

	Making Windows 1,500 DLHs	Processing Orders 3 orders	Customer Relations 1 customer	Total
Activity for Lynx Builders				
Indirect factory wages	$1,125.00	$360.00	$ 120.00	$1,605.00
Production equipment depreciation ...	3,750.00	0.00	0.00	3,750.00
Other factory costs	825.00	0.00	0.00	825.00
Administrative wages and salaries	0.00	180.00	420.00	600.00
Office expenses	0.00	36.00	90.00	126.00
Marketing expenses	0.00	0.00	1,050.00	1,050.00
Total cost	$5,700.00	$576.00	$1,680.00	$7,956.00

Example: $0.75 per DLH × 1,500 DLHs = $1,125.00

Activity rate for indirect wages for the activity of making windows.

Case 8-23 (continued)

2. d. The action analyses can be constructed using the row totals from the overhead cost analysis in part (2c) above.

Avon Construction

Sales...		$9,995.00
Green costs:		
Direct materials............................		3,400.00
Green margin		6,595.00
Yellow costs:		
Direct labour.................................	$4,500.00	
Indirect factory wages....................	547.50	
Production equipment		
depreciation	625.00	
Other factory costs.........................	137.50	
Office expenses..............................	114.00	
Marketing expenses........................	1,050.00	6,974.00
Yellow margin....................................		(379.00)
Red costs:		
Administrative wages and		
salaries		540.00
Red margin		$(919.00)

Case 8-23 (continued)

Lynx Builders

Sales...		$54,995
Green costs:		
Direct materials..............................		<u>17,200</u>
Green margin		37,795
Yellow costs:		
Direct labour.................................	$27,000	
Indirect factory wages....................	1,605	
Production equipment		
depreciation	3,750	
Other factory costs.........................	825	
Office expenses..............................	126	
Marketing expenses........................	<u>1,050</u>	<u>34,356</u>
Yellow margin...................................		3,439
Red costs:		
Administrative wages and		
salaries		<u>600</u>
Red margin		<u>$ 2,839</u>

Case 8-23 (continued)

3. According to the activity-based costing analysis, Victorian Windows may be losing money dealing with Avon Construction. Both the red and yellow margins are negative. This means that if Victorian Windows could actually avoid the yellow costs (or redeploy those resources to more profitable uses) by dropping Avon Construction as a customer, the company would be better off without this customer.

   The activity-based costing and traditional costing systems do not agree concerning the profitability of these two customers. The traditional costing system regards Avon Construction as a profitable customer and Lynx Builders as a money-losing customer. The activity-based costing system comes to exactly the opposite conclusion. The activity-based costing system provides more useful data for decision making for several reasons. First, the traditional costing system assigns all manufacturing costs to products—even costs that are not actually caused by the products such as costs of idle capacity and organization-sustaining costs. Second, the traditional costing system excludes all nonmanufacturing costs from product costs—even those that are caused by the product such as some office expenses. Third, the traditional costing system spreads manufacturing overhead uniformly among products based on direct labour-hours. This penalizes high-volume products with large amounts of direct labour-hours. Low-volume products with relatively small amounts of direct labour-hours benefit since the costs of batch-level activities like processing orders are pushed onto the high-volume products.

Case 8-25 (90 minutes)

1. The total direct labour-hours worked for the year would be:

   B-10: 60,000 units × 1 DLH per unit............ 60,000
   C-20: 10,000 units × 1.5 DLH per unit......... 15,000
          Total DLHs................................... 75,000

   The predetermined overhead rate for the year would therefore be:

   $$\frac{\text{Manufacturing overhead cost}}{\text{Direct labour-hours}} = \frac{\$3,600,000}{75,000 \text{ DLHs}}$$

   $$= \$48 \text{ per DLH}$$

2. The unit product costs would be:

	B-10	C-20
Direct materials (given)	$ 60	$ 90
Direct labour (given)	12	18
Manufacturing overhead:		
$48 per DLH × 1 DLH per unit, 1.5 DLH per unit	48	72
Total unit product cost	$120	$180

3. This part of the case is open-ended, but students should provide data such as given below.

   Overhead rates for the activities are:

Activity	(a) Estimated Overhead Costs	(b) Expected Activity	(a) ÷ (b) Predetermined Overhead Rate
Machine setups ...	$416,000	3,200 setups	$130 per setup
Quality control	$720,000	18,000 inspections	$40 per inspection
Purchase orders ..	$180,000	2,400 orders	$75 per order
Soldering	$900,000	400,000 joints	$2.25 per joint
Shipments...........	$264,000	1,200 shipments	$220 per shipment
Machine related...	$1,120,000	140,000 MHs	$8 per MH

Case 8-25 (continued)

Overhead cost assigned to each product:

	B-10 Expected Activity	B-10 Amount	C-20 Expected Activity	C-20 Amount
Machine setups, at $130 per setup	2,000	$ 260,000	1,200	$ 156,000
Quality inspections, at $40 per inspection...............	8,000	320,000	10,000	400,000
Purchase orders, at $75 per order	1,680	126,000	720	54,000
Soldering, at $2.25 per joint	120,000	270,000	280,000	630,000
Shipments, at $220 per shipment	800	176,000	400	88,000
Machine related, at $8 per MH	60,000	480,000	80,000	640,000
Total overhead cost (a)................		$1,632,000		$1,968,000
Number of units produced (b)		60,000		10,000
Overhead cost per unit (a) ÷ (b)...........		$27.20		$196.80

The unit product cost of each product under activity-based costing is given below. For comparison, the costs computed in Part 2 above are also provided.

	Activity-Based Costing B-10	Activity-Based Costing C-20	Direct Labour-Hour Base B-10	Direct Labour-Hour Base C-20
Direct materials	$60.00	$ 90.00	$ 60.00	$ 90.00
Direct labour	12.00	18.00	12.00	18.00
Manufacturing overhead	27.20	196.80	48.00	72.00
Total unit product cost........	$99.20	$304.80	$120.00	$180.00

Case 8-25 (continued)

As shown by the above analysis, unit product costs may have been distorted as a result of using direct labour-hours as the base for assigning overhead costs to products. These distorted costs may have had a major impact on management's pricing policies and on management's perception of the margin being realized on each product. According to the activity-based costing approach, Model C-20 is being sold at a loss:

	Activity-Based Costing		Direct Labour-Hour Base	
	B-10	C-20	B-10	C-20
Selling price per unit*	$200.00	$250.00	$200.00	$250.00
Less unit product cost (above)	99.20	304.80	120.00	180.00
Gross margin (loss).............	$100.80	$(54.80)	$ 80.00	$ 70.00

*Total sales ÷ the number of units sold.

4. It is not surprising that the C-20 "sells itself" since the company is selling it at an apparent loss of $54.80. This probably explains why Borst Company couldn't meet Hammer Products' price.

   In addition, Hammer Products' distorted unit costs explains why Borst Company is able to undercut Hammer's price on the B-10 units. Hammer's management *thinks* that the B-10 costs $120 per unit to manufacture, whereas it costs just $99.20 according to the more accurate activity-based costing approach.

5. Students may suggest many possible strategies—there is no single "right" answer. Two possible strategies are: (a) raise the selling price of the C-20 enough to provide a satisfactory margin; and (b) discontinue the C-20 and focus all available resources on the B-10. The price of the B-10 might even be decreased to increase the volume of sales, if the company has adequate capacity to do so. Before taking any action, an action analysis report should be prepared as discussed in Appendix 8A.

Group Exercise 8-27

An activity-based costing system typically reduces the amount of overhead cost that is allocated based on direct labour-hours—shifting the overhead to other cost pools. Under an activity-based costing system, some of the overhead will be allocated based on the number of batches run, the number of products in the company's active list, and so on. This results in shifting costs from high-volume products produced in large batches to low-volume products produced in small batches. Once this is understood, the answers to the questions posed in the group exercise can be easily answered.

1. The unit product cost of a low-volume product made in small batches will typically increase in an activity-based costing system. The batch-level and product-level costs are spread across a small number of units, increasing the average unit cost.

2. The unit product cost of a high-volume product made in large batches with automated equipment and few direct labour-hours will typically go up under activity-based costing. Because of the low direct labour-hour requirement for the product, the unit product cost under a traditional direct labour-based costing system would be artificially low. Under an activity-based costing system, the product would be charged for its use of automated equipment and for batch-level and product-level costs.

3. The unit product cost of a high-volume product that requires little machine work but a lot of direct labour typically will decrease under activity-based costing. Because of the high direct labour-hour requirement for the product, the unit product cost under a traditional direct labour-based costing system would be artificially high. The activity-based costing system would shift some of the overhead costs that had been assigned to this product to other products that are made in smaller volumes.

Chapter 9
Budgeting

Exercise 9-1 (20 minutes)

1.

	July	August	September	Total
May sales:				
$430,000 × 10%	$ 43,000			$ 43,000
June sales:				
$540,000 × 70%,				
10%	378,000	$ 54,000		432,000
July sales:				
$600,000 × 20%,				
70%, 10%	120,000	420,000	$ 60,000	600,000
August sales:				
$900,000 × 20%,				
70%		180,000	630,000	810,000
September sales:				
$500,000 × 20%			100,000	100,000
Total cash collections......	$541,000	$654,000	$790,000	$1,985,000

Notice that even though sales peak in August, cash collections peak in September. This occurs because the bulk of the company's customers pay in the month following sale. The lag in collections that this creates is even more pronounced in some companies. Indeed, it is not unusual for a company to have the least cash available in the months when sales are greatest.

2. Accounts receivable at September 30:

From August sales: $900,000 × 10%	$ 90,000
From September sales:	
$500,000 × (70% + 10%)	400,000
Total accounts receivable	$490,000

© McGraw-Hill Ryerson, 2004

Exercise 9-3 (15 minutes)

	Quarter—Year 2				Year 3
	First	Second	Third	Fourth	First
Required production of calculators	60,000	90,000	150,000	100,000	80,000
Number of chips per calculator	× 3	× 3	× 3	× 3	× 3
Total production needs—chips	180,000	270,000	450,000	300,000	240,000

	Year 2				
	First	Second	Third	Fourth	Year
Production needs—chips	180,000	270,000	450,000	300,000	1,200,000
Add desired ending inventory—chips*	54,000	90,000	60,000	48,000	48,000
Total needs—chips	234,000	360,000	510,000	348,000	1,248,000
Less beginning inventory—chips	36,000	54,000	90,000	60,000	36,000
Required purchases—chips	198,000	306,000	420,000	288,000	1,212,000
Cost of purchases at $2 per chip	$396,000	$612,000	$840,000	$576,000	$2,424,000

*20% × 270,000; 20% × 450,000; and so on.

Managerial Accounting, 6th Canadian Edition

Exercise 9-5 (15 minutes)

1.

Krispin Corporation
Manufacturing Overhead Budget

	1st Quarter	2nd Quarter	3rd Quarter	4th Quarter	Year
Budgeted direct labour-hours........	5,000	4,800	5,200	5,400	20,400
Variable overhead rate	x $1.75	x $1.75	x $1.75	x $1.75	x $1.75
Variable manufacturing overhead...	$ 8,750	$ 8,400	$ 9,100	$ 9,450	$ 35,700
Fixed manufacturing overhead.......	35,000	35,000	35,000	35,000	140,000
Total manufacturing overhead	43,750	43,400	44,100	44,450	175,700
Less depreciation	15,000	15,000	15,000	15,000	60,000
Cash disbursements for manufacturing overhead..............	$28,750	$28,400	$29,100	$29,450	$115,700

2.

Total budgeted manufacturing overhead for the year (a)...........	$175,700
Total budgeted direct labour-hours for the year (b)................	20,400
Predetermined overhead rate for the year (a) ÷ (b)	$ 8.61

Exercise 9-7 (20 minutes)

	Quarter (000 omitted)				Year
	1	2	3	4	
Cash balance, beginning	$ 9 *	$ 5	$ 5	$ 5	$ 9 *
Add collections from customers	76	90	125 *	100	391 *
Total cash available	85 *	95	130	105	400
Less disbursements:					
Purchase of inventory	40 *	58 *	36	32 *	166
Operating expenses	36	42 *	54 *	48	180 *
Equipment purchases	10 *	8 *	8 *	10	36 *
Dividends	2 *	2 *	2 *	2 *	8
Total disbursements	88	110 *	100	92	390
Excess (deficiency) of cash available over disbursements	(3)*	(15)	30 *	13	10
Financing:					
Borrowings	8	20 *	—	—	28
Repayments (including interest)	0	0	(25)	(7)*	(32)
Total financing	8	20	(25)	(7)	(4)
Cash balance, ending	$ 5	$ 5	$ 5	$ 6	$ 6

*Given.

Problem 9-9 (30 minutes)

1. September cash sales .... $ 7,400
   September collections on account:
      July sales: $20,000 × 18% 3,600
      August sales: $30,000 × 70% 21,000
      September sales: $40,000 × 10% 4,000
      Total cash collections $36,000

2. Payments to suppliers:
      August purchases (accounts payable) $16,000
      September purchases: $25,000 × 20% 5,000
      Total cash payments $21,000

3.

CALGON PRODUCTS
Cash Budget
For the Month of September

Cash balance, September 1		$ 9,000
Add cash receipts:		
Collections from customers		36,000
Total cash available before current financing		45,000
Less disbursements:		
Payments to suppliers for inventory	$21,000	
Selling and administrative expenses	9,000 *	
Equipment purchases	18,000	
Dividends paid	3,000	
Total disbursements		51,000
Excess (deficiency) of cash available over		
disbursements		(6,000)

Financing:

Borrowings..	11,000
Repayments	0
Interest...	0
Total financing	11,000
Cash balance, September 30...................	$ 5,000

*$13,000 – $4,000 = $9,000.

Managerial Accounting, 6th Canadian Edition

Problem 9-11 (30 minutes)

1.

Priston Company
Direct Materials Budget

	1st Quarter	2nd Quarter	3rd Quarter	4th Quarter	Year
Required production	6,000	7,000	8,000	5,000	26,000
Raw materials per unit	× 3	× 3	× 3	× 3	× 3
Production needs	18,000	21,000	24,000	15,000	78,000
Add desired ending inventory (20%)	4,200	4,800	3,000	3,700	3,700
Total needs	22,200	25,800	27,000	18,700	81,700
Less beginning inventory	3,600	4,200	4,800	3,000	3,600
Raw materials to be purchased	18,600	21,600	22,200	15,700	78,100
Cost of raw materials to be purchased at $2.50 per kilogram	$46,500	$54,000	$55,500	$39,250	$195,250

Schedule of Expected Cash Disbursements for Materials

	1st Quarter	2nd Quarter	3rd Quarter	4th Quarter	Year
Accounts payable, beginning balance	$11,775				$ 11,775
1st Quarter purchases*	32,550	$13,950			46,500
2nd Quarter purchases		37,800	$16,200		54,000
3rd Quarter purchases			38,850	$16,650	55,500
4th Quarter purchases			-	27,475	27,475
Total cash disbursements for materials	$44,325	$51,750	$55,050	$44,125	$195,250

*70% × $46,500; 30% × $46,500

Problem 9-11 (continued)

2.

Priston Company
Direct Labour Budget

	1st Quarter	2nd Quarter	3rd Quarter	4th Quarter	Year
Required production................	6,000	7,000	8,000	5,000	26,000
Direct labour-hours per unit.........	× 0.50	× 0.50	× 0.50	× 0.50	× 0.50
Total direct labour-hours needed	3,000	3,500	4,000	2,500	13,000
Direct labour cost per hour	$12.00	$12.00	$12.00	$12.00	$12.00
Total direct labour cost...............	$36,000	$42,000	$48,000	$30,000	$156,000

Problem 9-13 (60 minutes)

1. Schedule of cash receipts:

Cash sales—June	$ 60,000
Collections on accounts receivable:	
May 31 balance	72,000
June (50% × 190,000)	95,000
Total cash receipts	$227,000

Schedule of cash payments for purchases:

May 31 accounts payable balance	$ 90,000
June purchases (40% × 200,000)	80,000
Total cash payments	$170,000

PHOTOTEC, INC.
Cash Budget
For the Month of June

Cash balance, beginning	$ 8,000
Add receipts from customers (above)	227,000
Total cash available	235,000
Less disbursements:	
Purchase of inventory (above)	170,000
Operating expenses	51,000
Purchases of equipment	9,000
Total cash disbursements	230,000
Excess of receipts over disbursements	5,000
Financing:	
Borrowings—note	18,000
Repayments—note	(15,000)
Interest	(500)
Total financing	2,500
Cash balance, ending	$ 7,500

Problem 9-13 (continued)

2.

PHOTOTEC, INC.
Budgeted Income Statement
For the Month of June

Sales		$250,000
Cost of goods sold:		
Beginning inventory	$ 30,000	
Add purchases..	200,000	
Goods available for sale	230,000	
Ending inventory.....................................	40,000	
Cost of goods sold		190,000
Gross margin		60,000
Operating expenses ($51,000 + $2,000).....		53,000
Net operating income		7,000
Interest expense		500
Net income		$ 6,500

3.

PHOTOTEC, INC.
Budgeted Balance Sheet
June 30

Assets

Cash..	$ 7,500
Accounts receivable (50% × 190,000)	95,000
Inventory...	40,000
Buildings and equipment, net of depreciation	
($500,000 + $9,000 − $2,000)	507,000
Total assets...	$649,500

Liabilities and Equity

Accounts payable (60% × 200,000)	$120,000
Note payable..	18,000
Capital stock	420,000
Retained earnings ($85,000 + $6,500)	91,500
Total liabilities and equity...	$649,500

Problem 9-15 (45 minutes)

1. Stokes is using the budget as a club to pressure employees and as a way to find someone to blame rather than as a legitimate planning and control tool. His planning seems to consist of telling everyone to increase sales volume by 40%. This kind of "planning" requires no analysis, no intelligence, no business insight, and is very likely viewed with contempt by the employees of the company.

2. The way in which the budget is being used is likely to breed hostility, tension, mistrust, lack of respect, and actions designed to meet targets using any means available. Unreasonable targets imposed from the top, coupled with a "no excuses" policy and the threat of being fired, create an ideal breeding ground for questionable business practices. Managers who would not, under ordinary circumstances, cheat or cut corners may do so if put under this kind of pressure.

3. As the old saying goes, Keri Kalani is "between a rock and a hard place." The standards of ethical conduct states that management accountants have a responsibility to "disclose fully all relevant information that could reasonably be expected to influence an intended user's understanding of the reports, comments, and recommendations presented." Assuming that Keri helps prepare the Production Department's reports to top management, collaborating with her boss in hiding losses due to defective disk drives would clearly violate this standard. Apart from the misrepresentation on the accounting reports, the policy of shipping defective returned units to customers is bound to have a negative effect on the company's reputation. If this policy were to become widely known, it would very likely have a devastating effect on the company's future sales. Moreover, this practice may be illegal under statutes designed to protect consumers.

   Having confronted her boss with no satisfactory resolution of the problem, Keri must now decide what to do. The standards of ethical conduct suggests that Keri go to the next higher level in management to present her case. Unfortunately, in the prevailing moral climate at PrimeDrive, she is unlikely to win any blue ribbons for blowing the whistle on her boss. All of the managers below Stokes are likely to be in fear of losing their own jobs and many of them may have taken actions to meet Stokes' targets that they are not proud of either. It would

Problem 9-15 (continued)

take tremendous courage for Keri to take the problem all the way up to Stokes himself—particularly in view of his less-than-humane treatment of subordinates. And going to the Board of Directors is unlikely to work either since Stokes and his venture capital firm apparently control the Board. Resigning, with a letter of memorandum to the individual who is most likely to be concerned and to be able to take action, may be the only ethical course of action that is left open to Keri in this situation. Of course, she must pay her rent, so hopefully she has good alternative employment opportunities.

Note: This problem is very loosely based on the MiniScribe scandal reported in the December, 1992 issue of *Management Accounting* as well as in other business publications. After going bankrupt, it was discovered that managers at MiniScribe had perpetrated massive fraud as a result of the unrelenting pressure to meet unrealistic targets. Q. T. Wiles, the real chairman of MiniScribe, was reported to have behaved much as described in this problem. Keri Kalani is, alas, a fabrication. Hopefully, there were people like Keri at MiniScribe who tried to do something to stop the fraud.

Problem 9-17 (60 minutes)

1. Collections on sales:

	July	August	Sept.	Quarter
Cash sales..................................	$ 8,000	$14,000	$10,000	$ 32,000
Credit sales:				
May: $30,000 × 80% × 20% ...	4,800			4,800
June: $36,000 × 80% × 70%, 20%..........................	20,160	5,760		25,920
July: $40,000 × 80% × 10%, 70%, 20%..........................	3,200	22,400	6,400	32,000
Aug.: $70,000 × 80% × 10%, 70%.............................		5,600	39,200	44,800
Sept.: $50,000 × 80% × 10%.....................................			4,000	4,000
Total cash collections..................	$36,160	$47,760	$59,600	$143,520

2. a. Inventory purchases budget:

	July	August	Sept.	Oct.
Budgeted cost of goods sold	$24,000	$42,000	$30,000	$27,000
Add desired ending inventory*	31,500	22,500	20,250	
Total needs	55,500	64,500	50,250	
Less beginning inventory	18,000	31,500	22,500	
Required inventory purchases	$37,500	$33,000	$27,750	

   *75% of the next month's budgeted cost of goods sold.

b. Schedule of expected cash disbursements for inventory:

	July	August	Sept.	Quarter
Accounts payable, June 30..........	$11,700			$11,700
July purchases	18,750	$18,750		37,500
August purchases.......................		16,500	$16,500	33,000
September purchases			13,875	13,875
Total cash disbursements............	$30,450	$35,250	$30,375	$96,075

Problem 9-17 (continued)

3.

JANUS PRODUCTS, INC.
Cash Budget
For the Quarter Ended September 30

	July	August	Sept.	Quarter
Cash balance, beginning	$ 8,000	$ 8,410	$ 8,020	$ 8,000
Add collections from sales.........	36,160	47,760	59,600	143,520
Total cash available...............	44,160	56,170	67,620	151,520
Less disbursements:				
For inventory purchases	30,450	35,250	30,375	96,075
For selling expenses..............	7,200	11,700	8,500	27,400
For administrative expenses ...	3,600	5,200	4,100	12,900
For land	4,500	0	0	4,500
For dividends.......................	0	0	1,000	1,000
Total disbursements..................	45,750	52,150	43,975	141,875
Excess (deficiency) of cash available over disbursements	(1,590)	4,020	23,645	9,645
Financing:				
Borrowings..........................	10,000	4,000		14,000
Repayment..........................	0	0	(14,000)	(14,000)
Interest at 12%*	0	0	(380)	(380)
Total financing	10,000	4,000	(14,380)	(380)
Cash balance, ending	$ 8,410	$ 8,020	$ 9,265	$ 9,265

$$\begin{aligned} * \ \$10,000 \times 12\% \times 3/12 &= \$300 \\ \$ 4,000 \times 12\% \times 2/12 &= \underline{80} \\ &= \underline{\$380} \end{aligned}$$

Problem 9-19 (120 minutes)

1. Schedule of expected cash collections:

	April	May	June	Total
Cash sales..............	$14,000	$17,000	$18,000	$ 49,000
Credit sales	48,000	56,000	68,000	172,000
Total collections........	$62,000	$73,000	$86,000	$221,000

2. a. Inventory purchases budget:

	April	May	June	Total
Budgeted cost of goods sold	$42,000	$51,000	$54,000	$147,000
Add desired ending inventory* ..	15,300	16,200	9,000	9,000
Total needs	57,300	67,200	63,000	156,000
Less beginning inventory	12,600	15,300	16,200	12,600
Required purchases	$44,700	$51,900	$46,800	$143,400

*At April 30: $51,000 × 30% = $15,300.
At June 30: $50,000 July sales × 60% × 30% = $9,000.

b. Schedule of cash disbursements for purchases:

	April	May	June	Total
For March purchases	$18,300			$18,300
For April purchases.............	22,350	$22,350		44,700
For May purchases		25,950	$25,950	51,900
For June purchases			23,400	23,400
Total cash disbursements........	$40,650	$48,300	$49,350	$138,300

Problem 9-19 (continued)

3. Schedule of cash disbursements for operating expenses:

	April	May	June	Total
Salaries and wages	$ 7,500	$ 7,500	$ 7,500	$22,500
Shipping	4,200	5,100	5,400	14,700
Advertising	6,000	6,000	6,000	18,000
Other expenses	2,800	3,400	3,600	9,800
Total cash disbursements for operating expenses	$20,500	$22,000	$22,500	$65,000

4. Cash budget:

	April	May	June	Total
Cash balance, beginning	$ 9,000	$ 8,350	$ 8,050	$ 9,000
Add cash collections	62,000	73,000	86,000	221,000
Total cash available	71,000	81,350	94,050	230,000
Less disbursements:				
For inventory purchases	40,650	48,300	49,350	138,300
For operating expenses	20,500	22,000	22,500	65,000
For equipment purchases	11,500	3,000	0	14,500
For dividends	0	0	3,500	3,500
Total disbursements	72,650	73,300	75,350	221,300
Excess (deficiency) of cash	(1,650)	8,050	18,700	8,700
Financing:				
Borrowings	10,000	0	0	10,000
Repayments	0	0	(10,000)	(10,000)
Interest*	0	0	(300)	(300)
Total financing	10,000	0	(10,300)	(300)
Cash balance, ending	$ 8,350	$ 8,050	$ 8,400	$ 8,400

* $10,000 × 12% × 3/12 = $300.

Problem 9-19 (continued)

5. Income Statement:

NORDIC COMPANY
Income Statement
For the Quarter Ended June 30

Sales..		$245,000
Less cost of goods sold:		
Beginning inventory (given)........................	$ 12,600	
Add purchases (Part 2).............................	143,400	
Goods available for sale............................	156,000	
Ending inventory (Part 2)..........................	9,000	
		147,000
Gross margin...		98,000
Less operating expenses:		
Salaries and wages (Part 3).......................	22,500	
Shipping (Part 3)......................................	14,700	
Advertising (Part 3)..................................	18,000	
Depreciation..	6,000	
Other expenses (Part 3)............................	9,800	
		71,000
Net operating income.....................................		27,000
Less interest expense (Part 4).........................		300
Net income..		$ 26,700

Problem 9-19 (continued)

6. Balance sheet:

NORDIC COMPANY
Balance Sheet
June 30

Assets

Current assets:
Cash (Part 4)	$ 8,400
Accounts receivable (80% × $90,000)	72,000
Inventory (Part 2)	9,000
Total current assets	89,400
Buildings and equipment, net ($214,100 + $14,500 − $6,000)	222,600
Total assets	$312,000

Liabilities and Equity

Current liabilities:
Accounts payable (Part 2: 50% × $46,800)		$ 23,400
Shareholders' equity:		
Capital stock	$190,000	
Retained earnings*	98,600	288,600
Total liabilities and equity		$312,000

* Retained earnings, beginning	$ 75,400
Add net income	26,700
Total	102,100
Less dividends	3,500
Retained earnings, ending	$ 98,600

Problem 9-21 (90 minutes)

1.

	April	May	June	Quarter
Budgeted sales	20,000	35,000	50,000	105,000
Add desired ending inventory*	7,000	10,000	9,000	9,000
Total needs	27,000	45,000	59,000	114,000
Less beginning inventory	4,000	7,000	10,000	4,000
Required production	23,000	38,000	49,000	110,000

*20% of the next month's sales.

2. Material #208:

	April	May	June	Quarter
Required production—units	23,000	38,000	49,000	110,000
Material #208 per unit	× 4 kgs.	× 4 kgs.	× 4 kgs.	× 4 kgs.
Production needs—kilograms	92,000	152,000	196,000	440,000
Add desired ending inventory*	76,000	98,000	84,000	84,000
Total needs—kilograms	168,000	250,000	280,000	524,000
Less beginning inventory	46,000	76,000	98,000	46,000
Required purchases—kilograms	122,000	174,000	182,000	478,000
Required purchases at $5.00 per kilogram	$610,000	$870,000	$910,000	$2,390,000

* 50% of the following month's production needs. For June: July production 45,000 + 6,000 − 9,000 = 42,000 units; 42,000 units × 4 kgs. per unit = 168,000 kgs.; 168,000 kgs. × 50% = 84,000 kgs.

Problem 9-21 (continued)

Material #311:

	April	May	June	Quarter
Required production—units	23,000	38,000	49,000	110,000
Material #311 per unit	× 9 m	× 9 m	× 9 m	× 9 m
Production needs—metres	207,000	342,000	441,000	990,000
Add desired ending inventory*	114,000	147,000	126,000	126,000
Total needs—metres	321,000	489,000	567,000	1,116,000
Less beginning inventory	69,000	114,000	147,000	69,000
Required purchases—metres	252,000	375,000	420,000	1,047,000
Required purchases at $2.00 per metre	$504,000	$750,000	$840,000	$2,094,000

* 1/3 of the following month's production needs. For June:
July production 45,000 + 6,000 – 9,000 = 42,000 units;
42,000 units × 9 m. per unit = 378,000 m.;
378,000 m. × 1/3 = 126,000 m.

3. Direct labour budget:

	Units Produced	Direct Labour Hours Per Unit	Direct Labour Hours Total	Cost per DLH	Total Cost
Shaping	110,000	0.25	27,500	$18.00	$ 495,000

Assembly	110,000	0.70	77,000	$16.00	1,232,000
Finishing	110,000	0.10	11,000	$20.00	220,000
			115,500		$1,947,000

Problem 9-21 (continued)

4. Manufacturing overhead budget:

Expected production for the year	250,000
Actual production through March 31	32,000
Expected production, April through December	218,000
Variable manufacturing overhead rate per unit ($112,000 ÷ 32,000 units)	× $3.50
Variable manufacturing overhead	$ 763,000
Fixed manufacturing overhead ($4,628,000 × ¾)	3,471,000
Total manufacturing overhead	4,234,000
Less depreciation ($2,910,000 × ¾)	2,182,500
Cash disbursement for manufacturing overhead	$2,051,500

Problem 9-23 (40 minutes)

GABLES CO.
Cash Budget
June 2003

Cash balance, June 1, 2003			$ 3,500
Receipts:			
June	50% × 98% × $64,000	$ 31,360	
May	40% × $48,000	19,200	
April	7% × $32,000	2,240	52,800
			56,300
Disbursements for inventory purchases:			
May		$ 7,000	
June		22,500*	
		29,500	
Selling and administrative disbursements:			
Fixed (24,000 − 6,000) ÷ 12		1,500	
Variable (108,000 − 24,000) ×			
(64,000 ÷ 800,000)		6,720	37,720
Cash balance, June 30, 2003			$ 18,580

* Cost of goods sold ($64,000 ÷ $16)	4,000 units
Ending inventory (0.50 × ($56,000 ÷ $16))	1,750 units
	5,750 units
Less beginning inventory (0.50 × 4,000)	2,000 units
Purchases for June	3,750 units

75% of June's purchases, that is, (3,750 × $8) $30,000

© McGraw-Hill Ryerson, 2004

Managerial Accounting, 6th Canadian Edition

CGA Solution, adapted

Case 9-25 (75 minutes)

1. Before a cash budget can be prepared, the following supporting computations must be made:

Cash payments for skate purchases from the manufacturer:

Purchases:

	February	March	April	May	June	July	Quarter
Budgeted sales	$160,000	$164,000	$172,000	$176,000	$184,000	$190,000	
Cost of sales (75%)	120,000	123,000	129,000	132,000	138,000	142,500	
Purchases (one month in advance)	123,000	129,000	132,000	138,000	142,500		

Payments for purchases:

	February	March	April	May	June	July	Quarter
February purchases: $123,000 × 50%			$ 61,500				$ 61,500
March purchases: $129,000 × 50%, 50%			64,500	$ 64,500			129,000
April purchases: $132,000 × 50%, 50%				66,000	$ 66,000		132,000
May purchases: $138,000 × 50%					69,000		69,000
Total cash payments			$126,000	$130,500	$135,000		$391,500

Case 9-25 (continued)

Operating expenses:

	April	May	June	Quarter
Salaries and wages (1/12 of annual)	$10,000	$10,000	$10,000	$30,000
Advertising and promotion (1/12 of annual)	1,000	1,000	1,000	3,000
Property taxes			4,500	4,500
Insurance (1/12 of annual)	400	400	400	1,200
Utilities (1/12 of annual)	500	500	500	1,500
Depreciation (not a cash flow)	—	—	—	—
Total disbursements for operating expenses	$11,900	$11,900	$16,400	$40,200

Cash receipts from sales:

	April	May	June	Quarter
February sales: $160,000 × 70%	$112,000			$112,000
March sales: $164,000 × 30%, 70%	49,200	$114,800		164,000
April sales: $172,000 × 30%, 70%		51,600	$120,400	172,000
May sales: $176,000 × 30%			52,800	52,800
Total cash receipts	$161,200	$166,400	$173,200	$500,800

© McGraw-Hill Ryerson, 2004

Managerial Accounting, 6th Canadian Edition

Case 9-25 (continued)

Given the above data, the cash budget can be prepared as follows:

	April	May	June	Quarter
Cash balance, beginning	$ 20,000	$ 20,000	$ 20,000	$ 20,000
Add cash receipts (see above)	161,200	166,400	173,200	500,800
Total cash available	181,200	186,400	193,200	520,800
Less cash disbursements:				
Purchases (see above)	126,000	130,500	135,000	391,500
Operating expenses (see above)	11,900	11,900	16,400	40,200
Income taxes (given)	16,000			16,000
Equipment and facilities (given)	22,300	29,000		51,300
Total disbursements	176,200	171,400	151,400	499,000
Excess (deficiency) of cash available over disbursements	5,000	15,000	41,800	21,800
Financing:				
Borrowings	15,000	5,000	0	20,000
Repayments			(20,000)	(20,000)
Interest*			(550)	(550)
Invested funds			(1,250)	(1,250)
Total financing	15,000	5,000	(21,800)	(1,800)
Cash balance, ending	$ 20,000	$ 20,000	$ 20,000	$ 20,000

*($15,000 × 12% × 3/12) + ($5,000 × 12% × 2/12)

Case 9-25 (continued)

2. Cash budgeting is particularly important for a growing company like Roller, Ltd., because as sales grow, so do expenditures for inputs. These expenditures generally precede cash receipts, often by a considerable time period, and a growing company must be prepared to finance this gap between cash outflows and cash inflows. Thus, cash budgeting is essential because it will forewarn managers of impending cash problems. And, a cash budget will often be necessary documentation if it becomes necessary to arrange for financing.

Managerial Accounting, 6th Canadian Edition

Case 9-27 Solution

Lam Restaurant and Lounge
Instructor's Notes

Instructional Objectives:
1. to construct an interactive set of semi-annual financial statements
2. to investigate data necessary to prepare the forecasts
3. to undertake "what if" analysis of the results
4. to integrate the wide variety of materials necessary for a small business consulting assignment.

Issues:
1. interactive financial statements
2. empirical investigation of information
3. preparation of "what if" analysis for multiple assumptions
4. multiple product profit analysis.

Assumptions:
The restaurant serves food from 5pm to 9pm and the lounge is open from 9pm to 1:30am except Sunday when it is open until 12:30am. These assumptions aid in the formulation of hours worked. Minor adjustments can permit an allowance for preopening time for some employees.

Financing is required to cover the initial capital cost estimate. The cash, tables, chairs, dishes, kitchen, alarms, signage and leasehold improvements will be financed through a 5 year term loan at 12% interest for 90% of the required financing. Assume the owners contribute the remaining 10%.

The asset accounts of tables, chairs, dishes, kitchen, alarms and signage will be lumped into an equipment and furniture account and depreciated straight-line over 5 years. The leasehold improvements will be amortized over the same period and conditions.

The rent expense is assumed to be yearly because $6 per square foot is too high to be per month. We assumed that they would require 1500 square feet. The calculation in the solution shows the break-down of the numbers.

A number of assumptions were made regarding wages and salaries all of which determine the appropriate cost for the number of hours to be worked. The numbers that resulted are shown in the solution.

Case 9-27 Solution (continued)

Revenues are determined using the demographic figures given. The solution shows how these numbers all fit together to come up with a reasonable estimate of revenue. Year 2's revenue is determined by taking Year 1's figures and assuming a 10% increase in sales. Assume an initial market share of 20 percent.

April 1, 2003 is the starting date for forecasts and this date represents the forecast for the first six months of operation.

Calculations, Solutions and Income Statement Items

Sales:

The food and beverage figures for sales are determined using the demographic figures provided and the following formulas. Both figures are per year.

Food: $= \dfrac{\text{Population (19–39)}}{\text{Total pop. Halifax}} \times \begin{array}{c}\text{No. of households} \\ \text{in vicinity}\end{array} \times \begin{array}{c}\text{\% of households} \\ \text{that eat out}\end{array}$

$\times$ Food spending/Household $\times$ Lam's market share

$= \dfrac{52{,}815 + 69{,}610}{315{,}000} \times 4{,}000 \times 93\% \times \$630 \times 20\% = \$182{,}191$

Note: calculation rounded to $182,168 in spreadsheet.

Beverage: [{Pop (19–29) / Pop Hal} % in area × Beverage spending (19–29) } + {Same as above for 30–39 group}] × Market share

$= [\{\dfrac{69{,}610}{315{,}000} \times 4{,}000 \times 2 \times \$171.50\} + \{\dfrac{52{,}815}{315{,}000} \times 4{,}000 \times 2$

$\times \$100.50\}] \times 20\% = \$87{,}321$

Note: calculation rounded to $87,599.

Lotto Machine: $6,000 profit per month.

Door: Charge $5/person three nights a week during lounge hours (9 – 1:30). Capacity is 60 people per night. Assume that the bar runs at an average 70% of capacity during lounge hours and the turnover of people a night is 2.2

Managerial Accounting, 6th Canadian Edition

Case 9-27 Solution (continued)

$$\text{Revenue} = 60 \text{ people} \times 3 \text{ nights} \times 70\% \times 2.2 \times \$5$$
$$= \$1,386/\text{week}, \$5,544/\text{month}, \$66,528/\text{year}$$

Cost of Goods Sold:

Cost of goods sold was found by taking the mark-up on the food and beverage and using that to determine the individual cost of goods sold. The sales figures were then used to determine the weighted average cost of goods sold.

Food: Mark-up = 100%
  Cost of Goods Sold = $\dfrac{100}{200}$ = 50%
  Weight = 182,191/(182191 + 87321) = .676

Beverage: Mark-up = 80%
  Cost of Goods Sold = $\dfrac{100}{180}$ = 55.55%
  Weight = 87321/(182191 + 87321) = .324

So, the weighted average CGS = 50% (0.676) + 55.55 (0.324)
  = .338 + .18
  = 51.8%

Closing Inventory:

This was found using the inventory turnover ratio. This ratio is computed by dividing Cost of goods sold by Inventory. Then for the period required the cost of goods sold is divided by this ratio to arrive at the ending inventory.

Purchases:

Once the ending and beginning inventories and cost of goods sold are known then a purchases figure can be found.

Purchases = Cost of + Ending – Beginning
  goods sold inventory inventory

Case 9-27 Solution (continued)

<u>Expenses:</u>

Note all expenses are converted to monthly amounts to make them consistent.

<u>Interest Expense</u> (per month) = $\dfrac{\text{(Amount of loan} \times \text{Interest rate)}}{12}$

<u>Depreciation:</u>   Calculated for all assets and depreciate straight-line over 5 years with no residual value.

<u>Amortization:</u>   Leasehold improvements are amortized over 5 years straight-line.

<u>Rent Expense:</u> The rent is yearly and is based on $6/square foot.

Square footage required:		
20 tables	200	
60 seats	300	
kitchen and entrance	500	
stage and bar	300	
	1300	
Sundry extra	200	
	1500	sq. feet

<u>Wages:</u>

These expenses were calculated based on the hours allocated in the data section on a weekly basis.

Cooks:
   3 cooks × 4 hrs/day (5-9) × 7 days/week = 84 hours/week

Waiters and Waitresses:

4 w & w's × 4 hours	× 7 days =	112	hours
4 w & w's × 4.5 hours	× 6 days =	108	
4 w & w's × 3.5 hours	× 1 day =	14	
		234	hours

Case 9-27 Solution (continued)

Bartenders (2):

1 bartender × 4 hours	× 7 days	=	28	hours
2 bartender × 3.5 hours	× 1 day	=	7	
2 bartender × 4.5	× 3 days	=	27	
			62	hours

Cleaning:

5 hours/day × 7 days	=	35	hours/week

Doorman:

4.5 hours	× 6 days	=	27	hours
3.5 hours	× 1 day	=	3.5	
			30.5	hours

Hostess:

4 hours	× 7 days	=	28 hours

These hours are multiplied by their appropriate wage rate to determine the wage expenses.

Benefits: These are calculated by taking 7% of the wages paid.

Balance Sheet Solution Key

Cash: This figure is the cumulative amount of cash taken from the statement of cash flows.

Inventory: This figure represents the opening inventory found in the income statement.

Accounts Payable: This is determined using the accounts payable turnover; that is,

$$\text{Accounts Payable} = \frac{\text{Purchases}}{\text{A/P turnover ratio}}$$

$$\text{A/P turnover} = \frac{\text{Purchases}}{\text{Trade acct's pay.}}$$

Case 9-27 Solution (continued)

<u>Note Payable:</u> Required financing is $50,000 excluding cash and the bank will finance 90% making the note payable $45,000.

<u>Owner's Capital:</u> It is assumed that the owners will come up with the other 10% of capital needed which is $10,000 including $5,000 in cash.

LAM RESTAURANT AND LOUNGE

Data Analysis:

Capital Expenditures:		Operating Expenses (per month):	
Cash	$5,000	Advertising..................	$200
Inventory	$4,000	Office costs	$100
Tables, chairs, dishes.........	$15,000	Utilities	$600
Kitchen	$26,000	Entertainment	$1,200
Alarms, Signage.................	$2,000	Leasing Expense..........	$200
Leasehold Improvement.....	$3,000	Cleaning Expense	$300
Accounts Payable..............	$0	Rent Expense..............	$750
Note Payable (12%)	$45,000	Depreciation Expense ..	$717
Useful Life (years)	5	Employee Benefits.......	$1,004
Sq. Footage Rented	1500	Interest Expense	$450
Rent per sq. foot	$6.00	Wages Expense...........	$14,345
Loan Payback	$9,000	Amortization	$50
Accounts Receivable	0	Principal repayment.....	$750
Owner's Capital	$10,000		

Wages and Salaries:	Rate	Hours/week	Expense/wk
Waiters & Waitresses.........	$5.25	234.00	$1,229
Doorman..........................	$6.50	30.50	198
Cleaning...........................	$5.25	35.00	184
Bar Tenders	$6.20	62.00	384
Manager...........................			350
Bookkeeping......................			100
Cooks	$8.00	84.00	672
Hostess............................	$7.00	28.00	196
		Total	$3,313

Case 9-27 Solution (continued)

Demographics:		Revenues (per Year)	
Households (vicinity)...........	4,000.00	Beverages	$87,599
Population (Halifax)	315,000.00	Food	$182,168
Population (19-29).............	69,610.00	Lotto Machine	$72,000
Population (30-39).............	52,815.00	Door.......................	$66,528
Beverage Spending (19-29).	$171.50		
Beverage Spending (30-39).	$100.50	Weighted Avg. CG.....	51.804%
Food Spending/Household...	$630.00	Margin (food)...........	50.00%
Household % who eat out...	93.00%	Margin (beverages)...	55.56%
Avg. Person/Household	2	Accounts Receiv........	
Market Share (Food)..........	20.00%	Inventory Turnover ...	17.47
Market Share (Beverage)	20.00%	Accts. Pay. Turnover .	

Case 9-27 Solution (continued)

Financial Analysis:

LAM Restaurant and Lounge
Forecasted Income Statement
For the Period Ending

	Sep.1/03	Apr.1/04	Sep.1/04	Apr.1/05
Sales				
Food............................	$ 91,084	$ 91,084	$100,193	$100,193
Beverage....................	43,800	43,800	48,179	48,179
Total Sales	134,884	134,884	148,372	148,372
Cost of Goods Sold				
Opening Inventory.....	4,000	4,000	4,000	4,400
Purchases	69,875	69,875	77,263	76,863
	73,875	73,875	81,263	81,263
Closing Inventory	4,000	4,000	4,400	4,400
Cost of Goods Sold	69,875	69,875	76,863	76,863
Gross Margin	65,009	65,009	71,509	71,509
Other Income				
Door	33,264	33,264	33,264	33,264
Lotto Machine............	36,000	36,000	36,000	36,000
Gross Profit	134,273	134,273	140,773	140,773

Managerial Accounting, 6th Canadian Edition

Case 9-27 Solution (continued)

	Sep.1/03	Apr.1/04	Sep.1/04	Apr.1/05
Expenses				
Advertising..................	1,200	1,200	1,200	1,200
Office costs	600	600	600	600
Utilities	3,600	3,600	3,600	3,600
Entertainment	7,200	7,200	7,200	7,200
Leasing Expense..........	1,200	1,200	1,200	1,200
Cleaning Expense	1,800	1,800	1,800	1,800
Rent Expense	4,500	4,500	4,500	4,500
Depreciation Expense...	4,300	4,300	4,300	4,300
Amortization Expense ..	300	300	300	300
Employee Benefits	6,025	6,025	6,025	6,025
Interest Expense	2,700	2,700	2,700	2,700
Wages Expense	86,070	86,070	86,070	86,070
Total Expenses	119,495	119,495	119,495	119,495
Income before taxes	$14,778	$14,778	$21,278	$21,278

Case 9-27 Solution (continued)

Balance Sheet
At the Period Ending

	Opening Balance	Sep.1/03	Apr.1/04	Sep.1/04	Apr.1/05
Assets					
Current Assets:					
Cash	$ 5,000	$19,878	$34,756	$56,134	$77,112
Accts. Receivable......	0	0	0	0	0
Inventory	4,000	4,000	4,000	4,000	4,400
Total	9,000	23,878	38,756	60,134	81,512
Capital Assets:					
Equip. and Furniture .	43,000	43,000	43,000	43,000	43,000
Accum. Depreciation .	0	(4,300)	(8,600)	(12,900)	(17,200)
Leasehold Improvements	3,000	3,000	3,000	3,000	3,000
Accum. Amortization..........	0	(300)	(600)	(900)	(1,200)
Total	$55,000	$65,278	$75,556	$92,334	$109,112
Liabilities					
Current Liabilities:					
Accounts Payable......	$ 0	$ 0	$ 0	$ 0	$ 0
Wages Payable.........	0	0	0	0	0
Total	0	0	0	0	0
Long-term Liabilities:					
Note Payable............	45,000	40,500	36,000	31,500	27,000
Total	45,000	40,500	36,000	31,500	27,000
Shareholders' Equity					
Owners' Capital	10,000	10,000	10,000	10,000	10,000
Retained Earnings........	0	14,778	29,556	50,834	72,112
Total	10,000	24,778	39,556	60,834	82,112
Total Liabilities & Equity	$55,000	$65,278	$75,556	$92,334	$109,112

Case 9-27 Solution (continued)

Schedule of Estimated Cash Flows
For the Year Ending

	Opening Balance	Sep.1/03	Apr.1/04	Sep.1/04	Apr.1/05
Cash In					
Earnings		$14,778	$14,778	$21,278	$21,278
Add: Amortization.....		300	300	300	300
Add: Depreciation.....		4,300	4,300	4,300	4,300
		19,378	19,378	25,878	25,878
Increase (decrease) accts. payable		0	0	0	0
Decrease (increase) Inventory		0	0	0	(400)
		19,378	19,378	25,878	25,478
Cash Out:					
Principal Bank Loan ..		4,500	4,500	4,500	4,500
Purchases of assets ..		0	0	0	0
Periodic Cash Surplus (deficiency		14,878	14,878	21,378	20,978
Cumulative Cash Surplus	$5,000	$19,878	$34,756	$56,134	$77,112

Case 9-27 Solution (continued)

Break-Even Analysis
Lam Restaurant and Lounge

	$	%
Net Revenues......................	495,830	100.00%
Cost of Goods Sold	256,840	51.80%
Gross Profit	238,990	48.20%

Expenses:

Advertising.....................	$2,400
Office costs	1,200
Utilities	7,200
Entertainment	14,400
Leasing Expense.............	2,400
Cleaning Expense	3,600
Rent Expense	9,000
Depreciation Expense......	8,600
Amortization Expense	600
Employee Benefits	12,050
Interest Expense	5,400
Wages Expense..............	172,140

	$	%
Total Expenses..................	238,990	48.20%
Net Income	$ 0	

Case 9-27 Solution (continued)

What-if Analysis based on Market Share

	Mkt. Share (food)	Mkt. Share (bever.)	Total Sales (year)	Net Income (year)
1	5.00%	5.00%	$67,442	($67,957)
2	5.00%	10.00%	$89,342	($57,402)
3	5.00%	15.00%	$111,241	($46,848)
4	10.00%	5.00%	$112,984	($46,008)
5	5.00%	20.00%	$133,141	($36,293)
6	10.00%	10.00%	$134,884	($35,453)
7	10.00%	15.00%	$156,783	($24,848)
8	15.00%	5.00%	$158,526	($24,058)
9	10.00%	20.00%	$178,683	($14,343)
10	15.00%	10.00%	$180,426	($13,504)
11	15.00%	15.00%	$202,325	($2,999)
12	20.00%	5.00%	$204,068	($2,109)
13	15.00%	20.00%	$224,525	$7,606
14	20.00%	10.00%	$225,968	$8,446
15	15.00%	25.00%	$246,125	$18,161
16	20.00%	15.00%	$247,868	$19,001
17	25.00%	5.00%	$249,610	$19,841
18	20.00%	20.00%	$269,767	$29,556
19	25.00%	10.00%	$271,510	$30,395
20	20.00%	25.00%	$291,667	$40,110
21	25.00%	15.00%	$293,410	$40,950
22	25.00%	20.00%	$315,309	$51,505
23	25.00%	25.00%	$337,209	$62,060
24	30.00%	30.00%	$404,651	$94,564
25	35.00%	35.00%	$472,093	$127,068

Solution adapted with permission
of the Accounting Case Institute

Case 9-27 Solution (continued)

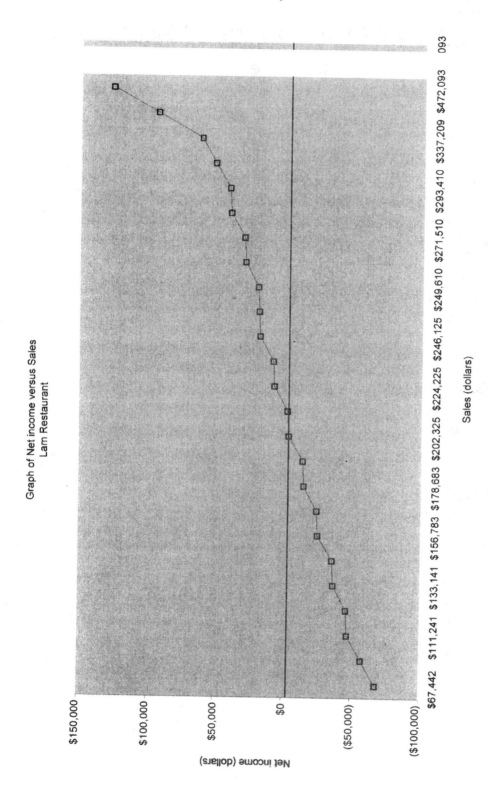

Graph of Net income versus Sales
Lam Restaurant

Managerial Accounting, 6th Canadian Edition

Chapter 10
Standard Costs and the Balanced Scorecard

Exercise 10-1 (20 minutes)

1. Cost per 2 kilogram container .... 6,000.00 Kr
   Less: 2% cash discount .... <u>120.00</u>
   Net cost.. 5,880.00
   Add freight cost per 2 kilogram container
      (1,000 Kr ÷ 10 containers)................................. <u>100.00</u>
   Total cost per 2 kilogram container (a).................... <u>5,980.00</u> Kr
   Number of grams per container
      (2 kilograms × 1000 grams per kilogram) (b)........ <u>2,000</u>
   Standard cost per gram purchased (a) ÷ (b)............ <u>2.99</u> Kr

2. Alpha SR40 required per capsule as per bill of materials .. 6.00 grams
   Add allowance for material rejected as unsuitable
      (6 grams ÷ 0.96 = 6.25 grams;
      6.25 grams − 6.00 grams = 0.25 grams)..................... <u>0.25</u> grams
   Total.. 6.25 grams
   Add allowance for rejected capsules
      (6.25 grams ÷ 25 capsules)................................. <u>0.25</u> grams
   Standard quantity of Alpha SR40 per salable capsule....... <u>6.50</u> grams

3.

Item	Standard Quantity per Capsule	Standard Price per Gram	Standard Cost per Capsule
Alpha SR40	6.50 grams	2.99 Kr	19.435 Kr

Exercise 10-3 (30 minutes)

1. a. Notice in the solution below that the materials price variance is computed on the entire amount of materials purchased, whereas the materials quantity variance is computed only on the amount of materials used in production.

Actual Quantity of Inputs, at Actual Price (AQ × AP)	Actual Quantity of Inputs, at Standard Price (AQ × SP)	Standard Quantity Allowed for Output, at Standard Price (SQ × SP)
70,000 diodes × $0.28 per diode = $19,600	70,000 diodes × $0.30 per diode = $21,000	40,000 diodes* × $0.30 per diode = $12,000

Price Variance,
$1,400 F

50,000 diodes × $0.30 per diode
= $15,000

Quantity Variance,
$3,000 U

*5,000 toys × 8 diodes per toy = 40,000 diodes

Alternative Solution:

Materials Price Variance = AQ (AP − SP)
70,000 diodes ($0.28 per diode − $0.30 per diode) = $1,400 F

Materials Quantity Variance = SP (AQ − SQ)
$0.30 per diode (50,000 diodes − 40,000 diodes) = $3,000 U

Exercise 10-3 (continued)

b. Direct labour variances:

Actual Hours of Input, at the Actual Rate (AH × AR)	Actual Hours of Input, at the Standard Rate (AH × SR)	Standard Hours Allowed for Output, at the Standard Rate (SH × SR)
$48,000	6,400 hours × $7 per hour = $44,800	6,000 hours* × $7 per hour = $42,000

Rate Variance, $3,200 U	Efficiency Variance, $2,800 U

Total Variance, $6,000 U

*5,000 toys × 1.2 hours per toy = 6,000 hours

Alternative Solution:

Labour Rate Variance = AH (AR − SR)
6,400 hours ($7.50* per hour − $7.00 per hour) = $3,200 U
    *$48,000 ÷ 6,400 hours = $7.50 per hour

Labour Efficiency Variance = SR (AH − SH)
$7 per hour (6,400 hours − 6,000 hours) = $2,800 U

Exercise 10-3 (continued)

2. A variance usually has many possible explanations. In particular, we should always keep in mind that the standards themselves may be incorrect. Some of the other possible explanations for the variances observed at Topper Toys appear below:

Materials Price Variance Since this variance is favourable, the actual price paid per unit for the material was less than the standard price. This could occur for a variety of reasons including the purchase of a lower grade material at a discount, buying in an unusually large quantity to take advantage of quantity discounts, a change in the market price of the material, and particularly sharp bargaining by the purchasing department.

Materials Quantity Variance Since this variance is unfavourable, more materials were used to produce the actual output than were called for by the standard. This could also occur for a variety of reasons. Some of the possibilities include poorly trained or supervised workers, improperly adjusted machines, and defective materials.

Labour Rate Variance Since this variance is unfavourable, the actual average wage rate was higher than the standard wage rate. Some of the possible explanations include an increase in wages that has not been reflected in the standards, unanticipated overtime, and a shift toward more highly paid workers.

Labour Efficiency Variance Since this variance is unfavourable, the actual number of labour hours was greater than the standard labour hours allowed for the actual output. As with the other variances, this variance could have been caused by any of a number of factors. Some of the possible explanations include poor supervision, poorly trained workers, low quality materials requiring more labour time to process, and machine breakdowns. In addition, if the direct labour force is essentially fixed, an unfavourable labour efficiency variance could be caused by a reduction in output due to decreased demand for the company's products.

Exercise 10-5 (20 minutes)

1.

Actual Quantity of Inputs, at Actual Price (AQ × AP)	Actual Quantity of Inputs, at Standard Price (AQ × SP)	Standard Quantity Allowed for Output, at Standard Price (SQ × SP)
20,000 grams × $2.40 per gram = $48,000	20,000 grams × $2.50 per gram = $50,000	18,000 grams* × $2.50 per gram = $45,000

Price Variance, $2,000 F	Quantity Variance, $5,000 U
Total Variance, $3,000 U	

*2,500 units × 7.2 grams per unit = 18,000 grams

Alternatively:

Materials Price Variance = AQ (AP − SP)
20,000 grams ($2.40 per gram − $2.50 per gram) = $2,000 F

Materials Quantity Variance = SP (AQ − SQ)
$2.50 per gram (20,000 grams − 18,000 grams) = $5,000 U

Exercise 10-5 (continued)

2.

Actual Hours of Input, at the Actual Rate (AH × AR)	Actual Hours of Input, at the Standard Rate (AH × SR)	Standard Hours Allowed for Output, at the Standard Rate (SH × SR)
$10,800	900 hours × $10 per hour = $9,000	1,000 hours* × $10 per hour = $10,000

Rate Variance, $1,800 U	Efficiency Variance, $1,000 F
Total Variance, $800 U	

*2,500 units × 0.4 hour per unit = 1,000 hours

Alternatively:

Labour Rate Variance = AH (AR − SR)
900 hours ($12 per hour* − $10 per hour) = $1,800 U
*10,800 ÷ 900 hours = $12 per hour

Labour Efficiency Variance = SR (AH − SH)
$10 per hour (900 hours − 1,000 hours) = 1,000 F

Exercise 10-7 (20 minutes)

1. If the total variance is $330 unfavourable, and if the rate variance is $150 favourable, then the efficiency variance must be $480 unfavourable, since the rate and efficiency variances taken together always equal the total variance.

   Knowing that the efficiency variance is $480 unfavourable, one approach to the solution would be:

   > Efficiency Variance = SR (AH − SH)
   > $6 per hour (AH − 420 hours*) = $480 U
   > $6 per hour × AH − $2,520 = $480**
   > $6 per hour × AH = $3,000
   > AH = 500 hours

   > * 168 batches × 2.5 hours per batch = 420 hours
   > ** When used with the formula, unfavourable variances are positive and favourable variances are negative.

2. Knowing that 500 hours of labour time were used during the week, the actual rate of pay per hour can be computed as follows:

   > Rate Variance = AH (AR − SR)
   > 500 hours (AR − $6 per hour) = $150 F
   > 500 hours × AR − $3,000 = -$150*
   > 500 hours × AR = $2,850
   > AR = $5.70 per hour

   > * When used with the formula, unfavourable variances are positive and favourable variances are negative.

Exercise 10-7 (continued)

An alternative approach to each solution would be to work from known to unknown data in the columnar model for variance analysis:

Actual Hours of Input, at the Actual Rate (AH × AR)	Actual Hours of Input, at the Standard Rate (AH × SR)	Standard Hours Allowed for Output, at the Standard Rate (SH × SR)
500 hours × $5.70 per hour = $2,850	500 hours × $6 per hour* = $3,000	420 hours§ × $6 per hour* = $2,520

Rate Variance, $150 F*	Efficiency Variance, $480 U
Total Variance, $330 U*	

§168 batches × 2.5 hours per batch = 420 hours
*Given

Managerial Accounting, 6th Canadian Edition

Exercise 10-9 (45 minutes)

1. a.

Actual Quantity of Inputs, at Actual Price (AQ × AP)	Actual Quantity of Inputs, at Standard Price (AQ × SP)	Standard Quantity Allowed for Output, at Standard Price (SQ × SP)
7,000 metres × $5.75 per metre = $40,250	7,000 metres × $6.00 per metre = $42,000	5,250 metres* × $6.00 per metre = $31,500

Price Variance, $1,750 F

6,000 metres × $6.00 per metre = $36,000

Quantity Variance, $4,500 U

*1,500 units × 3.5 metres per unit = 5,250 metres

Alternatively:

Materials Price Variance = AQ (AP − SP)
7,000 metres ($5.75 per metre − $6.00 per metre) = $1,750 F

Materials Quantity Variance = SP (AQ − SQ)
$6.00 per metre (6,000 metres − 5,250 metres) = $4,500 U

Exercise 10-9 (continued)

b. The journal entries would be:

Raw Materials (7,000 metres × $6 per metre)......... 42,000
    Materials Price Variance
      (7,000 metres × $0.25 F per metre)..............   1,750
    Accounts Payable
      (7,000 metres × $5.75 per metre).................   40,250

Work in Process (5,250 metres × $6 per metre) 31,500
Materials Quantity Variance
    (750 metres U × $6 per metre)......................... 4,500
      Raw Materials (6,000 metres × $6 per metre) ...   36,000

2. a.

Actual Hours of Input, at the Actual Rate (AH × AR)	Actual Hours of Input, at the Standard Rate (AH × SR)	Standard Hours Allowed for Output, at the Standard Rate (SH × SR)
$8,120	725 hours × $10 per hour = $7,250	600 hours* × $10 per hour = $6,000

Rate Variance, $870 U	Efficiency Variance, $1,250 U	
Total Variance, $2,120 U		

*1,500 units × 0.4 hour per unit = 600 hours

Alternatively:

Labour Rate Variance = AH (AR − SR)
725 hours ($11.20 per hour* − $10.00 per hour) = $870 U
*$8,120 ÷ 725 hours = $11.20 per hour

Labour Efficiency Variance = SR (AH − SH)
$10 per hour (725 hours − 600 hours) = $1,250 U

Exercise 10-9 (continued)

b. The journal entry would be:

Work in Process (600 hours × $10 per hour) 6,000
Labour Rate Variance
   (725 hours × $1.20 U per hour)........................... 870
Labour Efficiency Variance
   (125 U hours × $10 per hour).............................. 1,250
      Wages Payable (725 hours × $11.20 per hour)..... 8,120

3. The entries are: (a) purchase of materials; (b) issue of materials to production; and (c) incurrence of direct labour cost.

Raw Materials				Accounts Payable		
(a)	42,000	36,000	(b)		40,250	(a)
Bal.	6,000[1]					

Materials Price Variance				Wages Payable		
		1,750	(a)		8,120	(c)

Materials Quantity Variance				Labour Rate Variance		
(b)	4,500			(c)	870	

Work in Process				Labour Efficiency Variance		
(b)	31,500[2]			(c)	1,250	
(c)	6,000[3]					

[1]1,000 metres of material at a standard cost of $6.00 per metre
[2]Materials used
[3]Labour cost

Problem 10-11 (45 minutes)

1. The standard quantity of plates allowed for tests performed during the month would be:

Smears	2,700
Blood tests...............................	900
Total	3,600
Plates per test	× 3
Standard quantity allowed.........	10,800

The variance analysis for plates would be:

Actual Quantity of Inputs, at Actual Price (AQ × AP)	Actual Quantity of Inputs, at Standard Price (AQ × SP)	Standard Quantity Allowed for Output, at Standard Price (SQ × SP)
$38,400	16,000 plates × $2.50 per plate = $40,000	10,800 plates × $2.50 per plate = $27,000

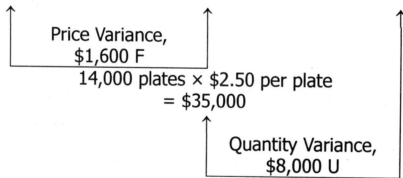

Price Variance,
$1,600 F

14,000 plates × $2.50 per plate
= $35,000

Quantity Variance,
$8,000 U

Alternative Solution:

Materials Price Variance = AQ (AP − SP)
16,000 plates ($2.40 per plate* − $2.50 per plate) = $1,600 F
  *$38,400 ÷ 16,000 plates = $2.40 per plate.

Materials Quantity Variance = SP (AQ − SQ)
$2.50 per plate (14,000 plates − 10,800 plates) = $8,000 U

Problem 10-11 (continued)

Note that all of the price variance is due to the clinic's 4% quantity discount. Also note that the $8,000 quantity variance for the month is equal to nearly 30% of the standard cost allowed for plates. This variance may be the result of using too many assistants in the lab.

2. a. The standard hours allowed for tests performed during the month would be:

Smears: 0.3 hour per test × 2,700 tests.......	810
Blood tests: 0.6 hour per test × 900 tests....	540
Total standard hours allowed......................	1,350

The variance analysis of labour would be:

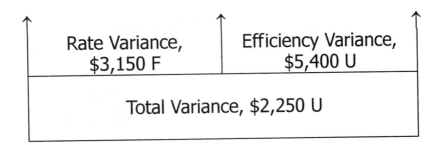

Actual Hours of Input, at the Actual Rate (AH × AR)	Actual Hours of Input, at the Standard Rate (AH × SR)	Standard Hours Allowed for Output, at the Standard Rate (SH × SR)
$18,450	1,800 hours × $12 per hour = $21,600	1,350 hours × $12 per hour = $16,200

Rate Variance, $3,150 F	Efficiency Variance, $5,400 U
Total Variance, $2,250 U	

Alternative Solution:

Labour Rate Variance = AH (AR − SR)
1,800 hours ($10.25 per hour* − $12.00 per hour) = $3,150 F
   *$18,450 ÷ 1,800 hours = $10.25 per hour

Labour Efficiency Variance = SR (AH − SH)
$12 per hour (1,800 hours − 1,350 hours) = $5,400 U

Problem 10-11 (continued)

  b. The policy probably should not be continued. Although the hospital is saving $1.75 per hour by employing more assistants relative to the number of senior technicians than other clinics, this savings is more than offset by other factors. Too much time is being taken in performing lab tests, as indicated by the large unfavourable labour efficiency variance. And, it seems likely that most (or all) of the hospital's unfavourable quantity variance for plates is traceable to inadequate supervision of assistants in the lab.

3. The variable overhead variances follow:

Actual Hours of Input, at the Actual Rate (AH × AR)	Actual Hours of Input, at the Standard Rate (AH × SR)	Standard Hours Allowed for Output, at the Standard Rate (SH × SR)
$11,700	1,800 hours × $6 per hour = $10,800	1,350 hours × $6 per hour = $8,100

Spending Variance, $900 U	Efficiency Variance, $2,700 U
Total Variance, $3,600 U	

Alternative Solution:

  Variable Overhead Spending Variance = AH (AR − SR)
  1,800 hours ($6.50 per hour* − $6.00 per hour) = $900 U
    *$11,700 ÷ 1,800 hours = $6.50 per hour

  Variable Overhead Efficiency Variance = SR (AH − SH)
  $6 per hour (1,800 hours − 1,350 hours) = $2,700 U

Yes, the two variances are related. Both are computed by comparing actual labour time to the standard hours allowed for the output of the period. Thus, if there is an unfavourable labour efficiency variance, there will also be an unfavourable variable overhead efficiency variance.

Problem 10-13 (45 minutes)

1. a.

Actual Quantity of Inputs, at Actual Price (AQ × AP)	Actual Quantity of Inputs, at Standard Price (AQ × SP)	Standard Quantity Allowed for Output, at Standard Price (SQ × SP)
25,000 kilograms × $2.95 per kilogram = $73,750	25,000 kilograms × $2.50 per kilogram = $62,500	20,000 kilograms* × $2.50 per kilogram = $50,000

Price Variance,
$11,250 U

19,800 kilograms × $2.50 per kilogram
= $49,500

Quantity Variance,
$500 F

*5,000 ingots × 4.0 kilograms per ingot = 20,000 kilograms

Alternatively:

Materials Price Variance = AQ (AP − SP)
25,000 kilograms ($2.95 per kilogram − $2.50 per kilogram) =
$11,250 U

Materials Quantity Variance = SP (AQ − SQ)
$2.50 per kilogram (19,800 kilograms − 20,000 kilograms) = $500 F

Problem 10-13 (continued)

b.

Actual Hours of Input, at the Actual Rate (AH × AR)	Actual Hours of Input, at the Standard Rate (AH × SR)	Standard Hours Allowed for Output, at the Standard Rate (SH × SR)
3,600 hours × $8.70 per hour = $31,320	3,600 hours × $9.00 per hour = $32,400	3,000 hours* × $9.00 per hour = $27,000

Rate Variance, $1,080 F	Efficiency Variance, $5,400 U
Total Variance, $4,320 U	

*5,000 ingots × 0.6 hour per ingot = 3,000 hours

Alternatively:

Labour Rate Variance = AH (AR − SR)
3,600 hours ($8.70 per hour − $9.00 per hour) = $1,080 F

Labour Efficiency Variance = SR (AH − SH)
$9.00 per hour (3,600 hours − 3,000 hours) = $5,400 U

Problem 10-13 (continued)

C.

Actual Hours of Input, at the Actual Rate (AH × AR)	Actual Hours of Input, at the Standard Rate (AH × SR)	Standard Hours Allowed for Output, at the Standard Rate (SH × SR)
$4,320	1,800 hours × $2.00 per hour = $3,600	1,500 hours* × $2.00 per hour = $3,000

Spending Variance, $720 U	Efficiency Variance, $600 U
Total Variance, $1,320 U	

*5,000 ingots × 0.3 hours per ingot = 1,500 hours

Alternatively:

Variable Overhead Spending Variance = AH (AR − SR)
1,800 hours ($2.40 per hour* − $2.00 per hour) = $720 U
 *$4,320 ÷ 1,800 hours = $2.40 per hour

Variable Overhead Efficiency Variance = SR (AH − SH)
$2.00 per hour (1,800 hours − 1,500 hours) = $600 U

Problem 10-13 (continued)

2. Summary of variances:

Material price variance............................	$11,250	U
Material quantity variance........................	500	F
Labour rate variance	1,080	F
Labour efficiency variance	5,400	U
Variable overhead spending variance.........	720	U
Variable overhead efficiency variance........	600	U
Net variance	$16,390	U

The net unfavourable variance of $16,390 for the month caused the plant's variable cost of goods sold to increase from the budgeted level of $80,000 to $96,390:

Budgeted cost of goods sold at $16 per ingot	$80,000
Add the net unfavourable variance (as above)	16,390
Actual cost of goods sold.....................................	$96,390

This $16,390 net unfavourable variance also accounts for the difference between the budgeted net operating income and the actual net loss for the month.

Budgeted net operating income..............................	$15,000
Deduct the net unfavourable variance added to cost of goods sold for the month.........................	16,390
Net operating loss..	$(1,390)

3. The two most significant variances are the materials price variance and the labour efficiency variance. Possible causes of the variances include:

Materials Price Variance:	Outdated standards, uneconomical quantity purchased, higher quality materials, high-cost method of transport.
Labour Efficiency Variance:	Poorly trained workers, poor quality materials, faulty equipment, work interruptions, inaccurate standards, insufficient demand.

Problem 10-15 (20 minutes)

1. Lanolin quantity standard:
Required per 100-litre batch	100 litres
Loss from rejected batches (100 litres × 1/20)	5 litres
Total quantity per good batch	105 litres

   Alcohol quantity standard:
Required per 100-litre batch	8.0 litres
Loss from rejected batches (8 litres × 1/20)	0.4 litres
Total quantity per good batch	8.4 litres

   Lilac powder quantity standard:
Required per 100-litre batch	200 grams
Loss from rejected batches (200 grams × 1/20) ...	10 grams
Total quantity per good batch	210 grams

2. Direct labour quantity standard:
Total hours per day	8 hours
Less lunch, rest breaks, and cleanup	2 hours
Productive time each day	6 hours

   $$\frac{\text{Productive time each day}}{\text{Time required per batch}} = \frac{6 \text{ hours per day}}{2 \text{ hours per batch}} = 3 \text{ batches per day}$$

Time required per batch	120 minutes
Lunch, rest breaks, and cleanup (120 minutes ÷ 3 batches)	40 minutes
Total	160 minutes
Loss from rejected batches (160 minutes × 1/20)	8 minutes
Total time per good batch	168 minutes

Problem 10-15 (continued)

3. Standard cost card:

	Standard Quantity or Time per Batch	Standard Price or Rate	Standard Cost per Batch
Lanolin	105 litres	€16 per litre	€1,680.00
Alcohol	8.4 litres	€2 per litre	16.80
Lilac powder	210 grams	€1 per gram	210.00
Direct labour..............	168 minutes	€0.20 per minute	33.60
Total standard cost per good batch........			€1,940.40

Managerial Accounting, 6th Canadian Edition

Problem 10-17 (30 minutes)

1. a. Materials Price Variance = AQ (AP − SP)
   6,000 kilograms ($2.75 per kilogram* − SP) = $1,500 F**
   $16,500 − 6,000 kilograms × SP = $1,500***
   6,000 kilograms × SP = $18,000
   SP = $3 per kilogram

   *$16,500 ÷ 6,000 kilograms = $2.75 per kilogram
   **$1,200 U + ? = $300 F; $1,200 U + $1,500 F = $300 F.
   ***When used with the formula, unfavourable variances are positive and favourable variances are negative.

   b. Materials Quantity Variance = SP (AQ − SQ)
   $3 per kilogram (6,000 kilograms − SQ) = $1,200 U
   $18,000 − $3 per kilogram × SQ = $1,200*
   $3 per kilogram × SQ = $16,800
   SQ = 5,600 kilograms

   *When used with the formula, unfavourable variances are positive and favourable variances are negative.

   Alternative approach to parts (a) and (b):

Actual Quantity of Inputs, at Actual Price (AQ × AP)	Actual Quantity of Inputs, at Standard Price (AQ × SP)	Standard Quantity Allowed for Output, at Standard Price (SQ × SP)
$16,500*	6,000 kilograms* × $3 per kilogram = $18,000	5,600 kilograms × $3 per kilogram = $16,800

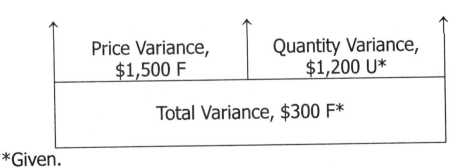

Price Variance, $1,500 F   Quantity Variance, $1,200 U*

Total Variance, $300 F*

   *Given.

   c. 5,600 kilograms ÷ 1,400 units = 4 kilograms per unit.

Problem 10-17 (continued)

2. a. Labour Efficiency Variance = SR (AH − SH)
$9 per hour (AH − 3,500 hours*) = $4,500 F
$9 per hour × AH − $31,500 = −$4,500**
$9 per hour × AH = $27,000
AH = 3,000 hours

> *1,400 units × 2.5 hours per unit = 3,500 hours
> **When used with the formula, unfavourable variances are positive and favourable variances are negative.

b. Labour Rate Variance = AH (AR − SR)
3,000 hours ($9.50 per hour* − $9.00 per hour) = $1,500 U

Alternative approach to parts (a) and (b):

Actual Hours of Input, at the Actual Rate (AH × AR)	Actual Hours of Input, at the Standard Rate (AH × SR)	Standard Hours Allowed for Output, at the Standard Rate (SH × SR)
3,000 hours × $9.50 per hour* = $28,500*	3,000 hours × $9.00 per hour** = $27,000	3,500 hours*** × $9.00 per hour** = $31,500

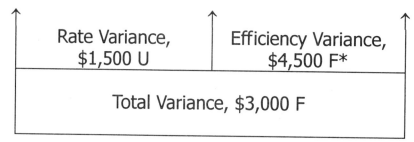

Rate Variance, $1,500 U	Efficiency Variance, $4,500 F*
Total Variance, $3,000 F	

> * $28,500 total labour cost ÷ 3,000 hours = $9.50 per hour
> ** Given
> *** 1,400 units × 2.5 hours per unit = 3,500 hours

Problem 10-19 (40 minutes)

1. Standard direct labour rate per hour:
   Actual direct labour cost .... $ 123,200
      Direct labour rate variance (unfavourable) .... (3,200)
   Actual direct labour cost at standard rate.................. 120,000
   Actual direct labour hours .... ÷ 7,500
   Standard direct labour rate per hour......................... $ 16

2. Standard direct labour cost per unit:
   Standard direct labour rate per hour [from part
      (a)]... $ 16
   Standard direct labour hours per unit .... ×   5
   Standard direct labour cost per unit........................... $ 80

3. Number of units produced:
   Actual direct labour cost at standard
      [from part (a)] $120,000
   Direct labour efficiency variance (favourable) 4,000
   Standard direct labour cost at standard rate.............. 124,000
   Standard direct labour rate per hour[from part (a)] ... ÷   16

   Standard direct labour hours..................................... 7,750
   Standard direct labour hours per unit .... ÷   5
   Number of units produced 1,550

4. Standard variable overhead cost per unit:
   Standard variable overhead cost per direct labour
      hour... $8
   Standard direct labour per unit.................................. ×   5
   Standard variable overhead per unit........................... $ 40

Problem 10-19 (continued)

5. Variable overhead spending variance:

Standard variable overhead cost per direct labour hour	$8
Actual direct labour hours...	× 7,500
Actual variable overhead cost at standard rate..............	60,000
Actual variable overhead cost	64,300
Variable overhead spending variance(unfavourable).........	$(4,300)

6. Direct materials usage variance:

Actual direct cost for 10,000 kilogram	$ 13,000
Direct materials price variance (unfavourable)	(500)
Standard cost of materials purchased...........................	12,500
Kilograms purchased	÷ 10,000
Standard cost of materials per kilogram	$ 1.25
Standard cost of materials per unit	$ 7.50
Standard cost of materials per kilogram(from above)	÷ 1.25
Standard kilograms used per unit...................................	6
Number of units produced [from part (c)].......................	× 1,550
Standard direct materials used (kilograms)	9,300
Actual direct materials used (kilograms)	9,000
Direct materials usage variance in kilograms(favourable)..	300
Standard cost of materials per kilogram(from above)	× 1.25
Direct materials usage variance (favourable)	$ 375

7. Variable overhead efficiency variance:

Standard direct labour hours [from part (c)].................	7,750
Actual direct labour hours...	7,500
Variable overhead efficiency variance in hours..............	250 F
Standard variable overhead cost per DL$	×$ 8
Variable overhead efficiency variance (favourable)...........	$ 2,000

CGA -Adapted

Managerial Accounting, 6th Canadian Edition

Problem 10-21 (60 minutes)

a. i.

Material	Actual Cost	Standard Cost	Price Variances
Alpha..........................	$325,565	$2 x 159,000	$5,565 U
Beta	290,102	$4 x 72,000	2,102 U
Gamma......................	435,000	$10 x 44,000	5,000 F
			$2,667 U

ii.

Material	Standard Cost x Actual Usage	Standard Cost x Standard Usage at Standard Mix*	Usage Variance
Alpha.......	$2 x 159,000 = $318,000	$2 x 140,000	$38,000 U
Beta	$4 x 72,000 = $288,000	$4 x 70,000	8,000 U
Gamma....	$10 x 44,000 = $440,000	$10 x 52,500	85,000 F
	275,000	262,500	$39,000 F

Actual Production (litres)	175,000
X Standard input per litre (150 ÷ 100)	1.5
Total standard litres of input	262,500

*Standard usage at standard mix:
   Alpha   80/150 x 262,000 = 140,000
   Beta   40/150 x 262,500 = 70,000
   Gamma 30/150 x 262,500 = 52,500

Problem 10-21 (continued)

iii.

Actual Quantity	Actual Quantity at standard Proportions	Difference × Standard Cost	Mix Variance
159,000	146,6667 (80 / 150)	$2 x 12,333 U	$24,666 U
72,000	73,333 (40 / 150)	$4 x 1,333 F	5,332 F
44,000	55,000 (30 / 150)	$10 x 11,000 F	110,000 F
275,000	275,000	-0-	$90,666 F

iv.
Actual yield (litres)........................... 175,000.00
Standard yield 183,333.33
(275,000 litres × 100 ÷ 150)
Difference .... (8,333.33)
× Cost per litre of output*................. $6.20
Yield variance.................................. $51,666.65 U

$$\frac{*(80 \times \$2) + (40 \times \$4) + (30 \times \$10)}{100} = \$6.20 \text{ / litre}$$

Check: Mix variance......................... $ 90,666 F
Yield variance................................. 51,666 U
Usage variance............................... $ 39,000 F

b. Labour efficiency variance:
[91,000 hrs − (50 hours ÷ 100 litres × 175,000)] × $15.00= $52,500U

Part of actual labour hours were used to transform the material that became part of the output yield loss. That amount is equal to:

½ hr. × (8,333 litres × $15 = $62,500 U)

Therefore, the production foreman is correct in arguing that his workers are operating *better* than standard.

(SMAC Solution, adapted)

Problem 10-23 (60 minutes)

1. a.

Actual Quantity of Inputs, at Actual Price (AQ × AP)	Actual Quantity of Inputs, at Standard Price (AQ × SP)	Standard Quantity Allowed for Output, at Standard Price (SQ × SP)
60,000 metres × $0.95 per metre = $57,000	60,000 metres × $1.00 per metre = $60,000	36,000 metres* × $1.00 per metre = $36,000

Price Variance, $3,000 F

38,000 metres × $1.00 per metre = $38,000

Quantity Variance, $2,000 U

*6,000 units × 6.0 metres per unit = 36,000 metres

Alternative approach:

Materials Price Variance = AQ (AP − SP)
60,000 metres ($0.95 per metre − $1.00 per metre) = $3,000 F

Materials Quantity Variance = SP (AQ − SQ)
$1.00 per metre (38,000 metres − 36,000 metres) = $2,000 U

b. Raw Materials (60,000 metres @ $1.00 per metre)... 60,000
   Materials Price Variance
      (60,000 metres @ $0.05 per metre F)............. 3,000
   Accounts Payable
      (60,000 metres @ $0.95 per metre) 57,000

   Work in Process (36,000 metres @ $1.00 per
      metre) 36,000
   Materials Quantity Variance
      (2,000 metres U @ $1.00 per metre) 2,000
      Raw Materials (38,000 metres @ $1.00 per
         metre) 38,000

Problem 10-23 (continued)

2. a.

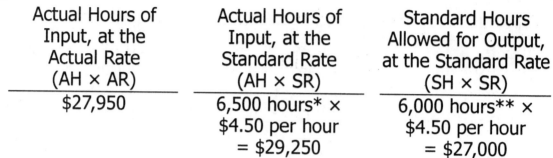

Actual Hours of Input, at the Actual Rate (AH × AR)	Actual Hours of Input, at the Standard Rate (AH × SR)	Standard Hours Allowed for Output, at the Standard Rate (SH × SR)
$27,950	6,500 hours* × $4.50 per hour = $29,250	6,000 hours** × $4.50 per hour = $27,000

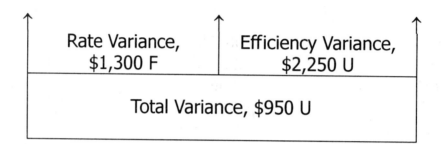

Rate Variance, $1,300 F	Efficiency Variance, $2,250 U
Total Variance, $950 U	

*The actual hours worked during the period can be computed through the variable overhead efficiency variance, as follows:

SR (AH − SH) = Efficiency Variance
$3 per hour (AH − 6,000 hours**) = $1,500 U
$3 per hour × AH − $18,000 = $1,500***
$3 per hour × AH = $19,500
AH = 6,500 hours

**6,000 units × 1.0 hour per unit = 6,000 hours
***When used with the formula, unfavourable variances are positive and favourable variances are negative.

Alternative approach:

Labour Rate Variance = AH × (AR − SR)
6,500 hours ($4.30 per hour* − $4.50 per hour) = $1,300 F

*$27,950 ÷ 6,500 hours = $4.30 per hour

Labour Efficiency Variance = SR (AH − SH)
$4.50 per hour (6,500 hours − 6,000 hours) = $2,250 U

Problem 10-23 (continued)

b. Work in Process
  (6,000 hours @ $4.50 per hour) 27,000
  Labour Efficiency Variance
  (500 hours U @ $4.50 per hour)...................... 2,250
    Labour Rate Variance
    (6,500 hours @ $0.20 per hour F) 1,300
    Wages Payable
    (6,500 hours @ $4.30 per hour) 27,950

3. a.

Actual Hours of Input, at the Actual Rate (AH × AR)	Actual Hours of Input, at the Standard Rate (AH × SR)	Standard Hours Allowed for Output, at the Standard Rate (SH × SR)
$20,475	6,500 hours × $3.00 per hour = $19,500	6,000 hours × $3.00 per hour = $18,000

Spending Variance, $975 U	Efficiency Variance, $1,500 U
Total Variance, $2,475 U	

Alternative approach:

Variable Overhead Spending Variance = AH × (AR − SR)
6,500 hours ($3.15 per hour* − $3.00 per hour) = $975 U

*$20,475 ÷ 6,500 hours = $3.15 per hour

Variable Overhead Efficiency Variance = SR (AH − SH)
$3.00 per hour (6,500 hours − 6,000 hours) = $1,500 U

Problem 10-23 (continued)

b. No. When variable manufacturing overhead is applied on the basis of direct labour-hours, it is impossible to have an unfavourable variable manufacturing overhead efficiency variance when the direct labour efficiency variance is favourable. The variable manufacturing overhead efficiency variance is the same as the direct labour efficiency variance except that the difference between actual hours and the standard hours allowed for the output is multiplied by a different rate. If the direct labour efficiency variance is favourable, the variable manufacturing overhead efficiency variance must also be favourable.

4: *For materials:*

Favourable price variance: Decrease in outside purchase prices, fortunate buy, inferior quality materials, unusual discounts due to quantity purchased, inaccurate standards.

Unfavourable quantity variance: Inferior quality materials, carelessness, poorly adjusted machines, unskilled workers, inaccurate standards.

For labour:

Favourable rate variance: Unskilled workers (paid lower rates), piecework, inaccurate standards.

Unfavourable efficiency variance: Poorly trained workers, poor quality materials, faulty equipment, work interruptions, fixed labour with insufficient demand to keep them all busy, inaccurate standards.

For variable overhead:

Unfavourable spending variance: Increase in supplier prices, inaccurate standards, waste, theft of supplies.

Unfavourable efficiency variance: See comments under direct labour efficiency variance.

Managerial Accounting, 6th Canadian Edition

Problem 10-25 (45 minutes)

The answers below are not the only possible answers. Ingenious people can figure out many different ways of making performance look better even though it really isn't. This is one of the reasons for a *balanced scorecard*. By having a number of different measures that ultimately are linked to overall financial goals, there will be less opportunity to "game" the system.

1. Speed-to-market can be improved by taking on less ambitious projects. Instead of working on major product innovations that require a great deal of time and effort, R&D may choose to work on small, incremental improvements in existing products. There is also a danger that in the rush to push products out the door, the products will be inadequately tested and developed.

2. Performance measures that are ratios or percentages present special dangers. A ratio can be increased either by increasing the numerator or by decreasing the denominator. Usually, the intention is to increase the numerator in the ratio, but a manager may react by decreasing the denominator instead. In this case (which actually happened), the managers pulled telephones out of the high-crime areas. This eliminated the problem for the managers, but was not what the CEO or the city officials had intended. They wanted the phones fixed, not eliminated.

3. In real life, the production manager simply added several weeks to the delivery cycle time. In other words, instead of promising to deliver an order in four weeks, the manager promised to deliver in six weeks. This increase in delivery cycle time did not, of course, please customers and drove some business away, but it dramatically improved the percentage of orders delivered on time.

Problem 10-25 (continued)

4. As stated above, ratios can be improved by changing either the numerator or the denominator. Managers who are under pressure to increase the revenue per employee may find it easier to eliminate employees than to increase revenues. Of course, eliminating employees may reduce total revenues and total profits, but the revenue per employee will increase as long as the percentage decline in revenues is less than the percentage cut in number of employees. Suppose, for example, that a manager is responsible for business units with a total of 1,000 employees, $120 million in revenues, and profits of $2 million. Further suppose that a manager can eliminate one of these business units that has 200 employees, revenues of $10 million, and profits of $1.2 million.

	Before eliminating the business unit	After eliminating the business unit
Total revenue................	$120,000,000	$110,000,000
Total employees............	1,000	800
Revenue per employee...................	$120,000	$137,500
Total profits.................	$2,000,000	$800,000

As these examples illustrate, performance measures should be selected with a great deal of care and managers should avoid placing too much emphasis on any one performance measure.

Problem 10-27 (45 minutes)

1. Students' answers may differ in some details from this solution.

+

2. The hypotheses underlying the balanced scorecard are indicated by the arrows in the diagram. Reading from the bottom of the balanced scorecard, the hypotheses are:
   o If the percentage of dining room staff who complete the hospitality course increases, then the average time to take an order will decrease.
   o If the percentage of dining room staff who complete the hospitality course increases, then dining room cleanliness will improve.
   o If the percentage of kitchen staff who complete the cooking course increases, then the average time to prepare an order will decrease.
   o If the percentage of kitchen staff who complete the cooking course increases, then the number of menu items will increase.
   o If the dining room cleanliness improves, then customer satisfaction with service will increase.
   o If the average time to take an order decreases, then customer satisfaction with service will increase.
   o If the average time to prepare an order decreases, then customer satisfaction with service will increase.
   o If the number of menu items increases, then customer satisfaction with menu choices will increase.
   o If customer satisfaction with service increases, sales will increase.
   o If customer satisfaction with menu choices increases, sales will increase.
   o If sales increase, total profits for the Lodge will increase.
   Each of these hypotheses is questionable to some degree. For example, even if the number of menu items increases, customer satisfaction with the menu choices may not increase. The items added to the menu may not appeal to customers. The fact that each of the hypotheses can be questioned does not, however, invalidate the balanced scorecard. If the scorecard is used correctly, management will be able to identify which, if any, of the hypotheses is incorrect. [See below.]

Problem 10-27 (continued)

3. Management will be able to tell if a hypothesis is false if an improvement in a performance measure at the bottom of an arrow does not, in fact, lead to improvement in the performance measure at the tip of the arrow. For example, if the number of menu items is increased, but customer satisfaction with the menu choices does not increase, management will immediately know that something was wrong with their assumptions.

Problem 10-29 (45 minutes)

This is a very difficult problem that is harder than it looks. Be sure your students have been thoroughly "checked out" in the variance formulas before assigning it.

1.

Actual Quantity of Inputs, at Actual Price (AQ × AP)	Actual Quantity of Inputs, at Standard Price (AQ × SP)	Standard Quantity Allowed for Output, at Standard Price (SQ × SP)
$36,000	6,000 metres × $6.50 per metre* = $39,000	5,600 metres** × $6.50 per metre* = $36,400

Price Variance, $3,000 F	Quantity Variance, $2,600 U

Total Variance, $400 F

  *$18.20 ÷ 2.8 metres = $6.50 per metre.
**2,000 units × 2.8 metres per unit = 5,600 metres

Alternative Solution:

Materials Price Variance = AQ (AP − SP)
6,000 metres ($6.00 per metre* − $6.50 per metre) = $3,000 F
  *$36,000 ÷ 6,000 metres = $6.00 per metre

Materials Quantity Variance = SP (AQ − SQ)
$6.50 per metre (6,000 metres − 5,600 metres) = $2,600 U

Problem 10-29 (continued)

2. Many students will miss parts 2 and 3 because they will try to use *product* costs as if they were *hourly* costs. Pay particular attention to the computation of the standard direct labour time per unit and the standard direct labour rate per hour.

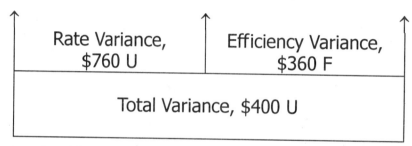

Actual Hours of Input, at the Actual Rate (AH × AR)	Actual Hours of Input, at the Standard Rate (AH × SR)	Standard Hours Allowed for Output, at the Standard Rate (SH × SR)
$7,600	760 hours × $9 per hour* = $6,840	800 hours** × $9 per hour* = $7,200

Rate Variance, $760 U	Efficiency Variance, $360 F

Total Variance, $400 U

* 780 standard hours ÷ 1,950 robes = 0.4 standard hour per robe.
$3.60 standard cost per robe ÷ 0.4 standard hours = $9 standard rate per hour.
** 2,000 robes × 0.4 standard hour per robe = 800 standard hours.

Alternative Solution:

Labour Rate Variance = AH (AR − SR)
760 hours ($10 per hour* − $9 per hour) = $760 U
 *$7,600 ÷ 760 hours = $10 per hour

Labour Efficiency Variance = SR (AH − SH)
$9 per hour (760 hours − 800 hours) = $360 F

Problem 10-29 (continued)

3.

Actual Hours of Input, at the Actual Rate (AH × AR)	Actual Hours of Input, at the Standard Rate (AH × SR)	Standard Hours Allowed for Output, at the Standard Rate (SH × SR)
$3,800	760 hours × $3 per hour* = $2,280	800 hours × $3 per hour* = $2,400

Spending Variance, $1,520 U	Efficiency Variance, $120 F

Total Variance, $1,400 U

*$1.20 standard cost per robe ÷ 0.4 standard hours = $3 standard rate per hour.

Alternative Solution:

Variable Overhead Spending Variance = AH (AR − SR)
760 hours ($5 per hour* − $3 per hour) = $1,520 U
   *$3,800 ÷ 760 hours = $5 per hour

Variable Overhead Efficiency Variance = SR (AH − SH)
$3 per hour (760 hours − 800 hours) = $120 F

Problem 10-31 (30 minutes)

1. The total hours for 1,600 units
   (1.344 x .80) 1,600 = 1,720.32 or 1,732 hours

2. The incremental assembly costs would be 1,720 x $15 = $25,800
   Less: (800 x 1.344) xx $15.................................... <u>16,128</u>
   Incremental cost of 800 .... <u>$ 9,672</u>

3.

	Y	Log Y	Q	Log Q
High	1075.2	3.0315	800	2.9031
Low	420.0	2.6232	200	2.3010

Formula for Linear Form:

Log Y = Log a + (b + 1) Log Q

(b +1) = (difference in Log Y)/(difference in Log Q)
$\qquad$ = (3.0315 - 2.6232)/ (2.9031 - 2.3010)
$\qquad$ = .4083/.6021 = .6781

Log a = Log Y - (b+1) Log Q
$\qquad$ = 3.0315 - .6781 (2.9031)
$\qquad$ = 3.0315 - 1.9686
$\qquad$ = 1.0629
$\quad$ a = $10^{1.0629}$ = 11.5585

Formula is:
$\qquad$ Y = (11.5585) $Q^{0.6781}$

Problem 10-31 (continued)

4. Total hours to produce 1,600:
$Y = 11.5585(1,600)^{0.6781} = 1,720.34$

Total hours to produce 1,700:
$Y = 11.5585 (1,700)^{0.6781} = 1,792.54$

Time to produce additional 100:
$1,792.54 - 1,720.34 = 72.20$ hours or 0.7220 hours per unit

The actual time was 0.90 hours per unit while the curve suggests 0.7220 per unit for the last 100 units. The deviation could result from inefficiency by the work force that is approaching the end of the contract.

The deviation could result because of deficient materials or poorly maintained equipment. The difference could also be caused because of inaccuracies in the estimates.

Case 10-33 (30 minutes)

This case, which is based on an actual situation, may be difficult for some students to grasp since it requires looking at standard costs from an entirely different perspective. In this case, standard costs have been inappropriately used as a means to manipulate reported earnings rather than as a way to control costs.

1. Lansing has evidently set very loose standards in which the standard prices and standard quantities are far too high. This will guarantee that favourable variances will ordinarily result from operations. If the standard costs are set artificially high, the standard cost of goods sold will be artificially high and thus the division's net operating income will be depressed until the favourable variances are recognized. If Lansing saves the favourable variances, he can release just enough in the second and third quarters to show some improvement and then he can release all of the rest in the last quarter, creating the annual "Christmas present."

2. Lansing should not be permitted to continue this practice for several reasons. First, it distorts the quarterly earnings for both the division and the company. The distortions of the division's quarterly earnings are troubling because the manipulations may mask real signs of trouble. The distortions of the company's quarterly earnings are troubling because they may mislead external users of the financial statements. Second, Lansing should not be rewarded for manipulating earnings. This sets a moral tone in the company that is likely to lead to even deeper trouble. Indeed, the permissive attitude of top management toward manipulation of earnings may indicate the existence of other, even more serious, ethical problems in the company. Third, a clear message should be sent to division managers like Lansing that their job is to manage their operations, not their earnings. If they keep on top of operations and manage well, the earnings should take care of themselves.

3. Stacy Cummins does not have any easy alternatives available. She has already taken the problem to the President, who was not interested. If she goes around the President to the Board of Directors, she will be putting herself in a politically difficult position with little likelihood that it will do much good if, in fact, the Board of Directors already knows what is going on.

On the other hand, if she simply goes along, she will be violating the "Objectivity" standard of ethical conduct for management accountants. The Home Security Division's manipulation of quarterly earnings does distort the entire company's quarterly reports. And the Objectivity standard clearly stipulates that "management accountants have a responsibility to disclose fully all relevant information that could reasonably be expected to influence an intended user's understanding of the reports, comments, and recommendations presented." Apart from the ethical issue, there is also a very practical consideration. If Merced Home Products becomes embroiled in controversy concerning questionable accounting practices, Stacy Cummins will be viewed as a responsible party by outsiders and her career is likely to suffer dramatically.

We would suggest that Ms. Cummins quietly bring the problem to the attention of the audit committee of the Board of Directors, carefully laying out in a non-confrontational manner the problems created by Lansing's practice of manipulating earnings. If the President and the Board of Directors are still not interested in dealing with the problem, she may reasonably conclude that the best alternative is to start looking for another job.

Case 10-35 (60 minutes)

1. Answers may differ concerning which category—learning and growth, internal business processes, customers, or financial—a particular performance measure belongs to.

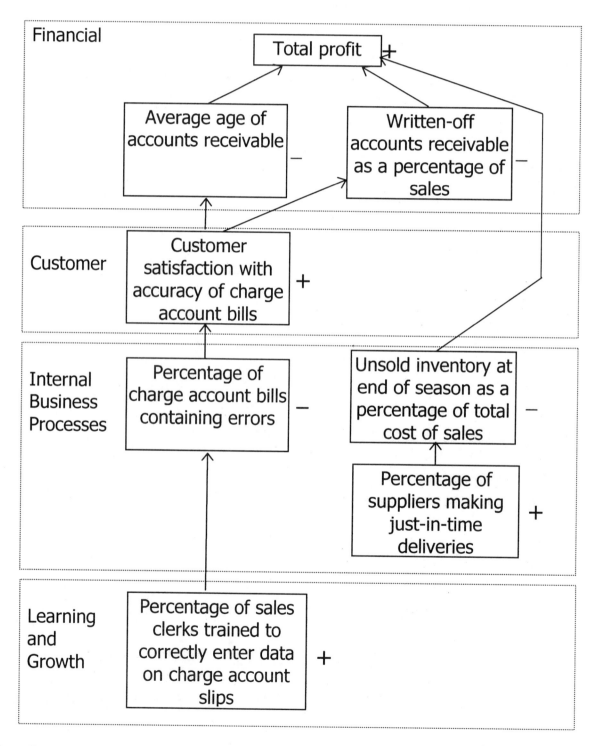

Case 10-35 (continued)

The performance measures that are not included above may have an impact on total profit, but they are not linked in any obvious way with the two key problems that have been identified by management—accounts receivables and unsold inventory. If every performance measure that potentially impacts profit is included in a company's balanced scorecard, it would become unwieldy and focus would be lost.

2. The results can be exploited for information about the company's strategy. Each link in the balanced scorecard should be regarded as a hypothesis of the form "If ..., then ...". For example, the balanced scorecard on the previous page contains the hypothesis "If customers express greater satisfaction with the accuracy of their charge account bills, then there will be improvement in the average age of accounts receivable." If customers in fact do express greater satisfaction with the accuracy of their charge account bills, but there is not an improvement in the average age of accounts receivable, this would have to be considered evidence that is inconsistent with the hypothesis. Management should try to figure out why there has been no improvement in the average age of receivables. (See the answer below for possible explanations.) The answer may suggest a shift in strategy.

In general, the most important results are those in which there has been an improvement in something that is supposed to lead to an improvement in something else, but none has occurred. This evidence contradicts a hypothesis underlying the company's strategy and provides invaluable feedback that can lead to modification of the strategy.

Case 10-35 (continued)

3. a. This evidence is inconsistent with two of the hypotheses underlying the balanced scorecard. The first of these hypotheses is "If customers express greater satisfaction with the accuracy of their charge account bills, then there will be improvement in the average age of accounts receivable." The second of these hypotheses is "If customers express greater satisfaction with the accuracy of their charge account bills, then there will be improvement in bad debts." There are a number of possible explanations. Two possibilities are that the company's collection efforts are ineffective and that the company's credit reviews are not working properly. In other words, the problem may not be incorrect charge account bills at all. The problem may be that the procedures for collecting overdue accounts are not working properly. Or, the problem may be that the procedures for reviewing credit card applications let through too many poor credit risks. If so, this would suggest that efforts should be shifted from reducing charge account billing errors to improving the internal business processes dealing with collections and credit screening. And in that case, the balanced scorecard should be modified.

   b. This evidence is inconsistent with three hypotheses. The first of these is "If the average age of receivables declines, then profits will increase." The second hypothesis is "If the written-off accounts receivable decrease as a percentage of sales, then profits will increase." The third hypothesis is "If unsold inventory at the end of the season as a percentage of cost of sales declines, then profits will increase."

   Again, there are a number of possible explanations for the lack of results consistent with the hypotheses. Managers may have decreased the average age of receivables by simply writing off old accounts earlier than was done previously. This would actually decrease reported profits in the short term. Bad debts as a percentage of sales could be decreased by drastically cutting back on extensions of credit to customers—perhaps even canceling some charge accounts. (There would be no bad debts at all if there were no credit sales.) This would have the effect of reducing bad debts, but might irritate otherwise loyal credit customers and reduce sales and profits.

Case 10-35 (continued)

The reduction in unsold inventories at the end of the season as a percentage of cost of sales could have occurred for a number of reasons that are not necessarily good for profits. For example, managers may have been too cautious about ordering goods to restock low inventories—creating stockouts and lost sales. Or, managers may have cut prices drastically on excess inventories in order to eliminate them before the end of the season. This may have reduced the willingness of customers to pay the store's normal prices. Or, managers may have gotten rid of excess inventories by selling them to discounters *before* the end of the season.

Group Exercise 10-37

The answers to the questions in this group exercise will depend on the particular company that is investigated.

Chapter 11
Flexible Budgets and Overhead Analysis

Exercise 11-1 (15 minutes)

AutoPutz, Gmbh
Flexible Budget

Overhead Costs	Cost Formula (per car)	Activity (cars) 7,000	8,000	9,000
Variable overhead costs:				
Cleaning supplies	€ 0.75	€ 5,250	€ 6,000	€ 6,750
Electricity	0.60	4,200	4,800	5,400
Maintenance	0.15	1,050	1,200	1,350
Total variable overhead costs	€ 1.50	10,500	12,000	13,500
Fixed overhead costs:				
Operator wages		10,000	10,000	10,000
Depreciation		20,000	20,000	20,000
Rent		8,000	8,000	8,000
Total fixed overhead costs		38,000	38,000	38,000
Total overhead costs		€ 48,500	€ 50,000	€ 51,500

Exercise 11-3 (15 minutes)

AutoPutz, Gmbh
Flexible Budget Performance Report
For the Month Ended August 31

Budgeted number of cars............. 8,200
Actual number of cars................. 8,300

Overhead Costs	Cost Formula (per car)	Actual Costs Incurred for 8,300 Cars	Budget Based on 8,300 Cars	Variance
Variable overhead costs:				
Cleaning supplies	€ 0.75	€ 6,350	€ 6,225	€ 125 U
Electricity............................	0.60	4,865	4,980	115 F
Maintenance	0.15	1,600	1,245	355 U
Total variable overhead costs ..	€ 1.50	12,815	12,450	365 U
Fixed overhead costs:				
Operator wages		10,050	10,000	50 U
Depreciation		20,200	20,000	200 U
Rent....................................		8,000	8,000	—
Total fixed overhead costs.......		38,250	38,000	250 U
Total overhead costs...............		€ 51,065	€ 50,450	€ 615 U

Students may question the variances for fixed costs. Operator wages can differ from what was budgeted for a variety of reasons including an unanticipated increase in the wage rate; changes in the mix of workers between those earning lower and higher wages; changes in the number of operators on duty; and overtime. Depreciation may have increased because of the acquisition of new equipment or because of a loss on equipment that must be scrapped—perhaps due to poor maintenance. (This assumes that the loss flows through the depreciation account on the performance report.)

Exercise 11-5 (20 minutes)

1.

Whaley Company
Variable Manufacturing Overhead Performance Report

Budgeted machine-hours 18,000
Actual machine-hours worked 16,000

Variable overhead costs:	Actual 16,000 hours	Budget 16,000 hours	Spending Variance
Utilities.....................................	$20,000	$19,200	$ 800 U
Supplies	4,700	4,800	100 F
Maintenance..............................	35,100	38,400	3,300 F
Rework time...............................	12,300	9,600	2,700 U
Total variable overhead cost	$72,100	$72,000	$ 100 U

2. Favourable variances can be as much a matter of managerial concern as unfavourable variances. In this case, the favourable maintenance variance undoubtedly would require investigation. Efforts should be made to determine if maintenance is not being carried out. In terms of percentage deviation from budgeted allowances, the rework time variance is even more significant (equal to 28% of the budget allowance). It may be that this unfavourable variance in rework time is a result of poor maintenance of machines. Some may say that if the two variances are related, then the trade-off is a good one, since the savings in maintenance cost is greater than the added cost of rework time. But this is shortsighted reasoning. Poor maintenance can reduce the life of equipment, as well as decrease overall output. These long-run costs may swamp any short-run savings.

Exercise 11-7 (20 minutes)

1. Overall rate: $\dfrac{\$33,200}{8,000 \text{ MHs}} = \$4.15 \text{ per MH}$

   Variable rate: $\dfrac{\$8,400}{8,000 \text{ MHs}} = \$1.05 \text{ per MH}$

   Fixed rate: $\dfrac{\$24,800}{8,000 \text{ MHs}} = \$3.10 \text{ per MH}$

2. The standard hours per unit of product are:
   8,000 MHs ÷ 3,200 units = 2.5 MHs per unit

   The standard hours allowed for the actual production would be:
   3,500 units × 2.5 MHs per unit = 8,750 MHs

3. Variable overhead
   spending variance = (AH × AR) – (AH × SR)
   = ($9,860) – (8,500 MHs × $1.05 per MH)
   = ($9,860) – ($8,925)
   = $935 U

   Variable overhead
   efficiency variance = SR (AH – SH)
   = $1.05 per MH (8,500 MHs – 8,750 MHs)
   = $262.50 F

Exercise 11-7 (continued)

Fixed overhead budget and volume variances:

Actual Fixed Overhead Cost	Budgeted Fixed Overhead Cost	Fixed Overhead Cost Applied to Work in Process
$25,100	$24,800*	8,750 standard MHs × $3.10 per MH = $27,125

Budget Variance, $300 U   Volume Variance, $2,325 F

Total Variance, $2,025 F

*8,000 denominator MHs × $3.10 per MH = $24,800.

Alternative approach to the budget variance:

Budget Variance = Actual Fixed Overhead Cost − Budgeted Fixed Overhead Cost

= $25,100 − $24,800 = $300 U

Alternative approach to the volume variance:

$$
\begin{array}{l}
\text{Volume} \\
\text{Variance}
\end{array}
=
\begin{array}{c}
\text{Fixed Portion of} \\
\text{the Predetermined} \\
\text{Overhead Rate}
\end{array}
\left(
\begin{array}{c}
\text{Denominator} \\
\text{Hours}
\end{array}
-
\begin{array}{c}
\text{Standard Hours} \\
\text{Allowed}
\end{array}
\right)
$$

$$
= \$3.10 \text{ per MH } (8{,}000 \text{ MHs} - 8{,}750 \text{ MHs}) = \$2{,}325 \text{ F}
$$

Exercise 11-9 (15 minutes)

1. 10,000 units × 0.8 DLH per unit = 8,000 DLHs.

2. and 3.

Actual Fixed Overhead Cost	Budgeted Fixed Overhead Cost	Fixed Overhead Cost Applied to Work in Process
$45,600*	$45,000	8,000 standard DLHs × $6 per DLH* = $48,000

Budget Variance, $600 U   Volume Variance, $3,000 F*

*Given.

4. $$\text{Fixed cost element of the predetermined overhead rate} = \frac{\text{Budgeted fixed overhead cost}}{\text{Denominator activity}}$$

$$= \frac{\$45,000}{\text{Denominator activity}} = \$6 \text{ per DLH}$$

Therefore, the denominator activity was 7,500 direct labour-hours.

Exercise 11-11 (10 minutes)

Company X: This company has an unfavourable volume variance because the standard direct labour-hours allowed for the actual output are less than the denominator activity.

Company Y: This company has an unfavourable volume variance because the standard direct labour-hours allowed for the actual output are less than the denominator activity.

Company Z: This company has a favourable volume variance because the standard direct labour-hours allowed for the actual output are greater than the denominator activity.

Managerial Accounting, 6th Canadian Edition

Problem 11-13 (30 minutes)

1. Direct materials, 4 kilograms at $2.60 per kg $10.40
   Direct labour, 2 DLHs at $9.00 per DLH 18.00
   Variable manufacturing overhead, 2 DLHs at $3.80 per DLH* 7.60
   Fixed manufacturing overhead, 2 DLHs at $7.00 per DLH** 14.00
   Standard cost per unit $50.00

     * $34,200 ÷ 9,000 DLHs = $3.80 per DLH
     ** $63,000 ÷ 9,000 DLHs = $7.00 per DLH

2. Materials variances:

   Materials Price Variance = AQ (AP − SP)
   30,000 kilograms ($2.50 per kg − $2.60 per kg) = $3,000 F

   Materials Quantity Variance = SP (AQ − SQ)
   $2.60 per kg (20,000 kilograms − 19,200 kilograms*) = $2,080 U
     *4,800 units × 4 kilograms per unit = 19,200 kilograms

   Labour variances:

   Labour Rate Variance = AH (AR − SR)
   10,000 DLHs ($8.60 per DLH − $9.00 per DLH) = $4,000 F

   Labour Efficiency Variance = SR (AH − SH)
   $9 per DLH (10,000 DLHs − 9,600 DLHs*) = $3,600 U
     *4,800 units × 2 DLHs per unit = 9,600 DLHs

Problem 11-13 (continued)

3. Variable manufacturing overhead variances:

Actual Hours of Input, at the Actual Rate (AH × AR)	Actual Hours of Input, at the Standard Rate (AH × SR)	Standard Hours Allowed for Output, at the Standard Rate (SH × SR)
$35,900	10,000 DLHs × $3.80 per DLH = $38,000	9,600 DLHs × $3.80 per DLH = $36,480

Spending Variance, $2,100 F

Efficiency Variance, $1,520 U

Total Variance, $580 F

Alternative solution for the variable overhead variances:

Variable Overhead Spending Variance = (AH × AR) − (AH × SR)
($35,900) − (10,000 DLHs × $3.80 per DLH) = $2,100 F

Variable Overhead Efficiency Variance = SR (AH − SH)
$3.80 per DLH (10,000 DLHs − 9,600 DLHs) = $1,520 U

Fixed manufacturing overhead variances:

Actual Fixed Overhead Cost	Budgeted Fixed Overhead Cost	Fixed Overhead Cost Applied to Work in Process
$64,800	$63,000	9,600 DLHs ×

Budget Variance,
$1,800 U

Volume Variance,
$4,200 F

$7 per DLH
= $67,200

Problem 11-13 (continued)

Alternative approach to the budget variance:

$$
\begin{array}{ccc}
\text{Budget} & = & \text{Actual Fixed} & - & \text{Budgeted Fixed} \\
\text{Variance} & & \text{Overhead Cost} & & \text{Overhead Cost}
\end{array}
$$

$$= \$64,800 - \$63,000 = \$1,800 \text{ U}$$

Alternative approach to the volume variance:

$$
\begin{array}{ccc}
\text{Volume} & = & \text{Fixed Portion of} & \left(\text{Denominator} - \text{Standard Hours} \right) \\
\text{Variance} & & \text{the Predetermined} & \quad \text{Hours} \qquad \text{Allowed} \\
& & \text{Overhead Rate} &
\end{array}
$$

$$= \$7 \text{ per DLH } (9,000 \text{ DLHs} - 9,600 \text{ DLHs}) = \$4,200 \text{ F}$$

4. The choice of a denominator activity level affects standard unit costs in that the higher the denominator activity level chosen, the lower standard unit costs will be. The reason is that the fixed portion of overhead costs is spread more thinly as the denominator activity figure rises.

The volume variance cannot be controlled by controlling spending. Rather, the volume variance simply reflects whether actual activity was greater or less than the denominator activity. Thus, the volume variance is controllable only through activity.

Problem 11-15 (45 minutes)

1. Direct materials price and quantity variances:

Direct Materials Price Variance = AQ (AP − SP)
78,000 metres ($3.75 per m − $3.50 per m) = $19,500 U

Direct Materials Quantity Variance = SP (AQ − SQ)
$3.50 per m (78,000 metres − 80,000 metres*) = $7,000 F

*20,000 units × 4 metres per unit = 80,000 metres

2. Direct labour rate and efficiency variances:

Direct Labour Rate Variance = AH (AR − SR)
32,500 DLHs ($11.80 per DLH − $12.00 per DLH) = $6,500 F

Direct Labour Efficiency Variance = SR (AH − SH)
$12.00 per DLH (32,500 DLHs − 30,000 DLHs*) = $30,000 U

*20,000 units × 1.5 DLHs per unit = 30,000 DLHs

3. a. Variable manufacturing overhead spending and efficiency variances:

Actual Hours of Input, at the Actual Rate (AH × AR)	Actual Hours of Input, at the Standard Rate (AH × SR)	Standard Hours Allowed for Output, at the Standard Rate (SH × SR)
$68,250	32,500 DLHs × $2 per DLH = $65,000	30,000 DLHs × $2 per DLH = $60,000

| Spending Variance, $3,250 U | Efficiency Variance, $5,000 U |

Alternative solution:

Variable Overhead Spending Variance = (AH × AR) − (AH × SR)
($68,250) − (32,500 DLHs × $2.00 per DLH) = $3,250 U

Variable Overhead Efficiency Variance = SR (AH − SH)
$2.00 per DLH (32,500 DLHs − 30,000 DLHs) = $5,000 U

Problem 11-15 (continued)

b. Fixed overhead budget and volume variances:

Actual Fixed Overhead Cost	Budgeted Fixed Overhead Cost	Fixed Overhead Cost Applied to Work in Process
$148,000	$150,000	30,000 DLHs × $6 per DLH = $180,000

Budget Variance, $2,000 F

Volume Variance, $30,000 F

Alternative approach to the budget variance:

$$\begin{array}{ccc} \text{Budget} \\ \text{Variance} \end{array} = \begin{array}{c} \text{Actual Fixed} \\ \text{Overhead Cost} \end{array} - \begin{array}{c} \text{Flexible Budget Fixed} \\ \text{Overhead Cost} \end{array}$$

$148,000 − $150,000 = $2,000 F

Alternative approach to the volume variance:

$$\begin{array}{c} \text{Volume} \\ \text{Variance} \end{array} = \begin{array}{c} \text{Fixed Portion of} \\ \text{the Predetermined} \\ \text{Overhead Rate} \end{array} \left(\begin{array}{c} \text{Denominator} \\ \text{Hours} \end{array} - \begin{array}{c} \text{Standard Hours} \\ \text{Allowed} \end{array} \right)$$

$6.00 per DLH (25,000 DLHs − 30,000 DLHs) = $30,000 F

Problem 11-15 (continued)

4. The total of the variances would be:

Direct materials variances:

Price variance	$19,500	U
Quantity variance	7,000	F

Direct labour variances:

Rate variance	6,500	F
Efficiency variance	30,000	U

Variable manufacturing overhead variances:

Spending variance	3,250	U
Efficiency variance	5,000	U

Fixed manufacturing overhead variances:

Budget variance	2,000	F
Volume variance	30,000	F
Total of variances	$12,250	U

Notice that the total of the variances agrees with the $12,250 unfavourable variance mentioned by the vice president.

It appears that not everyone should be given a bonus for good cost control. The materials price variance and the labour efficiency variance are 7.1% and 8.3%, respectively, of the standard cost allowed and thus would warrant investigation. In addition, the variable overhead spending variance is 5.0% of the standard cost allowed.

The reason the company's large unfavourable variances (for materials price and labour efficiency) do not show up more clearly is that they are offset for the most part by the company's favourable volume variance for the year. This favourable volume variance is the result of the company operating at an activity level that is well above the denominator activity level used to set predetermined overhead rates. (The company operated at an activity level of 30,000 standard DLHs; the denominator activity level set at the beginning of the year was 25,000 DLHs.) As a result of the large favourable volume variance, the unfavourable price and efficiency variances have been concealed in a small "net" figure. Finally, the large favourable volume variance may have been achieved by building up inventories.

Problem 11-17 (45 minutes)

1. The cost formulas below can be developed from the data in the problem using the simple high-low method. The completed flexible budget over an activity range of 80 to 100% of capacity would be:

Elgin Company
Flexible Budget

	Cost Formulas	Percentage of Capacity		
	per MH	80%	90%	100%
Overhead Costs				
Machine-hours		40,000	45,000	50,000
Variable overhead costs:				
Utilities.........	$0.80	$ 32,000	$ 36,000	$ 40,000
Supplies	0.10	4,000	4,500	5,000
Indirect labour	0.20	8,000	9,000	10,000
Maintenance.........	0.40	16,000	18,000	20,000
Total variable costs.........	$1.50	60,000	67,500	75,000
Fixed overhead costs:				
Utilities.........		9,000	9,000	9,000
Maintenance.........		21,000	21,000	21,000
Supervision		10,000	10,000	10,000
Total fixed costs		40,000	40,000	40,000
Total overhead costs.........		$100,000	$107,500	$115,000

2. The cost formula for all overhead costs would be $40,000 per month plus $1.50 per machine-hour.

Managerial Accounting, 6th Canadian Edition

Problem 11-17 (continued)

3.

Elgin Company
Performance Report
For the Month of May

Budgeted machine-hours 40,000
Standard machine-hours allowed 41,000
Actual machine-hours .... 43,000 *

Overhead Costs	Cost Formula per MH	Actual Cost 43,000 MH	Budgeted Cost 43,000 MH	Spending Variance
Variable overhead costs:				
Utilities........................	$0.80	$ 33,540 **	$ 34,400	$ 860 F
Supplies.........................	0.10	6,450	4,300	2,150 U
Indirect labour..................	0.20	9,890	8,600	1,290 U
Maintenance......................	0.40	14,190 **	17,200	3,010 F
Total variable costs............	$1.50	64,070	64,500	430 F
Fixed overhead costs:				
Utilities........................		9,000	9,000	—
Maintenance......................		21,000	21,000	—
Supervision		10,000	10,000	—
Total fixed costs		40,000	40,000	—
Total overhead costs........		$104,070	$104,500	$ 430 F

* 86% of 50,000 MHs = 43,000 MHs
** $42,540 − $9,000 fixed = $33,540
$35,190 − $21,000 fixed = $14,190

4. Assuming that variable overhead really should be proportional to actual machine-hours, the unfavourable spending variance could be the result either of price increases or of waste. Unlike the price variance for materials and the rate variance for labour, the spending variance for variable overhead measures both price and waste elements. This is why the variance is called a "spending" variance. Total spending can be affected as much by waste as it can by prices paid.

Problem 11-17 (continued)

5. Efficiency Variance = SR (AH − SH)
$1.50 per MH (43,000 MHs − 41,000 MHs) = $3,000 U

The overhead efficiency variance is really misnamed, since it does not measure efficiency (waste) in use of variable overhead items. The variance arises solely because of the inefficiency in the *base* underlying the incurrence of variable overhead cost. If the incurrence of variable overhead costs is directly tied to the actual machine-hours worked, then the excessive number of machine-hours worked during May has caused the incurrence of $3,000 in variable overhead costs that would have been avoided had production been completed in the standard time allowed. In short, the overhead efficiency variance is independent of any spillage, waste, or theft of overhead supplies or other variable overhead items that may take place during a month.

Problem 11-19 (30 minutes)

1.

The Durrant Company

Flexible Budget—Machining Department

Overhead Costs	Cost Formula per MH	10,000	15,000	20,000
			Machine-Hours	
Variable:				
Utilities.................	$0.70	$ 7,000	$ 10,500	$ 14,000
Lubricants	1.00	10,000	15,000	20,000
Machine setup	0.20	2,000	3,000	4,000
Indirect labour.......	0.60	6,000	9,000	12,000
Total variable cost	$2.50	25,000	37,500	50,000
Fixed:				
Lubricants		8,000	8,000	8,000
Indirect labour.......		120,000	120,000	120,000
Depreciation..........		32,000	32,000	32,000
Total fixed costs		160,000	160,000	160,000
Total overhead costs....		$185,000	$197,500	$210,000

Problem 11-19 (continued)

2.

The Durrant Company
Overhead Performance Report—Machining Department
For the Month of March

Budgeted machine-hours 20,000
Actual machine-hours 18,000

Overhead Costs	Cost Formula per MH	Actual 18,000 MHs	Budget 18,000 MHs	Spending Variance
Variable:				
Utilities...........	$0.70	$ 12,000	$ 12,600	$ 600 F
Lubricants.........	1.00	16,500 *	18,000	1,500 F
Machine setup........	0.20	4,800	3,600	1,200 U
Indirect labour........	0.60	12,500	10,800	1,700 U
Total variable cost	$2.50	45,800	45,000	800 U
Fixed:				
Lubricants...........		8,000	8,000	—
Indirect labour.......		120,000	120,000	—
Depreciation...........		32,000	32,000	—
Total fixed costs.........		160,000	160,000	—
Total overhead costs.....		$205,800	$205,000	$ 800 U

* $24,500 total lubricants – $8,000 fixed lubricants = $16,500 variable lubricants. The variable element of other costs is computed in the same way.

3. In order to compute an overhead efficiency variance, it would be necessary to know the standard hours allowed for the 9,000 units produced during March in the Machining Department.

Problem 11-21 (20 minutes)

Budgeted machine-hours.............................. 3,200
Actual machine-hours................................. 2,700
Standard machine-hours allowed .... 2,800 *

*14,000 units × 0.2 MH per unit = 2,800 MHs

Overhead Cost	Cost Formula (per MH)	Actual Costs Incurred, 2,700 MHs (1)	Budget Based on 2,700 MHs (2)	Budget Based on 2,800 MHs (3)	Total Variance (1) – (3)	Spending Variance (1) – (2)	Efficiency Variance (2) – (3)
Supplies...........	$0.70	$ 1,836	$ 1,890	$ 1,960	$124 F	$ 54 F	$ 70 F
Power	1.20	3,348	3,240	3,360	12 F	108 U	120 F
Lubrication	0.50	1,485	1,350	1,400	85 U	135 U	50 F
Wearing tools	3.10	8,154	8,370	8,680	526 F	216 F	310 F
Total	$5.50	$14,823	$14,850	$15,400	$577 F	$ 27 F	$550 F

Breakdown of the Total Variance

Problem 11-23 (45 minutes)

1. Total: $\dfrac{\$240,000}{30,000 \text{ DLHs}} = \$8 \text{ per DLH}$

   Variable: $\dfrac{\$60,000}{30,000 \text{ DLHs}} = \$2 \text{ per DLH}$

   Fixed: $\dfrac{\$180,000}{30,000 \text{ DLHs}} = \$6 \text{ per DLH}$

2.
Direct materials: 4 metres at $3 per m	$12.00
Direct labour: 1.5 DLHs at $12 per DLH...............	18.00
Variable overhead: 1.5 DLHs at $2 per DLH	3.00
Fixed overhead: 1.5 DLHs at $6 per DLH	9.00
Standard cost per unit...................................	$42.00

3. a. 22,000 units × 1.5 DLHs per unit = 33,000 standard DLHs.

   b.
   Manufacturing Overhead

Actual costs	244,000	264,000 *	Applied costs
		20,000	Overapplied overhead

   *33,000 standard DLHs × $8 per DLH = $264,000.

4. Variable overhead variances:

Actual Hours of Input, at the Actual	Actual Hours of Input, at the	Standard Hours Allowed for Output,

Rate (AH × AR)	Standard Rate (AH × SR)	at the Standard Rate (SH × SR)
$63,000	35,000 DLHs × $2 per DLH = $70,000	33,000 DLHs × $2 per DLH = $66,000

Spending Variance, $7,000 F

Efficiency Variance, $4,000 U

Problem 11-23 (continued)

Alternative solution:

Variable Overhead Spending Variance = (AH × AR) − (AH × SR) ($63,000) − (35,000 DLHs × $2 per DLH) = $7,000 F

Variable Overhead Efficiency Variance = SR (AH − SH) $2 per DLH (35,000 DLHs − 33,000 DLHs) = $4,000 U

Fixed overhead variances:

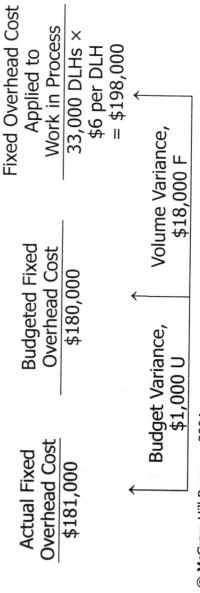

Actual Fixed Overhead Cost	Budgeted Fixed Overhead Cost	Fixed Overhead Cost Applied to Work in Process
$181,000	$180,000	33,000 DLHs × $6 per DLH = $198,000

Budget Variance, $1,000 U

Volume Variance, $18,000 F

Alternative approach to the budget variance:

$$\begin{array}{c} \text{Budget} \\ \text{Variance} \end{array} = \begin{array}{c} \text{Actual Fixed} \\ \text{Overhead Cost} \end{array} - \begin{array}{c} \text{Flexible Budget Fixed} \\ \text{Overhead Cost} \end{array}$$

$$\$181,000 - \$180,000 = \$1,000 \text{ U}$$

Alternative approach to the volume variance:

$$\begin{array}{c} \text{Volume} \\ \text{Variance} \end{array} = \begin{array}{c} \text{Fixed Portion of} \\ \text{the Predetermined} \\ \text{Overhead Rate} \end{array} \left(\begin{array}{c} \text{Denominator} \\ \text{Hours} \end{array} - \begin{array}{c} \text{Standard Hours} \\ \text{Allowed} \end{array} \right)$$

$$\$6 \text{ per DLH } (30,000 \text{ DLHs} - 33,000 \text{ DLHs}) = \$18,000 \text{ F}$$

Problem 11-23 (continued)

Summary of variances:

Variable overhead spending variance	$ 7,000 F
Variable overhead efficiency variance	4,000 U
Fixed overhead budget variance	1,000 U
Fixed overhead volume variance	18,000 F
Overapplied overhead—see part 3	$20,000

5. Only the volume variance would have changed. It would have been unfavourable, since the standard DLHs allowed for the year's production (33,000 DLHs) would have been less than the denominator DLHs (36,000 DLHs).

Problem 11-25 (60 minutes)
1. The computations of the cost formulas appear below.

	Cost	Variable with respect to	Activity level	Cost per unit of activity
Actors and directors' wages	$144,000	performances	60	$2,400
Stagehands' wages	27,000	performances	60	450
Ticket booth personnel and ushers' wages	10,800	performances	60	180
Scenery, costumes, and props	43,000	productions	5	8,600
Theatre hall rent	45,000	performances	60	750
Printed programs	10,500	performances	60	175
Publicity	13,000	productions	5	2,600
Administrative expenses (15%)	6,480	productions	5	1,296
Administrative expenses (10%)	4,320	performances	60	72
Fixed administrative expenses (75%)	32,400	—	—	—

Problem 11-25 (continued)

2. The performance report is clearest when it is organized by cost behaviour. The costs that are variable with respect to the number of productions come first, then the costs that are variable with respect to performances, then the administrative expenses as a special category.

The Munchkin Theater
Flexible Budget Performance Report

Actual number of productions................................. 4
Actual number of performances per production 16
Actual total number of performances 64

The performance report is continued on the next page.

Problem 11-25 (continued)

Costs	Cost Formula Per Unit of Activity	Actual Costs Incurred	Budget Based on Actual Activity	Variance
Variable costs of productions: (Flexible budget based on 4 productions)				
Scenery, costumes, and props	$ 8,600	$ 39,300	$ 34,400	$4,900 U
Publicity	2,600	12,000	10,400	1,600 U
Total variable cost per production*	$11,200	51,300	44,800	6,500 U
Variable costs of performances: (Flexible budget based on 64 performances)				
Actors and directors' wages	$2,400	148,000	153,600	5,600 F
Stagehands' wages	450	28,600	28,800	200 F
Ticket booth personnel and ushers' wages.....	180	12,300	11,520	780 U
Theatre hall rent..................	750	49,600	48,000	1,600 U
Printed programs	175	10,950	11,200	250 F
Total variable cost per performance*	$3,955	249,450	253,120	3,670 F
Administrative expenses:				
Variable per production	$1,296		5,184	
Variable per performance	72		4,608	
Fixed............			32,400	
Total administrative expenses		41,650	42,192	542 F
Total cost............		$342,400	$340,112	$2,288 U

*Excluding variable portion of administrative expenses

Problem 11-25 (continued)

3. The overall unfavourable variance is a very small percentage of the total cost, about 0.7%, which suggests that costs are under control. In addition, the largest unfavourable variance is for scenery, costumes, and props. This may indicate waste, but it may also indicate that more money was spent on these items, which are highly visible to theatre-goers, to ensure higher-quality productions.

4. The average costs may not be very good indicators of the additional costs of any particular production or performance. The averages gloss over considerable variations in costs. For example, a production of Peter the Rabbit may require only half a dozen actors and actresses and fairly simple costumes and props. On the other hand, a production of Cinderella may require dozens of actors and actresses and very elabourate and costly costumes and props. Consequently, both the production costs and the cost per performance will be much higher for Cinderella than for Peter the Rabbit. Managers of theatre companies know that they must estimate the costs of each new production individually—average costs are of little use for this purpose.

Case 11-27 (60 minutes)

1. The number of units produced can be computed by using the total standard cost applied for the period for *any* input (materials, labour, or overhead), or it can be computed by using the total standard cost applied for all inputs together. Using only the standard cost applied for materials, we have:

$$\frac{\text{Total standard cost applied}}{\text{Standard cost per unit}} = \frac{\$608,000}{\$32 \text{ per unit}} = 19,000 \text{ units}$$

Alternatively, the number of units can be obtained by dividing the $608,000 total standard cost applied by the $16 standard price per metre for materials, and then dividing the answer by the 2 metres standard quantity per unit:

$608,000 ÷ $16 per m = 38,000 metres;
38,000 metres ÷ 2 metres per unit = 19,000 units.

The same answer can be obtained by using any other cost input.

2. 40,000 metres; see below for a detailed analysis.

3. $15.71 per m; see below for a detailed analysis.

4. 61,000 DLHs; see below for a detailed analysis.

5. $5.14 per DLH; see below for a detailed analysis.

6. Standard variable overhead cost applied... $171,000
   Add: Overhead efficiency variance............   12,000 U (see analysis
   Deduct: Overhead spending variance........   3,700 F   below)
   Actual variable overhead cost incurred...... $179,300

7. Standard fixed overhead cost applied $456,000
   Add: Unfavourable volume variance..........   24,000 U
   Budgeted fixed overhead cost.................. $480,000

8. Budgeted fixed overhead cost (a)................................ $480,000
   Fixed portion of the predetermined overhead rate (b).... $8 per DLH
   Denominator activity (a) ÷ (b) .... 60,000 DLHs

Case 11-27 (continued)

Direct materials analysis:

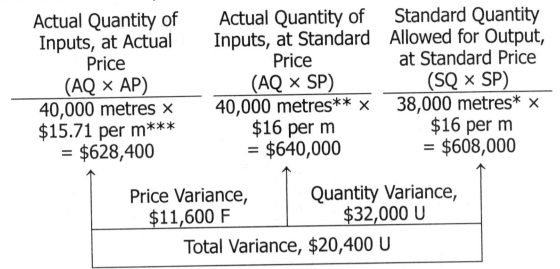

Actual Quantity of Inputs, at Actual Price (AQ × AP)	Actual Quantity of Inputs, at Standard Price (AQ × SP)	Standard Quantity Allowed for Output, at Standard Price (SQ × SP)
40,000 metres × $15.71 per m*** = $628,400	40,000 metres** × $16 per m = $640,000	38,000 metres* × $16 per m = $608,000

Price Variance, $11,600 F | Quantity Variance, $32,000 U

Total Variance, $20,400 U

    * 19,000 units × 2 metres per unit = 38,000 metres
  ** $640,000 ÷ $16 per m = 40,000 metres
*** $628,400 ÷ 40,000 metres = $15.71 per m

Direct labour analysis:

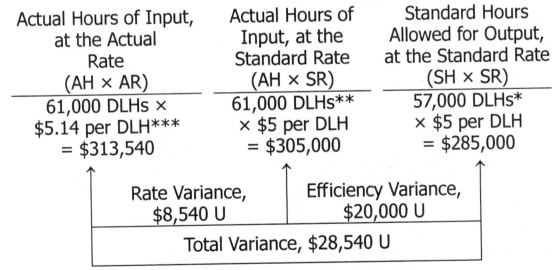

Actual Hours of Input, at the Actual Rate (AH × AR)	Actual Hours of Input, at the Standard Rate (AH × SR)	Standard Hours Allowed for Output, at the Standard Rate (SH × SR)
61,000 DLHs × $5.14 per DLH*** = $313,540	61,000 DLHs** × $5 per DLH = $305,000	57,000 DLHs* × $5 per DLH = $285,000

Rate Variance, $8,540 U | Efficiency Variance, $20,000 U

Total Variance, $28,540 U

    * 19,000 units × 3 DLHs per unit = 57,000 DLHs
  ** $305,000 ÷ $5 per DLH = 61,000 DLHs
*** $313,540 ÷ 61,000 DLHs = $5.14 per DLH

Case 11-27 (continued)

Variable overhead analysis:

Actual Hours of Input, at the Actual Rate (AH × AR)	Actual Hours of Input, at the Standard Rate (AH × SR)	Standard Hours Allowed for Output, at the Standard Rate (SH × SR)
$179,300**	61,000 DLHs × $3 per DLH = $183,000*	57,000 DLHs × $3 per DLH = $171,000

Spending Variance, $3,700 F	Efficiency Variance, $12,000 U

Total Variance, $8,300 U

   * Computed using 61,000 actual DLHs at the $3 per DLH standard rate.
** $183,000 − $3,700 = $179,300.

Fixed overhead analysis:

Actual Fixed Overhead Cost	Budgeted Fixed Overhead Cost	Fixed Overhead Cost Applied to Work in Process
$478,500**	$480,000*	57,000 DLHs × $8 per DLH = $456,000

Budget Variance, $1,500 F	Volume Variance, $24,000 U

   * $456,000 + $24,000 = $480,000.
** $480,000 − $1,500 = $478,500.

Case 11-29 (45 minutes for each company; 90 minutes in total)

(Note to the Instructor: You may wish to assign only one company.)

	Item	Company X	Company Y
1.	Denominator activity in machine-hours........	18,000*	30,000
2.	Standard machine-hours allowed for units produced	19,500	28,000*
3.	Actual machine-hours worked	20,000	27,500*
4.	Flexible budget variable overhead per machine-hour	$ 1.60*	$ 2.00
5.	Budgeted fixed overhead (total)..................	72,000	135,000
6.	Actual variable overhead cost.....................	30,000*	55,275*
7.	Actual fixed overhead cost..........................	72,500*	134,600*
8.	Variable overhead cost applied to production.......................................	31,200*	56,000
9.	Fixed overhead cost applied to production ...	78,000	126,000*
10.	Variable overhead spending variance...........	2,000F	275U
11.	Variable overhead efficiency variance	800U*	1,000F*
12.	Fixed overhead budget variance..................	500U*	400F
13.	Fixed overhead volume variance	6,000F	9,000U*
14.	Variable portion of the predetermined overhead rate..	1.60	2.00
15.	Fixed portion of the predetermined overhead rate..	4.00	4.50
16.	Underapplied or (overapplied) overhead	(6,700)	7,875

*Given.

Case 11-29 (continued)

Company X:

Variable overhead data:

Actual Hours of Input, at the Actual Rate (AH × AR)	Actual Hours of Input, at the Standard Rate (AH × SR)	Standard Hours Allowed for Output, at the Standard Rate (SH × SR)
$30,000*	20,000 MHs × $1.60 per MH* = $32,000	19,500 MHs × $1.60 per MH* = $31,200*

     Spending Variance, $2,000 F   Efficiency Variance, $800 U*

*Given.

Fixed overhead data:

Actual Fixed Overhead Cost	Budgeted Fixed Overhead Cost	Fixed Overhead Cost Applied to Work in Process
$72,500*	$72,000	19,500 MHs × $4 per MH = $78,000

     Budget Variance, $500 U*   Volume Variance, $6,000 F

*Given.

Computation of the fixed overhead rate:

$$\frac{\text{Budgeted fixed overhead cost}}{\text{Denominator activity}} = \frac{\$72,000}{18,000 \text{ MHs}} = \$4 \text{ per MH}$$

Overapplied overhead:

Variable overhead spending variance	$2,000	F
Variable overhead efficiency variance.........	800	U
Fixed overhead budget variance	500	U
Fixed overhead volume variance................	6,000	F
Overapplied overhead	$6,700	

Case 11-29 (continued)

Company Y:

Variable overhead data:

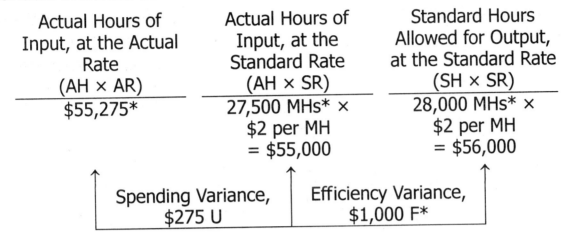

Actual Hours of Input, at the Actual Rate (AH × AR)	Actual Hours of Input, at the Standard Rate (AH × SR)	Standard Hours Allowed for Output, at the Standard Rate (SH × SR)
$55,275*	27,500 MHs* × $2 per MH = $55,000	28,000 MHs* × $2 per MH = $56,000

Spending Variance, $275 U   Efficiency Variance, $1,000 F*

Fixed overhead data:

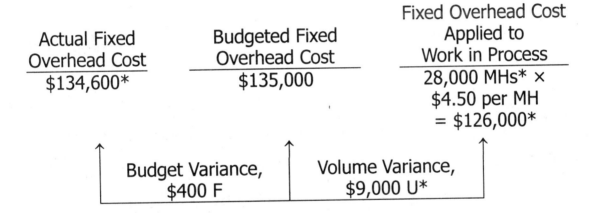

Actual Fixed Overhead Cost	Budgeted Fixed Overhead Cost	Fixed Overhead Cost Applied to Work in Process
$134,600*	$135,000	28,000 MHs* × $4.50 per MH = $126,000*

Budget Variance, $400 F   Volume Variance, $9,000 U*

Denominator activity in hours:

$$\text{Fixed portion of the pre-determined overhead rate} = \frac{\text{Budgeted fixed overhead cost}}{\text{Denominator activity}}$$

$$= \frac{\$135,000}{\text{Denominator activity}} = \$4.50 \text{ per MH}$$

Therefore, the denominator activity is:
$135,000 ÷ $4.50 per MH = 30,000 MHs.

*Given.

Case 11-29 (continued)

Underapplied overhead:

Variable overhead spending variance	$ 275	U
Variable overhead efficiency variance.....	1,000	F
Fixed overhead budget variance	400	F
Fixed overhead volume variance...........	9,000	U
Underapplied overhead	$7,875	

Case 11-31 (40 minutes)

Fixed overhead = denominator activity times fixed overhead per hour
$$= 60,000 \text{ hours} \times \$5.00 \text{ per hour}$$
$$= \$300,000$$

Sales Quantity*...........	27,500	30,000	37,500	50,000
Sales Price**..............	$75	$75	$67.5	$60
Total Sales	$2,062,500	$2,250,000	$2,531,250	$3,000,000
Cost of Sales				
Material $20	550,000	600,000	750,000	1,000,000
Direct labour $16.........	440,000	480,000	600,000	800,000
Variable overhead $6...	165,000	180,000	225,000	300,000
Fixed overhead $10	300,000	300,000	300,000	300,000
	1,455,000	1,560,000	1,875,000	2,400,000
Gross profit...............	$ 607,500	$ 690,000	$ 656,250	$ 600,000

The need to reduce the selling price to achieve practical or theoretical capacity levels yields a decline in income because the revenue drops more than the saving in fixed costs resulting from the capacity expansion. In addition, the added costs of the expansion of crews, the reduction of scheduled maintenance and the change in set ups has not been added beyond the change in variable costs indicated by the analysis above.

* 55,000 hours ÷ 2 hours per unit = 27,500 units
**$75 × .90 = $67.5; $75 × .80 = $60

Group Exercise 11-33

The solution will depend on the particular college or university that the students investigate.

Chapter 12
Segment Reporting

Exercise 12-1 (15 minutes)

	Total		CD		DVD	
	Amount	*%*	*Amount*	*%*	*Amount*	*%*
Sales	$750,000	100.0	$300,000 *	100	$450,000 *	100
Less variable expenses............	435,000	58.0	120,000	40	315,000	70
Contribution margin	315,000	42.0	180,000	60	135,000	30
Less traceable fixed expenses	183,000	24.4	138,000	46	45,000	10
Product line segment margin ..	132,000	17.6	$ 42,000	14	$ 90,000	20
Less common fixed expenses not traceable to products.............	105,000	14.0				
Net operating income...............	$ 27,000	3.6				

* CD: 37,500 packs × $8 per pack = $300,000;
  DVD: 18,000 packs × $25 per pack= $450,000.
  Variable expenses are computed in the same way.

Exercise 12-3 (15 minutes)

1. The company should focus its campaign on Landscaping Clients. The computations are:

	Construction Clients	Landscaping Clients
Increased sales......................................	$70,000	$60,000
Market CM ratio	× 35%	× 50%
Incremental contribution margin	24,500	30,000
Less cost of the campaign	8,000	8,000
Increased segment margin and net operating income for the company as a whole	$16,500	$22,000

2. The $90,000 in traceable fixed expenses in Exercise 12-2 is now partly traceable and partly common. When we segment St. John's by market, only $72,000 remains a traceable fixed expense. This amount represents costs such as advertising and salaries that arise because of the existence of the construction and landscaping market segments. The remaining $18,000 ($90,000 − $72,000) becomes a common cost when St. John's is segmented by market. This amount would include such costs as the salary of the manager of the St. John's office that could not be avoided by eliminating either of the two market segments.

Exercise 12-5 (20 minutes)

1.

	Total Company Amount	%	Geographic Market South Amount	%	Central Amount	%	North Amount	%
Sales	$1,500,000	100.0	$400,000	100	$600,000	100	$500,000	100
Less variable expenses	588,000	39.2	208,000	52	180,000	30	200,000	40
Contribution margin	912,000	60.8	192,000	48	420,000	70	300,000	60
Less traceable fixed expenses	770,000	51.3	240,000	60	330,000	55	200,000	40
Geographic market segment margin	142,000	9.5	$(48,000)	(12)	$ 90,000	15	$100,000	20
Less common fixed expenses not traceable to geographic markets*	175,000	11.7						
Net operating income (loss)	$ (33,000)	(2.2)						

*$945,000 – $770,000 = $175,000.

2.
Incremental sales ($600,000 × 15%)	$90,000
Contribution margin ratio	× 70%
Incremental contribution margin	63,000
Less incremental advertising expense	25,000
Incremental net operating income	$38,000

Yes, the advertising program should be initiated.

Exercise 12-7 (15 minutes)

1. ROI computations:

$$ROI = \frac{\text{Net operating income}}{\text{Sales}} \times \frac{\text{Sales}}{\text{Average operating assets}}$$

Eastern Division: $\dfrac{\$90,000}{\$1,000,000} \times \dfrac{\$1,000,000}{\$500,000} = 9\% \times 2 = 18\%$

Western Division: $\dfrac{\$105,000}{\$1,750,000} \times \dfrac{\$1,750,000}{\$500,000} = 6\% \times 3.5 = 21\%$

2. The manager of the Western Division seems to be doing the better job. Although her margin is three percentage points lower than the margin of the Eastern Division, her turnover is higher (a turnover of 3.5, as compared to a turnover of two for the Eastern Division). The greater turnover more than offsets the lower margin, resulting in a 21% ROI, as compared to an 18% ROI for the other division.

Notice that if you look at margin alone, then the Eastern Division appears to be the strongest division. This fact underscores the importance of looking at turnover as well as at margin in evaluating performance in an investment centre.

Exercise 12-9 (20 minutes)

1. ROI computations:

$$\text{ROI} = \frac{\text{Net operating income}}{\text{Sales}} \times \frac{\text{Sales}}{\text{Average operating assets}}$$

Perth: $\dfrac{\$630,000}{\$9,000,000} \times \dfrac{\$9,000,000}{\$3,000,000} = 7\% \times 3 = 21\%$

Darwin: $\dfrac{\$1,800,000}{\$20,000,000} \times \dfrac{\$20,000,000}{\$10,000,000} = 9\% \times 2 = 18\%$

2.

	Perth	Darwin
Average operating assets (a)	$3,000,000	$10,000,000
Net operating income..........................	$ 630,000	$ 1,800,000
Minimum required return on average operating assets—16% × (a)	480,000	$ 1,600,000
Residual income	$ 150,000	$ 200,000

3. No, the Darwin Division is simply larger than the Perth Division and for this reason one would expect that it would have a greater amount of residual income. Residual income can't be used to compare the performance of divisions of different sizes. Larger divisions will almost always look better, not necessarily because of better management but because of the larger dollar figures involved. In fact, in the case above, Darwin does not appear to be as well managed as Perth. Note from Part (1) that Darwin has only an 18% ROI as compared to 21% for Perth.

Exercise 12-11 (30 minutes)

1. a. The lowest acceptable transfer price from the perspective of the selling division, the Electrical Division, is given by the following formula:

$$\text{Transfer price} = \frac{\text{Variable cost}}{\text{per unit}} + \frac{\text{Total contribution margin on lost sales}}{\text{Number of units transferred}}$$

Since there is enough idle capacity to fill the entire order from the Motor Division, there are no lost outside sales. And since the variable cost per unit is $21, the lowest acceptable transfer price as far as the selling division is concerned is also $21.

$$\text{Transfer price} = \$21 + \frac{\$0}{10,000} = \$21$$

b. The Motor Division can buy a similar transformer from an outside supplier for $38. Therefore, the Motor Division would be unwilling to pay more than $38 per transformer.

Transfer price = Cost of buying from outside supplier = $38

c. Combining the requirements of both the selling division and the buying division, the acceptable range of transfer prices in this situation is:

$$\$21 < \text{Transfer price} \leq \$38$$

Assuming that the managers understand their own businesses and that they are cooperative, they should be able to agree on a transfer price within this range and the transfer should take place.

d. From the standpoint of the entire company, the transfer should take place. The cost of the transformers transferred is only $21 and the company saves the $38 cost of the transformers purchased from the outside supplier.

Exercise 12-11 (continued)

2. a. Each of the 10,000 units transferred to the Motor Division must displace a sale to an outsider at a price of $40. Therefore, the selling division would demand a transfer price of at least $40. This can also be computed using the formula for the lowest acceptable transfer price as follows:

$$\text{Transfer price} = \$21 + \frac{(\$40 - \$21) \times 10,000}{10,000}$$

$$= \$21 + (\$40 - \$21) = \$40$$

   b. As before, the Motor Division would be unwilling to pay more than $38 per transformer.

   c. The requirements of the selling and buying divisions in this instance are incompatible. The selling division must have a price of at least $40 whereas the buying division will not pay more than $38. An agreement to transfer the transformers is extremely unlikely.

   d. From the standpoint of the entire company, the transfer should not take place. By transferring a transformer internally, the company gives up revenue of $40 and saves $38, for a loss of $2.

Exercise 12-13 (20 minutes)

1. The lowest acceptable transfer price from the perspective of the selling division is given by the following formula:

$$\text{Transfer price} = \frac{\text{Variable cost}}{\text{per unit}} + \frac{\text{Total contribution margin on lost sales}}{\text{Number of units transferred}}.$$

There is no idle capacity, so each of the 20,000 units transferred from Division X to Division Y reduces sales to outsiders by one unit. The contribution margin per unit on outside sales is $20 (= $50 − $30).

$$\text{Transfer price} = (\$30 - \$2) + \frac{\$20 \times 20{,}000}{20{,}000}$$

$$= \$28 + \$20 = \$48$$

The buying division, Division Y, can purchase a similar unit from an outside supplier for $47. Therefore, Division Y would be unwilling to pay more than $47 per unit.

$$\text{Transfer price} = \text{Cost of buying from outside supplier} = \$47$$

The requirements of the two divisions are incompatible and no transfer will take place.

2. In this case, Division X has enough idle capacity to satisfy Division Y's demand. Therefore, there are no lost sales and the lowest acceptable price as far as the selling division is concerned is the variable cost of $20 per unit.

$$\text{Transfer price} = \$20 + \frac{\$0}{20{,}000} = \$20$$

The buying division, Division Y, can purchase a similar unit from an outside supplier for $34. Therefore, Division Y would be unwilling to pay more than $34 per unit.

$$\text{Transfer price} = \text{Cost of buying from outside supplier} = \$34$$

In this case, the requirements of the two divisions are compatible and a transfer will hopefully take place at a transfer price within the range:

$$\$20 < \text{Transfer price} \leq \$34$$

Problem 12-15 (60 minutes)

1. The segmented income statement follows:

	Total Company Amount	%	Wheat Cereal Amount	%	Pancake Mix Amount	%	Flour Amount	%
Sales	$600,000	100.0	$200,000	100.0	$300,000	100.0	$100,000	100
Less variable expenses:								
Materials, labour & other	204,000	34.0	60,000	30.0	126,000	42.0	18,000	18
Sales commissions	60,000	10.0	20,000	10.0	30,000	10.0	10,000	10
Total	264,000	44.0	80,000	40.0	156,000	52.0	28,000	28
Contribution margin	336,000	56.0	120,000	60.0	144,000	48.0	72,000	72
Less traceable fixed expenses:								
Advertising	123,000	20.5	48,000	24.0	60,000	20.0	15,000	15
Salaries	66,000	11.0	34,000	17.0	21,000	7.0	11,000	11
Equipment depreciation*	30,000	5.0	12,000	6.0	15,000	5.0	3,000	3
Warehouse rent**	12,000	2.0	4,000	2.0	7,000	2.3	1,000	1
Total	231,000	38.5	98,000	49.0	103,000	34.3	30,000	30
Product line segment margin	105,000	17.5	$ 22,000	11.0	$ 41,000	13.7	$ 42,000	42
Less common fixed expenses:								
General administration	90,000	15.0						
Net operating income	$ 15,000	2.5						

* $30,000 × 40%, 50%, and 10% respectively
** $4.50 per square metre × 889 square metres, 1,556 square metres, and 222 square metres respectively

Problem 12-15 (continued)

2. a. No, the wheat cereal should not be eliminated. The wheat cereal product is covering all of its own costs and is generating a $22,000 segment margin toward covering the company's common costs and toward profits. (Note: Problems relating to the elimination of a product line are covered in more depth in Chapter 13.)

   b. No, it is probably unwise to focus all available resources on promoting the pancake mix. The company is already spending nearly as much on the promotion of this line as it is on the other two lines together. Furthermore, the pancake mix has the lowest contribution margin ratio of the three products. Nevertheless, we cannot say for sure which product should be emphasized in this situation without more information. If the equipment is being fully utilized, increasing the production of any one product would probably require cutting back on one of the other products. In Chapter 13 we will discuss how to choose the most profitable product when there is a production constraint that forces such a trade-off between products.

3. At least three additional points should be brought to the attention of management:

   i. Compared to the other two products, salaries are very high for wheat cereal. This should be thoroughly investigated to find the reason for the wide difference in cost. If these salaries can be reduced, it would greatly enhance the profitability of the wheat cereal, as well as the profitability of the company as a whole.

   ii. The company pays a commission of 10% on the selling price of any product. Consideration should be given to revising the commission structure to base it on contribution margin, rather than on sales.

   iii. Management should consider JIT deliveries to reduce warehouse costs.

Managerial Accounting, 6th Canadian Edition

Problem 12-17 (30 minutes)

1. Breaking the ROI computation into two separate elements helps the manager to see important relationships that might remain hidden if net operating income were simply related to operating assets. First, the importance of turnover of assets as a key element to overall profitability is emphasized. Prior to use of the ROI formula, managers tended to allow operating assets to swell to excessive levels. Second, the importance of sales volume in profit computations is stressed and explicitly recognized. Third, breaking the ROI computation into margin and turnover elements stresses the possibility of trading one off for the other in attempts to improve the overall profit picture. That is, a firm may shave its margins slightly hoping for a great enough increase in turnover to increase the overall rate of return. Fourth, it permits a manager to reduce important profitability elements to ratio form, which enhances comparisons between units (divisions, etc.) of the organization.

2.

	Companies in the Same Industry		
	A	B	C
Sales..................................	$4,000,000*	$1,500,000*	$6,000,000
Net operating income............	560,000*	210,000*	210,000
Average operating assets	2,000,000*	3,000,000	3,000,000*
Margin	14%	14%	3.5%*
Turnover	2.0	0.5	2.0 *
Return on investment (ROI) ..	28%	7%*	7%

   *Given.

Because of differences in size between Company A and the other two companies (notice that B and C are equal in income and assets), it is difficult to say much about comparative performance by looking at net operating income and operating assets alone. That is, it is impossible to determine whether Company A's higher ROI is a result of its lower assets or its higher income. This points up the need to specifically include sales as an element in ROI computations. By including sales, light is shed on the comparative performance and possible problems in the three companies above.

Problem 12-17 (continued)

NAA Report No. 35 states (p. 35):

"Introducing sales to measure level of operations helps to disclose specific areas for more intensive investigation. Company B does as well as Company A in terms of profit margin, for both companies earn 14% on sales. But Company B has a much lower turnover of capital than does Company A. Whereas a dollar of investment in Company A supports two dollars in sales each period, a dollar investment in Company B supports only 50 cents in sales each period. This suggests that the analyst should look carefully at Company B's investment. Is the company keeping an inventory larger than necessary for its sales volume? Are receivables being collected promptly? Or did Company A acquire its fixed assets at a price level which was much lower than that at which Company B purchased its plant?"

Thus, by including sales specifically in ROI computations the manager is able to discover possible problems, as well as reasons underlying a strong or a weak performance. Looking at Company A compared to Company C, notice that C's turnover is the same as A's, but C's margin on sales is much lower. Why would C have such a low margin? Is it due to inefficiency, is it due to geographical location (thereby requiring higher salaries or transportation charges), is it due to excessive materials costs, or is it due to still other factors? ROI computations raise questions such as these, which form the basis for managerial action.

To summarize, in order to bring B's ROI into line with A's, it seems obvious that B's management will have to concentrate its efforts on increasing turnover, either by increasing sales or by reducing assets. It seems unlikely that B can appreciably increase its ROI by improving its margin on sales. On the other hand, C's management should concentrate its efforts on the margin element by trying to pare down its operating expenses.

Managerial Accounting, 6th Canadian Edition

Problem 12-19 (30 minutes)

1. Revenue per client analysis

	Actual**	Budget*	Actual Number of Clients	Total Revenue Variance
Residential	$1,785.71	$2,000	14	($3,000)
Commercial	42,500	36,000	4	26,000
Total	Favourable			$23,000

* $20,000 / 10 = $2,000 ; $180,000 / 5 = $36,000
** $25,000 / 14 = $1,785.71 ; $170,000 / 4 = $42,500

2. Revenue volume analysis
   Note : volume in this firm is number of clients.

	Actual	Budget	Budgeted CM per Client *	Total Contribution Margin
Residential	14	10	$1,500	$6,000
Commercial	4	5	$29,000	($29,000)
Total	unfavourable			($23,000)

* $15,000 / 10 = $1,500; $145,000 / 5 = $ 29,000

Depending of the objectives a mix and volume variance can be computed as follows:

Mix variance

	Actual Volume at Actual Mix	Actual Volume at Anticipated Mix *	Variance	Budgeted CM per Client	Total CM
Residential	14	12	2 F	$1,500	$3,000 F
Commercial	4	6	2 U	$29,000	($58,000) U
Total	18	18			($55,000) U

* 10/15 × 18 = 12; 5/15 × 18 = 6

Problem 12-19 (continued)

Volume variance

	Actual Volume at Anticipated Mix **	Budgeted Volume at Anticipated Mix	Variance	Budgeted CD per Client	Total CM	
Residential	12	10	2	$1,500	$3,000	F
Commercial	6	5	1	$29,000	$29,000	F
Total	18	15			$32,000	F

** See calculation in mix variance
Note mix total plus volume total equals the total volume variance
$55,000 U + $32,000 F = $23,000 U

3. Market analysis

	Market Volume Actual	Market Volume Budget *	Anticipated Market Share	Budgeted CM per Client	Total Contribution Margin	
Residential	150	125	10/125	$1,500	$3,000	F
Commercial	13.3	14.8	5/14.8	$29,000	($14,696)	U
Total	unfavourable				($11,696)	

*Residential $300,000 = 1.20 × budget. Budget market = $250,000 or 125 clients; Commercial $480,000 = .90 × budget. Budget market = $533,333 or 14.8 clients.

Market price has not changed. Revenue per client was not analyzed. Market share variance was not analyzed because of a lack of information.

Note: This problem provides an opportunity to discuss the use of averages per unit for analysis as well as the way simplification can be used to simplify analysis.

Problem 12-21 (45 minutes)

1. The lowest acceptable transfer price from the perspective of the selling division is given by the following formula:

$$\text{Transfer price} = \frac{\text{Variable cost}}{\text{per unit}} + \frac{\text{Total contribution margin on lost sales}}{\text{Number of units transferred}}$$

The Tuner Division has no idle capacity, so transfers from the Tuner Division to the Assembly Division would cut directly into normal sales of tuners to outsiders. Since the costs are the same whether a tuner is transferred internally or sold to outsiders, the only relevant cost is the lost revenue of $20 per tuner that could be sold to outsiders. This is confirmed below:

$$\text{Transfer price} = \$11 + \frac{(\$20 - \$11) \times 30{,}000}{30{,}000}$$

$$= \$11 + (\$20 - \$11) = \$20$$

Therefore, the Tuner Division will refuse to transfer at a price less than $20 per tuner.

The Assembly Division can buy tuners from an outside supplier for $20, less a 10% quantity discount of $2, or $18 per tuner. Therefore, the Division would be unwilling to pay more than $18 per tuner.

$$\text{Transfer price} = \text{Cost of buying from outside supplier} = \$18$$

The requirements of the two divisions are incompatible. The Assembly Division won't pay more than $18 and the Tuner Division will not accept less than $20. Thus, there can be no mutually agreeable transfer price and no transfer will take place.

2. The price being paid to the outside supplier, net of the quantity discount, is only $18. If the Tuner Division meets this price, then profits in the Tuner Division and in the company as a whole will drop by $60,000 per year:

Lost revenue per tuner	$20
Outside supplier's price..........................	$18
Loss in contribution margin per tuner	$2
Number of tuners per year	× 30,000
Total loss in profits...............................	$60,000

Problem 12-21 (continued)

Profits in the Assembly Division will remain unchanged, since it will be paying the same price internally as it is now paying externally.

3. The Tuner Division has idle capacity, so transfers from the Tuner Division to the Assembly Division do not cut into normal sales of tuners to outsiders. In this case, the minimum price as far as the Assembly Division is concerned is the variable cost per tuner of $11. This is confirmed in the following calculation:

$$\text{Transfer price} = \$11 + \frac{\$0}{30,000} = \$11$$

The Assembly Division can buy tuners from an outside supplier for $18 each and would be unwilling to pay more than that in an internal transfer. If the managers understand their own businesses and are cooperative, they should agree to a transfer and should settle on a transfer price within the range:

$$\$11 < \text{Transfer price} \leq \$18$$

4. Yes, $16 is a bona fide outside price. Even though $16 is less than the Tuner Division's $17 "full cost" per unit, it is within the range given in Part 3 and therefore will provide some contribution to the Tuner Division.

If the Tuner Division does not meet the $16 price, it will lose $150,000 in potential profits:

Price per tuner	$16
Less variable costs....................................	11
Contribution margin per tuner	$ 5

30,000 tuners × $5 per tuner = $150,000 potential increased profits

This $150,000 in potential profits applies to the Tuner Division and to the company as a whole.

5. No, the Assembly Division should probably be free to go outside and get the best price it can. Even though this would result in suboptimization for the company as a whole, the buying division should probably not be forced to purchase inside if better prices are available outside.

Problem 12-21 (continued)

6. The Tuner Division will have an increase in profits:

Selling price	$20
Less variable costs......................................	11
Contribution margin per tuner	$ 9

30,000 tuners × $9 per tuner = $270,000 increased profits

The Assembly Division will have a decrease in profits:

Inside purchase price..................................	$20
Outside purchase price	16
Increased cost per tuner.............................	$ 4

30,000 tuners × $4 per tuner = $120,000 decreased profits

The company as a whole will have an increase in profits:

Increased contribution margin in the Tuner Division..........	$ 9
Decreased contribution margin in the Assembly Division ...	4
Increased contribution margin per tuner	$ 5

30,000 tuners × $5 per tuner = $150,000 increased profits

So long as the selling division has idle capacity and the transfer price is greater than the selling division's variable costs, profits in the company as a whole will increase if internal transfers are made. However, there is a question of *fairness* as to how these profits should be split between the selling and buying divisions. The inflexibility of management in this situation damages the profits of the Assembly Division and greatly enhances the profits of the Tuner Division.

Problem 12-23 (60 minutes)

1.

	Total Company Amount	%	District A Amount	%	District B Amount	%	District C Amount	%
Sales (15,000, 25,000 and 10,000 units @ $20)	$1,000,000	100.0	$300,000	100.0	$500,000	100.0	$200,000	100.0
Less variable expenses:								
Cost of goods sold @ $9	450,000	45.0	135,000	45.0	225,000	45.0	90,000	45.0
Shipping	51,250	5.1	11,250	3.7	25,000	5.0	15,000	7.5
Sales commissions	60,000	6.0	18,000	6.0	30,000	6.0	12,000	6.0
Order processing expense*	25,000	2.5	15,000	5.0	7,500	1.5	2,500	1.3
Total variable expenses	586,250	58.6	179,250	59.7	287,500	57.5	119,500	59.8
Contribution margin	413,750	41.4	120,750	40.3	212,500	42.5	80,500	40.2
Less traceable fixed expenses:								
Sales salaries	30,000	3.0	12,000	4.0	10,000	2.0	8,000	4.0
District advertising	75,000	7.5	20,000	6.7	25,000	5.0	30,000	15.0
District management salaries	40,000	4.0	12,000	4.0	15,000	3.0	13,000	6.5
Warehouse rent**	80,000	8.0	30,000	10.0	40,000	8.0	10,000	5.0
Total traceable fixed expenses	225,000	22.5	74,000	24.7	90,000	18.0	61,000	30.5
District segment margin	188,750	18.9	$ 46,750	15.6	$122,500	24.5	$ 19,500	9.7

Problem 12-23 (continued)

	Total Company	
	Amount	%
Less common fixed expenses:		
National advertising	115,000	11.5
Central office administrative		
expense***	75,000	7.5
Total common fixed expenses ..	190,000	19.0
Net operating loss	$ (1,250)	(0.1)

* $25,000 order processing costs ÷ 5,000 orders = $5.00 per order
$5.00 per order × 3,000 orders; 1,500 orders; and 500 orders

** $80,000 warehouse rent ÷ 17,778 square metres = $4.50 per square metre
$4.50 per square metre × 6,667 square metres; 8,889 square metres; and 2,222 square
metres

*** $100,000 – $25,000 variable order processing expense = $75,000 fixed

Problem 12-23 (continued)

2.

	District A	District B	District C
Contribution margin (a)	$120,750	$212,500	$80,500
Number of orders (b).......................	3,000	1,500	500
Contribution margin per order (a) ÷ (b)	$40.25	$141.67	$161.00

District A is taking many small orders, resulting in a contribution margin per order that is only one fourth that of District C. Given the high variable administrative cost of processing an order ($5), the sales staff should try to get customers to order less frequently in larger amounts. Apparently, it is possible to get fewer orders in larger amounts, as shown by the experience in both Districts B and C. If District A had written large enough orders during March to provide a contribution margin of $150 per order, then only 805 orders would have to be written during the month ($120,750 contribution margin ÷ $150 per order = 805 orders), rather than 3,000 orders. This would have reduced variable order processing costs by $10,975—enough to put the company in the black for the month:

Orders actually written	3,000
Orders that could have been written, at $150 contribution margin per order (above)	805
Difference...	2,195
Variable cost to process an order	× $5
Potential savings in processing costs	$10,975

However, this approach is contrary to the JIT trend that emphasizes smaller, more frequent orders. A better solution may be to use process re-engineering to reduce the costs of processing an order.

3.

Incremental sales	$100,000
Contribution margin ratio	× 0.425
Incremental contribution margin.............................	42,500
Less incremental advertising expense.....................	25,000
Incremental segment margin (and company net operating income)...	$ 17,500

Problem 12-23 (continued)

Yes, the expenditures would be justified. Note that the contribution margin ratio should be used in the computation, rather than the segment margin ratio. This answer assumes no change in the average size of an order in District B.

4. The following points should be brought to the attention of management:

a. The large number of orders in District A, as discussed above.

b. The sales staffs in Districts A and C are far less effective than the sales staff in District B, as shown below:

	District A	District B	District C
District sales (a).....................	$300,000	$500,000	$200,000
Number of salespersons (b)......	6	5	4
Dollar sales per salesperson (a) ÷ (b).............................	$ 50,000	$100,000	$ 50,000

c. Although District C has the least sales of any district, it has the highest district advertising expense. This may be indicative of poorly directed or ineffective advertising. Perhaps the district advertising programs should be coordinated through an advertising manager to ensure consistency and effectiveness in overall advertising efforts.

d. Districts B and C have high shipping costs compared to District A. Shipping costs per unit in the three districts are:

	District A	District B	District C
Shipping expense (a)	$11,250	$25,000	$15,000
Number of units sold (b)	15,000	25,000	10,000
Shipping costs per unit (a) ÷ (b).............................	$0.75	$1.00	$1.50

Perhaps company policy should determine the shipping method rather than allowing the sales staff to specify the shipping method. This might avoid unnecessary use of the more expensive shipping methods.

Problem 12-23 (continued)

e. Districts A and C have lower contribution margin ratios than District B, as a result of the higher ordering costs in District A and the higher shipping costs in District C. One advantage of the segmented statement as shown in Part (1) above is that it permits the computation of contribution margins and contribution margin ratios, as well as segment margins, thus providing management with more detailed information.

f. Sales in both Districts A and C are substantially lower than in District B. This may be a result of the low productivity per salesperson in these districts, combined with ineffective advertising in District C and perhaps insufficient advertising in District A.

In conclusion, unprofitable operations may be caused by a number of small problems rather than a single, large problem. Statements in the segmented format help to focus on potential small problem areas, such as shown above.

Managerial Accounting, 6th Canadian Edition

Problem 12-25 (30 minutes)

1. $ROI = \dfrac{\text{Net operating income}}{\text{Sales}} \times \dfrac{\text{Sales}}{\text{Average operating assets}}$

$$= \dfrac{\$80,000}{\$1,000,000} \times \dfrac{\$1,000,000}{\$500,000}$$

$$= 8\% \times 2 = 16\%$$

2. $ROI = \dfrac{\$90,000}{\$1,000,000} \times \dfrac{\$1,000,000}{\$500,000}$

$$= \quad 9\% \quad \times \quad 2 \quad = \quad 18\%$$

$$\text{(Increase)} \quad \text{(Unchanged)} \quad \text{(Increase)}$$

3. $ROI = \dfrac{\$80,000}{\$1,000,000} \times \dfrac{\$1,000,000}{\$400,000}$

$$= \quad 8\% \quad \times \quad 2.5 \quad = \quad 20\%$$

$$\text{(Unchanged)} \quad \text{(Increase)} \quad \text{(Increase)}$$

4. The company has a contribution margin ratio of 40% ($20 CM per unit, divided by $50 selling price per unit). Therefore, a $100,000 increase in sales would result in a new net operating income of:

Sales...	$1,100,000	100%
Less variable expenses	660,000	60
Contribution margin	440,000	40%
Less fixed expenses	320,000	
Net operating income..............................	$ 120,000	

Problem 12-25 (continued)

$$ROI = \frac{\$120,000}{\$1,100,000} \times \frac{\$1,100,000}{\$500,000}$$

$$= 10.91\% \times 2.2 = 24\%$$

(Increase)   (Increase)   (Increase)

A change in sales affects *both* the margin and the turnover.

5. Interest is a financing expense and thus is not used to compute net operating income.

$$ROI = \frac{\$85,000}{\$1,000,000} \times \frac{\$1,000,000}{\$625,000}$$

$$= 8.5\% \times 1.6 = 13.6\%$$

(Increase)   (Decrease)   (Decrease)

6.
$$ROI = \frac{\$80,000}{\$1,000,000} \times \frac{\$1,000,000}{\$320,000}$$

$$= 8\% \times 3.125 = 25\%$$

(Unchanged)   (Increase)   (Increase)

7.
$$ROI = \frac{\$60,000}{\$1,000,000} \times \frac{\$1,000,000}{\$480,000}$$

$$= 6\% \times 2.08 = 12.5\%$$

(Decrease)   (Increase)   (Decrease)

Problem 12-27 (45 minutes)

1. The Consumer Products Division will probably reject the $400 price because it is below the division's variable cost of $420 per DVD player. This variable cost includes the $190 transfer price from the Board Division, which in turn includes $30 per unit in fixed costs. However, from the viewpoint of the Consumer Products Division, the entire $190 transfer price is a variable cost. Consequently, the Consumer Products Division will reject the $400 price offered by the overseas distributor.

2. If both the Board Division and the Consumer Products Division have idle capacity, then from the standpoint of the entire company the $400 offer should be accepted. By rejecting the $400 price, the company will lose $50 per DVD player in potential contribution margin:

Price offered per player		$400
Less variable costs per player:		
Board Division	$120	
Consumer Products Division	230	350
Potential contribution margin per player		$ 50

3. If the Board Division is operating at capacity, any boards transferred to the Consumer Products Division to fill the overseas order will have to be diverted from outside customers. Whether a board is sold to outside customers or is transferred to the Consumer Products Division, its production cost is the same. However, if a board is diverted from outside sales, the Board Division (and the entire company) loses the $190 in revenue. As a consequence, as shown below, there would be a net loss of $20 on each player sold for $400.

Price offered per player		$400
Less:		
Lost revenue from sales of boards to outsiders	$190	
Variable cost of Consumer Products Division	230	420
Net loss per player		($ 20)

Problem 12-27 (continued)

4. When the selling division has no idle capacity, as in part (3), market price works very well as a transfer price. The cost to the company of a transfer when there is no idle capacity is the lost revenue from sales to outsiders. If the market price is used as the transfer price, the buying division will view the market price of the transferred item as its cost — which is appropriate since that is the cost to the company. As a consequence, the manager of the buying division should be motivated to make decisions that are in the best interests of the company.

When the selling division has idle capacity, the cost to the company of the transfer is just the variable cost of producing the item. If the market price is used as the transfer price, the manager of the buying division will view that as his/her cost rather than the real cost to the company, which is just variable cost. Hence, the manager will have the wrong cost information for making decisions as we observed in parts (1) and (2).

Managerial Accounting, 6th Canadian Edition

Case 12-29 (75 minutes)

1. See the segmented statement that follows. Supporting computations for the statement are given below:

Revenues:

Membership dues (10,000 × $60)	$600,000
Assigned to the Journal (10,000 × $15)......................	150,000
Assigned to Membership Service	$450,000
Non-member journal subscriptions (1,000 × $20)........	$ 20,000
Advertising (given)	$ 50,000
Books and reports (given).......................................	$ 70,000
Continuing education courses (given)	$230,000

Occupancy costs:

Membership Services ($100,000 × 0.3 + $20,000)	$ 50,000
Journal ($100,000 × 0.1)..	10,000
Books and Reports ($100,000 × 0.1).........................	10,000
Continuing Education ($100,000 × 0.2)	20,000
Central staff ($100,000 × 0.3).................................	30,000
Total occupancy costs	$120,000

Printing costs:

Journal (11,000 × $4)	$ 44,000
Books and Reports (given).......................................	25,000
Continuing Education (plug).....................................	13,000
Total printing costs	$ 82,000

Mailing costs:

Journal (11,000 × $1)	$ 11,000
Books and Reports (given).......................................	8,000
Central staff (plug)	5,000
Total mailing costs..	$ 24,000

Case 12-29 (continued)

	Total	Membership Services	Journal	Books and Reports	Continuing Education
Revenues:					
Membership dues............................	$600,000	$450,000	$150,000		
Non-member journal subscriptions.........	20,000		20,000		
Advertising..................................	50,000		50,000		
Books and reports.........................	70,000			$ 70,000	
Continuing education courses.............	230,000				$230,000
Total revenues..............................	970,000	450,000	220,000	70,000	230,000
Expenses traceable to segments:					
Salaries.....................................	320,000	170,000	60,000	40,000	50,000
Occupancy costs...........................	90,000	50,000	10,000	10,000	20,000
Distributions to local chapters............	210,000	210,000			
Printing.....................................	82,000		44,000	25,000	13,000
Mailing......................................	19,000		11,000	8,000	
Continuing education instructors' fees....	60,000				60,000
Total traceable expenses..................	781,000	430,000	125,000	83,000	143,000
Program segment margin...................	189,000	$ 20,000	$ 95,000	$ (13,000)	$ 87,000

(The segmented income statement is continued on the next page.)

Case 12-29 (continued)

Less common expenses:

Salaries—corporate staff	120,000
Occupancy costs	30,000
Mailing	5,000
General administrative	27,000
Total common expenses	182,000
Excess of revenues over expenses	$ 7,000

Note: Some may argue that apart from the $20,000 in rental cost directly attributed to Membership Services, occupancy costs are common costs that should not be allocated to programs. The correct treatment of the occupancy costs depends on whether they could be avoided in part by eliminating a program. We have assumed that they could be avoided.

2. While we do not favour the allocation of common costs to segments, the reason most often given for this practice is that segment managers need to be aware of the fact that common costs exist and that they must be covered.

Arguments against allocation of common costs include:

- Allocation bases must be chosen arbitrarily since there is no cause-and-effect relationship between common costs and the segments to which they are allocated.

- Management may be misled into eliminating a profitable segment that appears to be unprofitable because of allocated common costs.

- Segment managers usually have little control over the common costs. They should not be held accountable for costs over which they have little or no control.

- Allocations of common costs tend to undermine the credibility of performance reports.

Case 12-31 (90 minutes)

1.

	Total Amount	%	Line A Amount	%	Line B Amount	%	Line C Amount	%
Sales	$1,000,000	100.0	$400,000	100.0	$250,000	100	$350,000	100.0
Less variable expenses:								
Production	242,500	24.3	80,000	20.0	75,000	30	87,500	25.0
Selling	50,000	5.0	20,000	5.0	12,500	5	17,500	5.0
Total	292,500	29.3	100,000	25.0	87,500	35	105,000	30.0
Contribution margin	707,500	70.7	300,000	75.0	162,500	65	245,000	70.0
Less traceable fixed expenses:								
Production	200,000	20.0	107,000	26.8	30,000	12	63,000	18.0
Selling	100,000	10.0	40,000	10.0	10,000	4	50,000	14.3
Total	300,000	30.0	147,000	36.8	40,000	16	113,000	32.3
Product line segment margin	407,500	40.7	$153,000	38.2	$122,500	49	$132,000	37.7
Less common fixed expenses:								
Production*	300,000	30.0						
Administrative	150,000	15.0						
Total	450,000	45.0						
Net operating loss	$ (42,500)	(4.3)						

* Total fixed production costs.............. $500,000
Less traceable fixed production costs.............. 200,000
Common fixed production costs.............. $300,000

Case 12-31 (continued)

2. No, production of Line B, not Line A, should be cut back. Under the conditions posed, it does not appear that the company will be able to avoid any fixed costs (either traceable or common) when production is cut back. Both Lines A and B sell for $100 per unit. Since the contribution margin ratio of Line A is 75%, its unit contribution margin is $75. And since the contribution margin ratio of Line B is 65%, its unit contribution margin is $65. Since the company must choose between using a B4 chip to produce one unit of Line A or one unit of Line B, Line A is clearly the better choice since its unit contribution margin is $10 higher.

   Some students will disagree with this analysis, and state that Mr. Aiken is correct in cutting back production of Line A. These students will base their argument on Line B's higher segment margin percentage (notice from the income statement in part (1) that Line B has a segment margin ratio of 49%, as compared to only 38.2% for Line A). However the segment margin should not be used for decision-making. Unlike contribution margin percentages, the segment margin percentages are unstable because fixed cost is included in the segment margin. Thus, as total sales change, the segment margin percentages change also.

3. Line C should not be eliminated. Notice from the income statement in part (1) that the line is covering all of its own traceable costs, and is generating a segment margin of $132,000 per month. If the line is discontinued, all of this segment margin will be lost to the company and the overall monthly loss will worsen.

Case 12-31 (continued)

4. a.

	Total		Home Market		Foreign Market	
	Amount	%	Amount	%	Amount	%
Sales	$350,000	100.0	$300,000	100.0	$50,000	100.0
Less variable expenses:						
Production	87,500	25.0	75,000	25.0	12,500	25.0
Selling	17,500	5.0	15,000	5.0	2,500	5.0
Total	105,000	30.0	90,000	30.0	15,000	30.0
Contribution margin	245,000	70.0	210,000	70.0	35,000	70.0
Less traceable fixed expenses:						
Selling	50,000	14.3	10,000	3.3	40,000	80.0
Market segment margin	195,000	55.7	$200,000	66.7	$ (5,000)	(10.0)
Less common fixed expenses:						
Production	63,000	18.0				
Product line segment margin	$132,000	37.7				

b. At least the following three points should be brought to the attention of management:

1. Compared to the home market, sales in the foreign market are very low.

2. Fixed selling expenses are very high in the foreign market, totaling four times as much each month as in the home market. Why?

3. The foreign market is not covering all of its own traceable fixed expenses, and thus the market is showing a negative segment margin. If sales cannot be increased sufficiently in future months for the foreign market to cover its own traceable expenses, then consideration should be given to eliminating the market.

Case 12-33

TEACHING NOTES[*]

Contribution of the Case

The HCS case extends the accounting literature by providing instructors an effective teaching tool to incorporate the balanced scorecard into a variety of courses. The case focuses on the selection, design, collection, and monitoring of appropriate performance measures for the construction of a balanced scorecard in the "real-world" setting of a knowledge-based firm. Two other balanced scorecard cases in the extant literature also provide "real-world" settings, but from a different perspective than the HCS case.[1] Frigo et al. (1999) address assurance services related to performance measurement systems, primarily focusing on the definition of corporate vision and strategy as the key element to developing a balanced scorecard. Carr (1999) emphasizes evaluation and improvement of an existing balanced scorecard measurement system. Neither of these cases includes requirements that allow students to complete the process of performance measurement design, collection, and monitoring. The HCS case extends both Frigo et al. (1999) and Carr (1999) by focusing on the role of the managerial accountant who has primary responsibility for the design and implementation of a firm's performance measurement system.

Learning Objectives

Completing the HCS case enables students to (1) gain experience in selecting appropriate performance measures for a balanced scorecard (case requirement 1), (2) gain familiarity working with both financial and nonfinancial measures (case requirements 1 and 2), and (3) gain practice in developing a reporting and monitoring process for the measures selected (case requirement 2). Secondary learning objectives are for students to: (1) gain insight into the difficulties of aligning performance measures with compensation, and (2) integrate what they have learned

---

[*] Adapted from Chris Moore, Beverly J. Rowe, and Sally K. Widener. "HCS: Designing a Balanced Scorecard in a Knowledge-Based Firm." *Issues in Accounting Education*, Volume 16, No. 4, November 2001, pp 569 to 601, with permission.

[1] In addition, in a noncase article, Chang and Chow (1999) show how the balanced scorecard can be used effectively within academic instructions.

Case 12-33 (continued)

in the HCS case with prior knowledge in order to expand their overall business knowledge.

Core competencies that accountants need in order to be successful (AICPA 1997, 1998) include: strategic and critical-thinking skills (e.g., ability to transform information into knowledge and bring the necessary insight to bear on strategic decisions); interpretation of converging information (e.g., ability to interpret and broaden the context of financial and nonfinancial information); and focus on the customer, client, and market (e.g., ability to anticipate and meet the rapidly changing and increasingly complex needs of clients, employees, customers and markets). Each of these core competencies is addressed by one or more of the HCS case requirements.

Requirements 1 and 2 provide students the opportunity to build strategic and critical-thinking skills as well as integrating converging information. To complete the task of designing, collecting, and monitoring performance measures for each of HCS' strategic objectives and core values, students must integrate data given in the case to build knowledge about HCS, its strategy, and the task at hand. Once the knowledge has been acquired, students can then form insights that guide their choice of measures, which by design are linked to the firm's strategy. Students should select nonfinancial as well as financial performance indicators, which lead them to consider measures in a broader context than in the traditional financial accounting environment. Requirements 1 and 2 allow students to practice interpreting converging information by linking HCS' strategic objectives to both financial and nonfinancial measures. The HCS case also requires students to move outside the thinking norm for accounting students, and expand their thoughts and ideas into the concept of a knowledge-based firm in a niche market. As such, students must consider how the performance measurement system addresses the needs of HCS (client), its staff (employees), and HCS' strategy for the niche market.

In addition, the HCS case exposes students to some of the nontraditional services now being performed by management accountants. The Institute of Management Accountants states that management accountants are becoming "strategic partners" in firms (Siegel and Sorenson 1999, 18). Long-term strategic planning and performance evaluation are two of the most critical work activities identified for management accountants (Siegel 1996). By designing a performance-evaluation system within the context of HCS' strategic environment,

Case 12-33 (continued)

students gain experience in a value-added work activity for management accountants.

DISCUSSION OF REQUIREMENTS

Requirement 1

Students are required to recommend both financial and nonfinancial measures that are designed to provide information on the degree to which the underlying strategic objectives and core values are being accomplished (addressing the first two learning objectives). Figure 3 illustrates how the strategic objectives and the core values relate to HCS' customer-intimacy strategy and its primary strategic resource: human capital. Each strategic objective and core value has been linked to a balanced scorecard perspective. To assist students in understanding the essential links between strategy, strategic resources, and the development of the strategic objectives and the core values, the instructor may review Figure 3 with the class prior to the small groups beginning work on the case. Alice is determined to achieve growth using a customer-intimacy strategy, which requires long-standing customer relationships. For HCS, the key to developing and maintaining a necessary customer-relationship centres on attracting, retaining, and facilitating a highly knowledgeable and effective staff. HCS' open and collaborative culture is the primary ingredient to achieving staff retention. As Figure 3 illustrates, HCS' strategic objectives and core values focus the firm on these essential elements (growth, customer relationships, staff, and culture), which are necessary to succeed using the customer-intimacy strategy.

The strategic objectives and core values as shown on Figure 3 are listed for the students in column (1) of Figure 4 under the appropriate balanced scorecard perspective. Completing Figure 4 allows students to gain experience in recommending appropriate performance measures (both financial and nonfinancial) that are linked to the firm's strategic and core values.

One suggested solution is illustrated in Appendix 1. The solution includes numerous performance measures to aid the instructor. Students' solutions may reflect performance measures that are not included in the suggested solution. The important issue is not whether the students recommend the same measures that are illustrated in the suggested solution, but rather whether the measures students recommend are

Case 12-33 (continued)

appropriate for gaining information about how well the firm is achieving its strategic objectives and maintaining its core values.

The instructor may want to ask students to describe their reasoning for recommending a particular measure. Do the students understand how the measure they recommended will provide management with information about the degree to which a strategic objective is being accomplished or a core value is being maintained (e.g., know and understand the customer needs)? A discussion at this point may also include the notion of lead/lag indicators. Students may be asked how one measure in their balanced scorecard not only provides managers with information related to a strategic objective or core value, but is also part of a lead/lag (or casual) relation. For example, consider the measure of customer satisfaction. A component of customer satisfaction is a question asking customers to respond to how well HCS identified their needs within the context of their business. Asking this question will provide HCS with insights about whether they are achieving their strategic objective: to know and understand customers' needs. As HCS develops a thorough understanding of customer needs, customers will be more satisfied and will likely contract for increased services. Thus, customer satisfaction is a leading indicator of another measure: growth in profitability.

Requirement 2

HCS must achieve a balance between effective monitoring of key performance measures and the costs associated with monitoring. Therefore, the collection and monitoring procedures should be customized based on the type of measures being collected. For example, employee satisfaction scores will be collected through a survey of the employees. This indicator might be collected on a quarterly basis since the data collection is a time-intensive process and employee opinions are not likely to change quickly. Other measures such as instances of successful conflict resolution may be collected on an ongoing basis and documented each time a successful resolution occurs. This could be done on a standardized form, initiated by the most senior employee, and initialed by all employees involved.

The student tasks is to complete the worksheet shown in Figure 5. For each measure selected by the group, students will have to indicate how they would measure the performance indicator (column (2)), how they would collect the measure and how often (column (3)), and how they

Managerial Accounting, 6th Canadian Edition

Case 12-33 (continued)

would monitor the measure (column (4)). Thus, this requirement addresses the third learning objective.

One suggested solution is illustrated in Appendix 2. The instructor may want to focus on the following key issues:

- Is the measurement of the performance indicator possible?
- Is the timing of the data collection appropriate and tailored to each performance indicator (e.g., is it appropriate to survey employees daily to gauge employee satisfaction)?
- Did the students use appropriate benchmarking or continuous improvement ideas?

Note: Reference sources for the authors listed in the preceding discussion can be found in the text description for this case.

Case 12-33 (continued)

APPENDIX 1
One Possible Balanced Scorecard

Firm Strategy: Customer-intimacy—*Create and maintain customer loyalty through customized services*

Strategic Objectives and Core Values	Possible Performance Measures
Financial	**Financial**
1. To "grow" the company	1a. Growth in profitability
	1b. Customer margins
	1c. Number of new clients
	1d. Revenue from new clients
Customer	**Customer**
1. To know and understand our customer's needs	1a. Number of face-to-face meetings with client
	1b. Customer satisfaction scores—how well did we identify customer needs within context of customer's business?
2. To engage in service over self-interest, which provides that the client will come first (service over self-interest)	2a. Number of system implementations completed on time.
	2b. Customer satisfaction scores—how well did we meet our customer's unique needs?
Internal Business Process	**Internal Business Process**
1. To encourage and promote knowledge sharing	1a. Number of team-implemented systems solutions
	1b. Number of additions of internal knowledge-generated ideas and solutions to company's intranet

Case 12-33 (continued)

APPENDIX 1 (continued)

Strategic Objectives and Core Values	Possible Performance Measures
2. To be authentic, which ensures that we have timely, honest, and accurate communication (authenticity) within the company	2a. Instances of successful conflict resolutions. 2b. Employee satisfaction survey—ranking of communication within the company
3. To empower the employees, which will enable them to make decisions that benefit the client (empowerment)	3a. Number of successful employee-generated solutions 3b. Ratio of managers to employees
Learning and Growth 1. To maintain an open and collaborative culture in order to attract and retain employees	Learning and Growth 1a. Employee satisfaction 1b. Voluntary turnover
2. To seek diversity among our employees (diversity)	2a. Diversity of undergraduate degrees 2b. Variety of skills and interests represented (obtained through employee survey)
3. To ensure that our employees have achieved a sense of balance in order to give us the ongoing energy to be efficient and effective (balance)	3a. Employee satisfaction score (obtained through employee survey) 3b. Amount of overtime hours worked 3c. Amount of vacation time taken

Case 12-33 (continued)

APPENDIX 2
Reporting and Monitoring of Performance Measures

Measures	Definition of Measures	Collection of Measures	Monitoring of Measures
Growth in profitability	Ratio, calculated as change in profitability divided by prior-period profitability	This indicator will be calculated monthly as part of the financial accounting system.	Distributed in the monthly reporting package. Managers will investigate variances, calculated as the difference between budget and actual. Margins will be benchmarked against industry standards.
Customer margins	Financial measure, calculated as customer billings less costs charged to the customer's job	This indicator will be calculated monthly as part of the financial accounting system.	Distributed in the monthly reporting package. Managers will investigate variances, calculated as the difference between budget and actual. Margins will be benchmarked against industry standards.
Number of new clients	Count of new clients	This indicator will be collected on an ongoing basis each time the firm gains a new client.	Discussed in weekly management/operations meeting. The measure will be tracked against a budgeted target.
Revenue from new clients	Financial measure, calculated as customer billings	This indicator will be calculated monthly as part of the financial accounting system.	Distributed in the monthly reporting package. Managers will investigate variances, calculated as the difference between budget and actual.
Number of face-to-face meetings with client	Count of the number of meetings with the client in person	This indicator will be collected on an ongoing basis each time a face-to-face meeting occurs.	Discussed in weekly management/operations meeting. The measure will be tracked against a budgeted target.
Customer satisfaction scores	Measured on a seven-point scale through mailed survey to customers	For short jobs a survey will be administered at the completion of each job. For long jobs (> 3-month implementations) a survey will be administered midway through the job and at the completion of the job.	Discussed in the closing conference at the completion of each job. The firm will strive for continuous improvement in this area, thus monitoring a trend of customer satisfaction scores.

Case 12-33 (continued)

APPENDIX 2 (continued)

Measures	Definition of Measures	Collection of Measures	Monitoring of Measures
On-time delivery	Count of the number of items the completion of the project was either on time or before the promised/ schedule date	This indicator will be calculated at the end of each month.	Distributed in the monthly reporting package. This measure will be benchmarked against industry standards.
Number of team-implemented systems solutions	Count of the number of solutions implemented that came from teams of employees	This indicator will be collected on an ongoing basis. Each time a solution is implemented a form will be checked to indicate the originator of the solution.	Discussed in weekly management/operations meeting. The measure will be tracked against a budgeted target.
Number of additions to intranet	Count of the number of additions to the firm's intranet site	This indicator will be collected electronically on an ongoing basis.	Discussed in weekly management/operations meeting. The measure will be tracked against a budgeted target.
Instances of successful conflict resolution	Count of successful resolutions. The employee will document the count on a form designed to monitor this indicator.	This indicator will be collected on an ongoing basis (at the time of conflict resolution).	Discussed in weekly management/operations meeting. The measure will be tracked against a budgeted target.
Employee satisfaction	Measurement on a seven-point scale through survey of employees. Data will be collected through a mailed survey.	Employee satisfaction scores will be collected via a mailed survey to all employees on an annual basis. Responses will be anonymous.	Discussed in quarterly management meetings. Continuous improvement is the goal for this area, so management will track the trend in employee satisfaction scores.
Number of successful employee-generated solutions	Count of successful employee-generated solutions. The employee will document the count on a form designed specifically to monitor this indicator.	This indicator will be collected on an ongoing basis (at the time the solution is generated).	Discussed in weekly management/operations meeting. The measure will be tracked against a budgeted target.
Ratio of managers to employees	Measured as the number of managers divided by the number of employees.	This indicator will be calculated monthly.	Distributed in the monthly reporting package. Managers will investigate variances, calculated as the difference between budget and actual.

Case 12-33 (continued)

APPENDIX 2 (continued)

Measures	Definition of Measures	Collection of Measures	Monitoring of Measures
Voluntary turnover	Ratio, measured as the number of employees who voluntarily leave to the total number of employees.	This indicator will be calculated monthly.	Distributed in the monthly reporting package. Managers will investigate variances, calculated as the difference between budget and actual.
Diversity of undergraduate degrees	Measured as a count of college degrees by major and minor field	This indicator will be updated (recalculated) each time an employee leaves the company or starts with the company.	Discussed in quarterly meetings. Continuous improvement is the goal for this area, so management will track the diversity of degrees.
Variety of skills and interests	Measured through a question on the employee survey	This indicator will be collected through a question on the employee survey on an annual basis.	Discussed in quarterly meetings. Continuous improvement is the goal for this area, so management will track the trend in the variety of skills and interests of its employees.
Amount of overtime hours worked	Measured as the number of overtime hours worked by employees	This indicator will be calculated monthly.	Distributed in the monthly reporting package. Managers will investigate variances, calculated as the difference between budget and actual.
Amount of vacation time taken	Measured as the hours of vacation time taken by employees	This indicator will be calculated monthly.	Distributed in the monthly reporting package. Managers will investigate variances, calculated as the difference between budget and actual.

Chapter 13
Relevant Costs for Decision Making

Exercise 13-1 (15 minutes)

	Case 1		Case 2	
Item	Relevant	Not Relevant	Relevant	Not Relevant
a. Sales revenue	X			X
b. Direct materials	X		X	
c. Direct labour	X			X
d. Variable manufacturing overhead	X			X
e. Book value—Model A3000 machine		X		X
f. Disposal value—Model A3000 machine		X	X	
g. Depreciation—Model A3000 machine		X		X
h. Market value—Model B3800 machine (cost)....	X		X	
i. Fixed manufacturing overhead		X		X
j. Variable selling expense ...	X			X
k. Fixed selling expense	X			X
l. General administrative overhead	X			X

Exercise 13-3 (30 minutes)

1. No, the housekeeping program should not be discontinued. It is actually generating a positive program segment margin and is, of course, providing a valuable service to seniors. Computations to support this conclusion follow:

   Contribution margin lost if the housekeeping $(80,000)

program is dropped ....
Fixed costs that can be avoided:
    Liability insurance $15,000
    Program administrator's salary............................ 37,000   52,000
Decrease in net operating income for the
    organization as a whole....................................... $(28,000)

Depreciation on the van is a sunk cost and the van has no salvage value because it would be donated to another organization. The general administrative overhead is allocated and none of it would be avoided if the program were dropped; thus it is not relevant to the decision.

The same result can be obtained with the alternative analysis below:

	Current Total	Total If House-keeping Is Dropped	Difference: Net Operating Income Increase or (Decrease)
Revenues....................................	$900,000	$660,000	$(240,000)
Less variable expenses	490,000	330,000	160,000
Contribution margin......................	410,000	330,000	(80,000)
Less fixed expenses:			
Depreciation*............................	68,000	68,000	0
Liability insurance	42,000	27,000	15,000
Program administrators' salaries .	115,000	78,000	37,000
General administrative overhead.	180,000	180,000	0
Total fixed expenses.....................	405,000	353,000	52,000
Net operating income (loss)	$ 5,000	$(23,000)	$ (28,000)

*Includes pro-rated loss on disposal of the van if it is donated to a charity.

Exercise 13-3 (continued)

2. To give the administrator of the entire organization a clearer picture of the financial viability of each of the organization's programs, the general administrative overhead should not be allocated. It is a common cost that should be deducted from the total program segment margin. Following the format introduced in Chapter 12 for a segmented income statement, a better income statement would be:

	Total	Home Nursing	Meals on Wheels	House-keeping
Revenues............................	$900,000	$260,000	$400,000	$240,000
Less variable expenses	490,000	120,000	210,000	160,000
Contribution margin...............	410,000	140,000	190,000	80,000
Less traceable fixed expenses:				
Depreciation.......................	68,000	8,000	40,000	20,000
Liability insurance	42,000	20,000	7,000	15,000
Program administrators' salaries............................	115,000	40,000	38,000	37,000
Total traceable fixed expenses...........................	225,000	68,000	85,000	72,000
Program segment margins	185,000	$ 72,000	$105,000	$ 8,000
General administrative overhead............................	180,000			
Net operating income (loss) ...	$ 5,000			

Exercise 13-5 (15 minutes)

Only the incremental costs and benefits are relevant. In particular, only the variable manufacturing overhead and the cost of the special tool are relevant overhead costs in this situation. The other manufacturing overhead costs are fixed and are not affected by the decision.

	Per Unit	Total 10 bracelets
Incremental revenue	$349.95	$3,499.50
Incremental costs:		
Variable costs:		
Direct materials	143.00	1,430.00
Direct labour	86.00	860.00
Variable manufacturing overhead	7.00	70.00
Special filigree	6.00	60.00
Total variable cost	$242.00	2,420.00
Fixed costs:		
Purchase of special tool		465.00
Total incremental cost		2,885.00
Incremental net operating income		$ 614.50

Even though the price for the special order is below the company's regular price for such an item, the special order would add to the company's net operating income and should be accepted. This conclusion would not necessarily follow if the special order affected the regular selling price of bracelets or if it required the use of a constrained resource.

Exercise 13-7 (10 minutes)

	Product X	Product Y	Product Z
Sales value after further processing	$80,000	$150,000	$75,000
Sales value at split-off point.................	50,000	90,000	60,000
Incremental revenue...........................	30,000	60,000	15,000
Cost of further processing	35,000	40,000	12,000
Incremental profit (loss)......................	$(5,000)	20,000	3,000

Products Y and Z should be processed further, but not Product X.

Exercise 13-9 (30 minutes)

No, the overnight cases should not be discontinued. The computations are:

Contribution margin lost if the cases are discontinued...		$(260,000)
Less fixed costs that can be avoided if the cases are discontinued:		
Salary of the product line manager...............	$ 21,000	
Advertising	110,000	
Insurance on inventories.............................	9,000	140,000
Net disadvantage of dropping the cases.............		$(120,000)

The same solution can be obtained by preparing comparative income statements:

	Keep Overnight Cases	Drop Overnight Cases	Difference: Net Operating Income Increase or (Decrease)
Sales..	$450,000	$ 0	$(450,000)
Less variable expenses:			
Variable manufacturing expenses .	130,000	0	130,000
Sales commissions.......................	48,000	0	48,000
Shipping	12,000	0	12,000
Total variable expenses	190,000	0	190,000
Contribution margin	260,000	0	(260,000)
Less fixed expenses:			
Salary of line manager.................	21,000	0	21,000
General factory overhead..............	104,000	104,000	0
Depreciation of equipment...........	36,000	36,000	0
Advertising—traceable	110,000	0	110,000
Insurance on inventories..............	9,000	0	9,000
Purchasing department expenses .	50,000	50,000	0
Total fixed expenses	330,000	190,000	140,000
Net operating loss..........................	$ (70,000)	$(190,000)	$(120,000)

Exercise 13-11 (15 minutes)

1.

$$\text{Markup percentage on absorption cost} = \frac{\left(\begin{array}{c}\text{Required ROI} \\ \times \text{ Investment}\end{array}\right) + \text{SG\&A expenses}}{\text{Unit sales} \times \text{Unit product cost}}$$

$$= \frac{(18\% \times \$500,000) + \$60,000}{12,500 \text{ units} \times \$30 \text{ per unit}}$$

$$= \frac{\$150,000}{\$375,000}$$

$$= 40\%$$

2. Unit product cost...................... $30
   Markup: 40% × $30................. 12
   Target selling price per unit....... $42

Exercise 13-13 (15 minutes)

1. Time rate to be used:

Plumbers' wages and fringe benefits
($340,000 ÷ 20,000 hours) $17
Other repair costs ($160,000 ÷ 20,000 hours)........... 8
Desired profit per hour of plumber time 5
Total charging rate per hour for service.................... $30

Material loading charge:

Ordering, handling, and storage cost .... 15% of invoice cost
Desired profit on parts............................. 30% of invoice cost
Material loading charge............................ 45% of invoice cost

2. Time charge: 3 hours × $30 per hour............. $ 90
   Material charge:
   Invoice cost of parts $40
   Material loading charge (45% × $40)........... 18   58
   Billed cost of the job..................................... $148

Problem 13-15 (60 minutes)

1. Contribution margin lost if the Bath Department is dropped:

Lost from the Bath Department	$700,000
Lost from the Kitchen Department (10% × $2,400,000)	240,000
Total lost contribution margin	940,000
Less avoidable fixed costs ($900,000 − $370,000)	530,000
Decrease in overall net operating income	$410,000

2. Merifulon should be processed further:

Sales value after further processing	$60,000
Sales value at the split-off point	40,000
Incremental revenue from further processing	20,000
Cost of further processing	13,000
Profit from further processing	$ 7,000

The $10,000 in allocated common costs (1/3 × $30,000) will be the same regardless of which alternative is selected, and hence is not relevant to the decision.

3. The company should accept orders first for Z, second for X, and third for Y. The computations are:

	X	Y	Z
(a) Direct materials required per unit	$24.00	$15.00	$9.00
(b) Cost per kilogram	$3.00	$3.00	$3.00
(c) Kilograms required per unit (a) ÷ (b)	8	5	3
(d) Contribution margin per unit	$32.00	$14.00	$21.00
Contribution margin per kilogram of materials used (d) ÷ (c)	$4.00	$2.80	$7.00

Problem 13-15 (continued)

Since Z uses the least amount of material per unit of the three products, and since it is the most profitable of the three in terms of its use of this constrained resource, some students will immediately assume that this is an infallible relationship. That is, they will assume that the way to spot the most profitable product is to find the one using the least amount of the constrained resource. The way to dispel this notion is to point out that product X uses more material (the constrained resource) than does product Y, but yet it is preferred over product Y. *The key factor is not how much of a constrained resource a product uses, but rather how much contribution margin the product generates per unit of the constrained resource.*

4.

| | Relevant Costs | |
Item	Make	Buy
Direct materials (60,000 @ $4.00)	$240,000	
Direct labour (60,000 @ $2.75)	165,000	
Variable manufacturing overhead (60,000 @ $0.50)	30,000	
Fixed manufacturing overhead, traceable (1/3 of $180,000)	60,000	
Cost of purchasing from outside supplier (60,000 @ $10)		$600,000
Total cost	$495,000	$600,000

The two-thirds of the traceable fixed manufacturing overhead costs that cannot be eliminated, and all of the common fixed manufacturing overhead costs, are irrelevant.

The company would save $105,000 per year by continuing to make the parts itself.

Managerial Accounting, 6th Canadian Edition

Problem 13-15 (continued)

5. Monthly profits would be increased by $9,000:

	Per Unit	Total for 2,000 Units
Incremental revenue	$12.00	$24,000
Incremental costs:		
Variable costs:		
Direct materials	2.50	5,000
Direct labour	3.00	6,000
Variable manufacturing overhead	0.50	1,000
Variable selling and administrative	1.50	3,000
Total variable cost	$ 7.50	15,000
Fixed costs:		
None affected by the special order		0
Total incremental cost		15,000
Incremental net operating income		$ 9,000

6. The relevant cost is $1.50 (the variable selling and administrative costs). All other variable costs are sunk, since the units have already been produced. The fixed costs would not be relevant, because they would not be affected by the sale of leftover units.

Problem 13-17 (45 minutes)

1. Product MJ-7 yields a contribution margin of $3.50 per litre ($8.75 − $5.25 = $3.50). If the plant closes, this contribution margin will be lost on the 88,000 litres (44,000 litres per month × 2 = 88,000 litres) that could have been sold during the two-month period. However, the company will be able to avoid certain fixed costs as a result of closing down. The analysis is:

Contribution margin lost by closing the plant for two months ($3.50 per litre × 88,000 litres)........		$(308,000)
Costs avoided by closing the plant for two months:		
Fixed manufacturing overhead cost ($230,000 − $170,000 = $60,000; $60,000 × 2 months = $120,000)...................$120,000		
Fixed selling costs ($310,000 × 10% × 2 months)........................	62,000	182,000
Net disadvantage of closing, before start-up costs...		(126,000)
Add start-up costs..		(14,000)
Disadvantage of closing the plant.........................		$(140,000)

No, the company should not close the plant; it should continue to operate at the reduced level of 44,000 litres produced and sold each month. Closing will result in a $140,000 greater loss over the two-month period than if the company continues to operate. Additional factors are the potential loss of goodwill among the customers who need the 44,000 litres of MJ-7 each month and the adverse effect on employee morale. By closing down, the needs of customers will not be met (no inventories are on hand), and their business may be permanently lost to another supplier.

Problem 13-17 (continued)

Alternative Solution:

	Plant Kept Open	Plant Closed	Difference— Net Operating Income Increase (Decrease)
Sales (44,000 litres × $8.75 per litre × 2)	$ 770,000	$ 0	$(770,000)
Less variable expenses (44,000 litres × $5.25 per litre × 2)	462,000	0	462,000
Contribution margin	308,000	0	(308,000)
Less fixed costs:			
Fixed manufacturing overhead cost ($230,000 × 2; $170,000 × 2)	460,000	340,000	120,000
Fixed selling cost ($310,000 × 2; $310,000 × 90% × 2)	620,000	558,000	62,000
Total fixed cost	1,080,000	898,000	182,000
Net operating loss before start-up costs	(772,000)	(898,000)	(126,000)
Start-up costs		(14,000)	(14,000)
Net operating loss	$ (772,000)	$(912,000)	$(140,000)

Problem 13-17 (continued)

2. Ignoring the additional factors cited in part (1) above, Hallas Company should be indifferent between closing down or continuing to operate if the level of sales drops to 48,000 litres (24,000 litres per month) over the two-month period. The computations are:

Cost avoided by closing the plant for two months
(see above) $182,000
Less start-up costs.. 14,000
Net avoidable costs.. $168,000

$$\frac{\text{Net avoidable costs}}{\text{Contribution margin per litre}} = \frac{\$168,000}{\$3.50 \text{ per litre}}$$

$$=48,000 \text{ litres}$$

Verification:

	Operate at 48,000 Litres for Two Months	Close for Two Months
Sales (48,000 litres × $8.75 per litre)..............	$ 420,000	$ 0
Less variable expenses (48,000 litre × $5.25 per litre)...	252,000	0
Contribution margin	168,000	0
Less fixed expenses:		
Manufacturing overhead ($230,000 and $170,000 × 2 months)...............................	460,000	340,000
Selling ($310,000 and $279,000 × 2 months)...	620,000	558,000
Total fixed expenses	1,080,000	898,000
Start-up costs...	0	14,000
Total costs..	1,080,000	912,000
Net operating loss...	$ (912,000)	$(912,000)

Problem 13-19 (30 minutes)

1. Incremental revenue:
Fixed fee (10,000 pairs × 4 ε per pair)................ 40,000 ε
Reimbursement for costs of production:
(Variable production cost of 16 ε plus fixed   210,000

overhead cost of 5 ε equals 21 ε per pair;
10,000 pairs × 21 ε per pair) ....

Total incremental revenue 250,000

Incremental costs:
  Variable production costs (10,000 pairs × 16 ε
    per pair) .... <u>160,000</u>

Increase in net operating income .... <u>90,000</u> ε

2. Sales revenue through regular channels
    (10,000 pairs × 32 ε per pair) .... 320,000 ε

Sales revenue from the army (above) .... <u>250,000</u>

Decrease in revenue received............................... 70,000

Less variable selling expenses avoided if the
  army's offer is accepted (10,000 pairs × 2 ε per
  pair) .... <u>20,000</u>

Net decrease in net operating income with the
  army's offer... <u>50,000</u> ε

Problem 13-21 (60 minutes)

1. The $2.00 per unit general overhead cost is not relevant to the decision, because the total general company overhead cost will be the same regardless of whether the company decides to make or buy the subassemblies. Also, the depreciation on the old equipment is not a relevant cost since it represents a sunk cost and the old equipment is worn out and must be replaced. The cost of supervision is relevant because this cost can be avoided by buying the subassemblies.

	Differential Costs Per Unit		Total Differential Costs for 40,000 Units	
	Make	Buy	Make	Buy
Outside supplier's price.............		$8.00		$320,000
Direct materials........................	$2.75		$110,000	
Direct labour ($4.00 × 0.75).....	3.00		120,000	
Variable overhead ($0.60 × 0.75)......................	0.45		18,000	
Supervision..............................	0.75		30,000	
Equipment rental*....................	1.50		60,000	
Total......................................	$8.45	$8.00	$338,000	$320,000
Difference in favour of buying ...	$0.45		$18,000	

* $60,000 per year ÷ 40,000 units per year = $1.50 per unit

Managerial Accounting, 6th Canadian Edition

Problem 13-21 (continued)

2. a. Notice that unit costs for both supervision and equipment rental will change if the company needs 50,000 subassemblies each year. These fixed costs will be spread over a larger number of units, thereby decreasing the cost per unit.

	Differential Costs Per Unit		Total Differential Costs—50,000 Units	
	Make	Buy	Make	Buy
Outside supplier's price..............		$8.00		$400,000
Direct materials........................	$2.75		$137,500	
Direct labour	3.00		150,000	
Variable overhead.....................	0.45		22,500	
Supervision ($30,000 ÷ 50,000 units)	0.60		30,000	
Equipment rental ($60,000 ÷ 50,000 units)	1.20		60,000	
Total.......................................	$8.00	$8.00	$400,000	$400,000
Difference...............................	$0		$0	

The company would be indifferent between the two alternatives if 50,000 subassemblies were needed each year.

© McGraw-Hill Ryerson, 2004

Problem 13-21 (continued)

b. Again, notice that the unit costs for both supervision and equipment rental decrease with the greater volume of units.

	Differential Costs Per Unit		Total Differential Costs—60,000 Units	
	Make	Buy	Make	Buy
Outside supplier's price.............		$8.00		$480,000
Direct materials........................	$2.75		$165,000	
Direct labour............................	3.00		180,000	
Variable overhead	0.45		27,000	
Supervision ($30,000 ÷ 60,000 units).......	0.50		30,000	
Equipment rental ($60,000 ÷ 60,000 units).......	1.00		60,000	
Total......................................	$7.70	$8.00	$462,000	$480,000
Difference in favour of making ..	$0.30		$18,000	

The company should purchase the new equipment and make the subassemblies if 60,000 units per year are needed.

Managerial Accounting, 6th Canadian Edition

Problem 13-21 (continued)

3. Other factors that the company should consider include:

   a. Will volume in future years be increasing, or will it remain constant at 40,000 units per year? (If volume increases, then buying the new equipment becomes more desirable, as shown in the computations above.)

   b. Can quality control be maintained if the subassemblies are purchased from the outside supplier?

   c. Does the company have some other profitable use for the space now being used to produce the subassemblies? Does production of the subassemblies require use of a constrained resource?

   d. Will the outside supplier be dependable in meeting shipping schedules?

   e. Can the company begin making the subassemblies again if the supplier proves to be undependable, or are there alternative suppliers?

   f. If the outside supplier's offer is accepted and the need for subassemblies increases in future years, will the supplier have the capacity to provide more than 40,000 subassemblies per year?

Problem 13-23 (45 minutes)

1. Only the avoidable costs are relevant in a decision to drop the Kensington product line. These costs are:

Direct materials	£ 32,000
Direct labour	200,000
Fringe benefits (30% of labour)	60,000
Variable manufacturing overhead.............................	30,000
Royalties (5% of sales)	24,000
Product-line managers' salaries	8,000
Sales commissions (10% of sales)	48,000
Fringe benefits (30% of salaries and commissions).....	16,800
Shipping	10,000
Advertising...	15,000
Total avoidable cost	£443,800

The following costs are not relevant in this decision:

Cost	Reason not relevant
Building rent and maintenance	All products use the same facilities; no space would be freed up if a product were dropped.
Depreciation	All products use the same equipment so no equipment can be sold. Furthermore, the equipment does not wear out through use.
General administrative expenses	Dropping the Kensington product line would have no effect on total general administrative expenses.

Managerial Accounting, 6th Canadian Edition

Problem 13-23 (continued)

Having determined the costs that can be avoided if the Kensington product line is dropped, we can now make the following computation:

Sales revenue lost if the Kensington line is dropped......	£480,000
Less costs that can be avoided (see above)..................	443,800
Decrease in overall company net operating income if the Kensington line is dropped.................................	£ 36,200

Thus, the Kensington line should not be dropped unless the company can find more profitable uses for the resources consumed by the Kensington line.

2. To determine the minimum acceptable sales level, we must first classify the avoidable costs into variable and fixed costs as follows:

	Variable	Fixed
Direct materials...	£ 32,000	
Direct labour..	200,000	
Fringe benefits (30% of labour)	60,000	
Variable manufacturing overhead.................	30,000	
Royalties (5% of sales)	24,000	
Product-line managers' salaries		£ 8,000
Sales commissions (10% of sales)	48,000	
Fringe benefits (30% of salaries and commissions)............	14,400	2,400
Shipping	10,000	
Advertising...		15,000
Total cost..	£418,400	£25,400

The Kensington product line should be retained as long as its contribution margin covers its avoidable fixed costs. Break-even analysis can be used to find the sales volume where the contribution margin just equals the avoidable fixed costs.

The contribution margin ratio is computed as follows:

$$CM \text{ ratio} = \frac{\text{Contribution margin}}{\text{Sales}}$$

$$= \frac{£480,000 - £418,400}{£480,000} = 12.83\% \text{ (rounded)}$$

And the break-even sales volume can be found using the break-even formula:

$$\text{Break-even point} = \frac{\text{Fixed expenses}}{\text{CM ratio}}$$

$$= \frac{£25,400}{0.1283} = £198,000 \text{ (rounded)}$$

Therefore, as long as the sales revenue from the Kensington product line exceeds £198,000, it is covering its own avoidable fixed costs and is contributing toward covering the common fixed costs and toward the profits of the entire company.

Problem 13-25 (45 minutes)

1. A product should be processed further so long as the incremental revenue from the further processing exceeds the incremental costs. The incremental revenue from further processing of the honey is:

Selling price of a container of honey drop candies	$4.40
Selling price of 345 grams of honey ($6.60 × .345)...	2.28
Incremental revenue per container	$2.12

The incremental variable costs are:

Decorative container	$0.40
Other ingredients...	0.25
Direct labour	0.20
Variable manufacturing overhead.............................	0.10
Commissions (5% × $4.40)......................................	0.22
Incremental variable cost per container...................	$1.17

Therefore, the incremental contribution margin is $0.95 per container ($2.12 − $1.17). The cost of purchasing the honeycombs is not relevant because those costs are incurred regardless of whether the honey is sold outright or processed further into candies.

2. The only avoidable fixed costs of the honey drop candies are the master candy maker's salary and the fixed portion of the salesperson's compensation. Therefore, the number of containers of the candy that must be sold each month to justify continued processing of the honey into candies is determined as follows:

Master candy maker's salary.................................	$3,700
Salesperson's fixed compensation.........................	2,000
Avoidable fixed costs	$5,700

$$\frac{\text{Avoidable fixed costs}}{\text{Incremental CM per container}} = \frac{\$5,700}{\$0.95 \text{ per container}} = 6,000 \text{ containers}$$

If the company can sell more than 6,000 containers of the candies each month, then profits will be higher than if the honey were simply sold outright. If the company cannot sell at least 6,000 containers of the candies each month, then profits will be higher if the company discontinues making honey drop candies. To verify this, we show below the total contribution to profits of sales of 5,000, 6,000, and 7,000 containers of candies, contrasted to sales of equivalent amounts of honey. For example, instead of selling 2,070 kilograms of honey, this same amount of honey can be processed into 6,000 containers of candy.

Sales of candies:

	5,000	6,000	7,000
Containers sold per month	5,000	6,000	7,000
Sales revenue @ $4.40 per container	$22,000	$26,400	$30,800
Less incremental variable costs @ $1.17 per container	5,850	7,020	8,190
Incremental contribution margin	16,150	19,380	22,610
Less avoidable fixed costs	5,700	5,700	5,700
Total contribution to profits	$10,450	$13,680	$16,910

Sales of equivalent amount of honey:

Kilograms sold per month*	1,725	2,070	2,415
Sales revenue @ $6.60 per kilogram	$11,385	$13,662	$15,939

* 5,000 containers × 345 grams per container = 1,725,000 grams
  6,000 containers × 345 grams per container = 2,070,000 grams
  7,000 containers × 345 grams per container = 2,415,000 grams

If there is a choice between selling 1,725 kilograms of honey or selling 5,000 containers of candies, profits would be higher selling the honey outright ($11,385 versus $10,450). The company should be largely indifferent between selling 2,070 kilograms of honey or 6,000 containers of candy. In either case, the contribution to profits would be nearly $13,700. On the other hand, if faced with a choice of selling 2,415 kilograms of honey or 7,000 containers of candies, profits would be higher processing the honey into candies ($16,910 versus $15,939).

Problem 13-27 (45 minutes)

1.
Projected sales (80 machines × $3,795 per machine)	$303,600
Less desired profit (20% × $50,000)	10,000
Target cost for 80 machines	$293,600

Target cost per machine ($293,600 ÷ 80 machines)	$3,670
Less Choice Culinary Supply's variable selling cost per machine	350
Maximum allowable purchase price per machine	$3,320

2. The relation between the purchase price of the machine and ROI can be developed as follows:

$$ROI = \frac{\text{Total projected sales} - \text{Total cost}}{\text{Investment}}$$

$$= \frac{\$303,600 - (\$350 + \text{Purchase price of machines}) \times 80}{\$50,000}$$

The above formula can be used to compute the ROI for purchase prices between $2,400 and $3,400 (in increments of $100):

Purchase price	ROI
$2,400	167.2%
$2,500	151.2%
$2,600	135.2%
$2,700	119.2%
$2,800	103.2%
$2,900	87.2%
$3,000	71.2%
$3,100	55.2%
$3,200	39.2%
$3,300	23.2%
$3,400	7.2%

Problem 13-27 (continued)

Using the above data, the relation between purchase price and ROI can be plotted as follows:

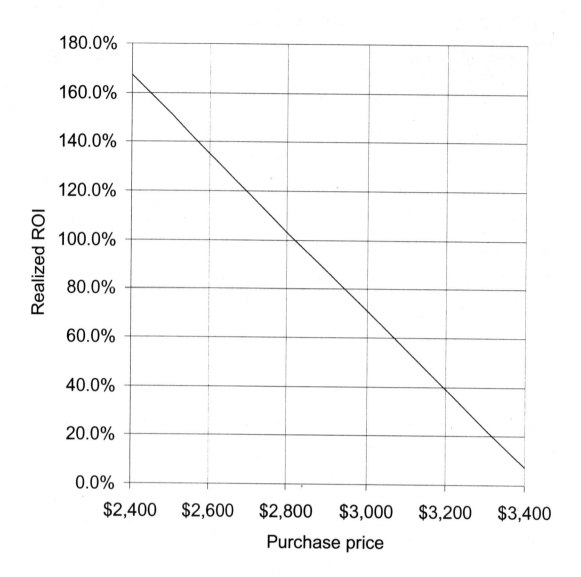

Problem 13-27 (continued)

3. A number of options are available in addition to simply giving up on adding the new gelato machines to the company's product lines. These options include:

- Check the projected unit sales figures. Perhaps more units could be sold at the $3,795 price. However, management should be careful not to indulge in wishful thinking just to make the numbers come out right.

- Modify the selling price. This does not necessarily mean increasing the projected selling price. Decreasing the selling price may generate enough additional unit sales to make carrying the gelato machines more profitable.

- Improve the selling process to decrease the variable selling costs.

- Rethink the investment that would be required to carry this new product. Can the size of the inventory be reduced? Are the new warehouse fixtures really necessary?

- Does the company really need a 20% ROI? Does it cost the company this much to acquire more funds?

Problem 13-29 (60 minutes)

1. Supporting computations:

Number of pads produced per year:
  100,000 labour-hours ÷ 2 labour-hours per pad = 50,000 pads

Standard cost per pad:
  $4,000,000 cost of goods sold ÷ 50,000 pads = $80 cost per pad

Fixed manufacturing overhead cost per pad:
  $1,750,000 ÷ 50,000 pads = $35 per pad

Manufacturing overhead cost per pad:
  $7 variable cost per pad + $35 fixed cost per pad = $42 per pad

Direct labour cost per pad:
  $80 − ($30 + $42) = $8

Given the computations above, the completed standard cost card follows:

	Standard Quantity or Hours	Standard Price or Rate	Standard Cost
Direct materials	5 metres	$ 6 per metre	$30
Direct labour	2 hours	4 per hour *	8
Manufacturing overhead.....	2 hours	21 per hour **	42
Total standard cost per pad			$80

  * $8 ÷ 2 hours = $4 per hour.
 ** $42 ÷ 2 hours = $21 per hour.

Managerial Accounting, 6th Canadian Edition

Problem 13-29 (continued)

2. a.

$$\text{Markup percentage on absorption cost} = \frac{\left(\begin{matrix}\text{Required ROI} \\ \times \text{ Investment}\end{matrix}\right) + \text{ SG\&A expenses}}{\text{Unit sales} \times \text{Unit product cost}}$$

$$= \frac{(24\% \times \$3,500,000) + \$2,160,000}{50,000 \text{ pads} \times \$80 \text{ per pad}}$$

$$= \frac{\$3,000,000}{\$4,000,000}$$

$$= 75\%$$

b.

Direct materials	$30
Direct labour	8
Manufacturing overhead	42
Unit product cost	80
Add markup: 75%	60
Target selling price	$140

c.

Sales (50,000 pads × $140 per pad)	$7,000,000
Less cost of goods sold (50,000 pads × $80 per pad)	4,000,000
Gross margin	3,000,000
Less selling, general, and administrative expense	2,160,000
Net operating income	$ 840,000

$$\text{ROI} = \frac{\text{Net operating income}}{\text{Sales}} \times \frac{\text{Sales}}{\text{Average operating assets}}$$

$$= \frac{\$840,000}{\$7,000,000} \times \frac{\$7,000,000}{\$3,500,000} = 12\% \times 2 = 24\%$$

Problem 13-29 (continued)

3. Total fixed cost:

Manufacturing overhead..	$1,750,000
Selling, general, and administrative	
[$2,160,000 – (50,000 pads × $5 variable per pad)].	1,910,000
Total fixed cost...	$3,660,000

Variable cost per pad:	
Direct materials	$30
Direct labour	8
Variable manufacturing overhead...............................	7
Variable selling	5
Total variable cost...	$50

To achieve the 24% ROI, the company would have to sell at least the 50,000 units assumed in part (2) above. The break-even volume can be computed as follows:

$$\frac{\text{Break-even point}}{\text{in units sold}} = \frac{\text{Fixed expenses}}{\text{Unit contribution margin}}$$

$$= \frac{\$3,660,000}{\$140 \text{ per pad} - \$50 \text{ per pad}}$$

$$= 40,667 \text{ pads}$$

Managerial Accounting, 6th Canadian Edition

Case 13-31 (75 minutes)

This is a difficult case that will challenge the best students. Part of the challenge is simply to understand the alternatives. As an aid, a diagram of the two alternatives, which we will call Alternatives A and B, is show below, together with the relevant data.

Alternative A

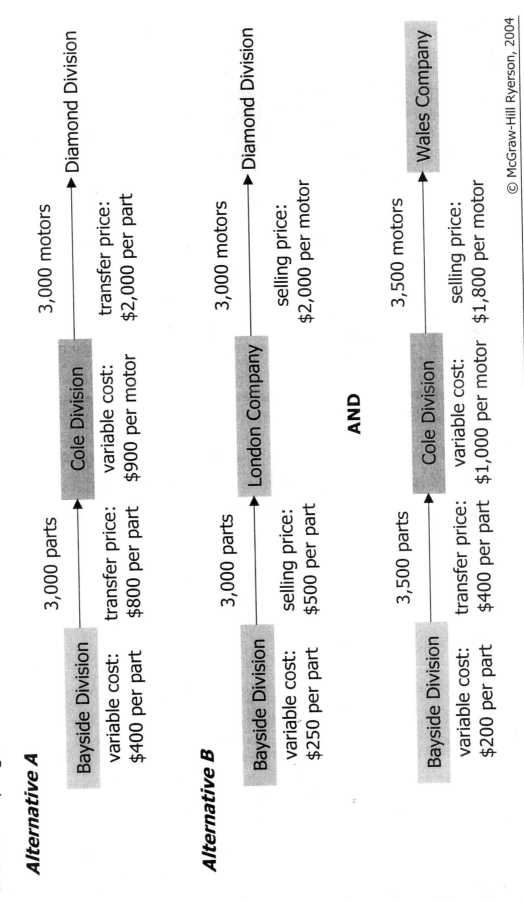

Bayside Division
variable cost: $400 per part

3,000 parts
transfer price: $800 per part

Cole Division
variable cost: $900 per motor

3,000 motors
transfer price: $2,000 per part

→ Diamond Division

Alternative B

Bayside Division
variable cost: $250 per part

3,000 parts
selling price: $500 per part

London Company

3,000 motors
selling price: $2,000 per motor

→ Diamond Division

AND

Bayside Division
variable cost: $200 per part

3,500 parts
transfer price: $400 per part

Cole Division
variable cost: $1,000 per motor

3,500 motors
selling price: $1,800 per motor

→ Wales Company

Case 13-31 (continued)

In both parts of the case the general fixed overhead costs are irrelevant since they are allocated costs that will remain the same regardless of which alternative is accepted. Also note that the same amount of total machine time would be consumed in both the Bayside Division's plant and the Cole Division's plant regardless of which order is accepted. Thus, the amount of machine time that would be required is not a factor in the decision.

Bayside's plant:
  Diamond Division order:
    3,000 motors × 3.5 hours per motor = 10,500 hours.
  Wales Company order:
    3,500 motors × 3.0 hours per motor = 10,500 hours.

Cole's plant:
  Diamond Division order:
    3,000 motors × 7.0 hours per motor = 21,000 hours.
  Wales Company order:
    3,500 motors × 6.0 hours per motor = 21,000 hours.

1. The Cole Division would accept the order from the Wales Company. Computations to support this conclusion follow:

Expected contribution margin from the Diamond Division order:

Sales revenue to Cole Division		
(3,000 motors × $2,000 per motor)		$6,000,000
Less variable costs:		
Transfer price to Bayside Division		
(3,000 parts × $800 per part)	$2,400,000	
Other variable costs		
(3,000 motors × $900 per motor)	2,700,000	5,100,000
Contribution margin................................		$ 900,000

Case 13-31 (continued)

Expected contribution margin from the Wales Company order:

Sales revenue to Cole Division (3,500 motors × $1,800 per motor)		$6,300,000
Less variable costs:		
Transfer price to Bayside Division (3,500 parts × $400 per part)	$1,400,000	
Other variable costs (3,500 motors × $1,000 per motor).....	3,500,000	4,900,000
Contribution margin.................................		$1,400,000

Thus, the Cole Division will net $500,000 ($1,400,000 − $900,000) more in contribution margin by accepting the order from Wales Company.

2. From the perspective of the company as a whole, the situation is at once simpler and more complex. It is simpler because transfer prices are irrelevant. Whatever one division pays, the other receives. From the standpoint of the entire company, money is taken out of one pocket and put into the other. The situation is more complex in that the company must take into account that if Cole Division accepts the order from Wales Company, Diamond Division will need to acquire its motors from London Company rather than from Cole Division. This is Alternative B in the diagram on the first page of the solution. But let's start with Alternative A, the simpler alternative. From the standpoint of the entire company, the cost of the motors transferred to Diamond Division is $1,300 per motor, the variable costs of Bayside Division plus the variable costs of Cole Division. The total cost of the motors would be $3,900,000 (3,000 motors @ $1,300 per motor). This is restated in slightly different form below:

Alternative A
   Diamond Division acquires motors from Cole Division, which acquires parts from Bayside Division

Bayside Division's variable expenses (3,000 parts × $400 per part).............................	$1,200,000
Cole Division's variable expenses (3,000 motors × $900 per motor)	2,700,000
Total cost of Alternative A	$3,900,000

Case 13-31 (continued)

Alternative B

This alternative is more complex than Alternative A. There are really two parts to this alternative. In the first part, Diamond Division purchases the required motors from London Company, which purchases parts from Bayside Division. In the second part, Cole Division sells motors to Wales Company using parts supplied by Bayside Division. (Refer back to the diagram.) We will compute the financial consequences of these two parts separately and then combine them.

Part 1: Diamond Division's purchase of motors

Diamond Division's payment to London Company	
(3,000 motors × $2,000 per motor)	$6,000,000
London Company's payments to Bayside Division	
(3,000 parts × $500 per part).............................	(1,500,000)
Bayside Division's variable expenses	
(3,000 parts × $250 per part).............................	750,000
Total cost (a)..	$5,250,000

Part 2: Wale Company's purchase of motors

Wales Company's payments to Cole Division	
(3,500 motors × $1,800 per motor)	$6,300,000
Cole Division's variable expenses	
(3,500 motors × $1,000 per motor)	(3,500,000)
Bayside Division's variable expenses	
(3,500 motors × $200 per motor)	(700,000)
Total contribution margin (b)..................................	$2,100,000
Net cost to the company of Alternative B (a) − (b)....	$3,150,000

Since the $3,150,000 cost of Alternative B is less than the $3,900,000 cost of Alternative A, it is the preferred alternative.

Managerial Accounting, 6th Canadian Edition

Case 13-33 (45 minutes)

1. Yes, milling of flour should be discontinued if the price remains at $625, but not for the reason given by the sales manager. The reason it should be discontinued is that the *added* contribution margin that can be obtained from milling a tonne of cracked wheat into flour is *less* than the contribution margin that can be obtained from using the milling capacity to produce another tonne of cracked wheat and selling it as cereal. The analysis is:

Selling price per tonne of cracked wheat.................................. $490
Less variable expenses ($390 materials and $20 labour)........... 410
Contribution margin per tonne of cracked wheat .... $ 80

Added revenue from further milling of cracked wheat into
   flour ($625 − $490).. $135
Less costs of further milling ($80 materials and $20 labour)* 100
Contribution margin per tonne of flour....................................... $ 35

> * The overhead costs are not relevant, since they are fixed and will remain the same whether the milling capacity is used to produce cracked wheat or flour.

Therefore, the company makes more money using its milling capacity to produce cracked wheat than flour.

2. Since the demand for the two products is unlimited and both require the same amount of milling time, the company should process the cracked wheat into flour only if the contribution margin for flour is at least as large as the contribution margin for cracked wheat. In algebraic form:

$$\begin{array}{c} \text{Added revenue from} \\ \text{milling cracked wheat} \\ \text{into flour} \end{array} - \begin{array}{c} \text{Costs of} \\ \text{further} \\ \text{processing} \end{array} = \begin{array}{c} \text{Contribution margin} \\ \text{of} \\ \text{cracked wheat} \end{array}$$

(Selling price of flour − $490) − $100 = $80

Selling price of flour = $80 + $490 + $100 = $670

Therefore, the selling price of flour should be at least $670; otherwise, the mill should be used to produce cracked wheat.

Case 13-35 (120 minutes)

1. The product margins computed by the accounting department for the drums and mountain bike frames should not be used in the decision of which product to make. The product margins are lower than they should be due to the presence of allocated fixed common costs that are irrelevant in this decision. Moreover, even after the irrelevant costs have been removed, what matters is the profitability of the two products in relation to the amount of the constrained resource—welding time—that they use. A product with a very low margin may be desirable if it uses very little of the constrained resource. In short, the financial data provided by the accounting department are pretty much useless for making this decision.

2. Students may have answered this question assuming that direct labour is a variable cost, even though the case strongly hints that direct labour is a fixed cost. The solution is shown here assuming that direct labour is fixed. The solution assuming that direct labour is variable will be shown in part (4).

Solution assuming direct labour is fixed

| | | Manufactured | |
	Purchased XSX Drums	XSX Drums	Mountain Bike Frames
Selling price	$154.00	$154.00	$65.00
Less variable costs:			
Materials	120.00	44.50	17.50
Variable manufacturing overhead	0.00	1.05	0.60
Variable selling and administrative	0.85	0.85	0.40
Total variable cost	120.85	46.40	18.50
Contribution margin	$ 33.15	$107.60	$46.50

Case 13-35 (continued)

3. Since the demand for the welding machine exceeds the 2,000 hours that are available, products that use the machine should be prioritized based on their contribution margin *per welding hour*. The computations are carried out below under the assumption that direct labour is a fixed cost and then under the assumption that it is a variable cost.

Solution assuming direct labour is fixed

	Manufactured	
	XSX Drums	Mountain Bike Frames
Contribution margin per unit (above) (a)	$107.60	$46.50
Welding hours per unit (b).................................	0.8 hour	0.2 hour
Contribution margin per welding hour (a) ÷ (b)	$134.50 per hour	$232.50 per hour

Case 13-35 (continued)

Since the contribution margin per unit of the constrained resource (i.e., welding time) is larger for the mountain bike frames than for the XSX drums, the frames make the most profitable use of the welding machine. Consequently, the company should manufacture as many mountain bike frames as possible up to demand and then use any leftover capacity to produce XSX drums. Buying the drums from the outside supplier can fill any remaining unsatisfied demand for XSX drums. The necessary calculations are carried out below.

Analysis assuming direct labour is a fixed cost

	(a) Quantity	(b) Unit Contribution Margin	(c) Welding Time per Unit	(a) × (c) Total Welding Time	Balance of Welding Time	(a) × (b) Total Contribution
Total hours available...........					2,000	
Mountain bike frames produced......	3,500	$ 46.50	0.20	700	1,300	$162,750
XSX Drums—make............	1,625	107.60	0.80	1,300	0	174,850
XSX Drums—buy..............	1,375	33.15				45,581
Total contribution margin........						383,181
Less: Contribution margin from present operations: 2,500 drums × $107.60 CM per drum....						269,000
Increased contribution margin and net operating income..........						$114,181

Case 13-35 (continued)

4. The computation of the contribution margins and the analysis of the best product mix are repeated here under the assumption that direct labour costs are variable.

Solution assuming direct labour is a variable cost

		Manufactured	
	Purchased XSX Drums	XSX Drums	Mountain Bike Frames
Selling price.............................	$154.00	$154.00	$65.00
Less variable costs:			
Materials.................................	120.00	44.50	17.50
Direct labour	0.00	4.50	22.50
Variable manufacturing overhead................................	0.00	1.05	0.60
Variable selling and administrative........................	0.85	0.85	0.40
Total variable cost	120.85	50.90	41.00
Contribution margin	$ 33.15	$103.10	$24.00

Solution assuming direct labour is a variable cost

		Manufactured
	XSX Drums	Mountain Bike Frames
Contribution margin per unit (above) (a)	$103.10	$24.00
Welding hours per unit (b)...................................	0.8 hour	0.2 hour
Contribution margin per welding hour (a) ÷ (b)	$128.88 per hour	$120.00 per hour

When direct labour is assumed to be a variable cost, the conclusion is reversed from the case in which direct labour is assumed to be a fixed cost—the XSX drums appear to be a better use of the constraint than the mountain bike frames. The assumption about the behaviour of direct labour really does matter.

Case 13-35 (continued)

Solution assuming direct labour is a variable cost

	(a)	(b) Unit Contri-bution Margin	(c) Welding Time per Unit	(a) × (c) Total Welding Time	Balance of Welding Time	(a) × (b) Total Contri-bution
	Quantity					
Total hours available............					2,000	
XSX Drums—make.................	2,500	$103.10	0.80	2,000	0	$257,750
Mountain bike frames produced.....	0	24.00	0.20	0	0	0
XSX Drums—buy	500	33.15				16,575
Total contribution margin						274,325
Less: Contribution margin from present operations: 2,500 drums × $103.10 CM per drum.....						257,750
Increased contribution margin and net operating income.............						$ 16,575

Case 13-35 (continued)

5. The case strongly suggests that direct labour is fixed: "The mountain bike frames could be produced with existing equipment and personnel." Nevertheless, it would be a good idea to examine how much labour time is really needed under the two opposing plans.

	Production	Direct Labour-Hours Per Unit	Total Direct Labour-Hours
Plan 1:			
Mountain bike frames	3,500	1.25*	4,375
XSX drums	1,625	0.25**	406
			4,781
Plan 2:			
XSX drums	2,500	0.25**	625

* $22.50 ÷ $18.00 per hour = 1.25 hours
** $4.50 ÷ $18.00 per hour = 0.25 hour

Some caution is advised. Plan 1 assumes that direct labour is a fixed cost. However, this plan requires over 4,000 more direct labour-hours than Plan 2 and the present situation. A full-time employee works about 1,900 hours a year, so the added workload is about equivalent to two full-time employees. Does the plant really have that much idle time at present? If so, and if shifting workers over to making mountain bike frames would not jeopardize operations elsewhere, then Plan 1 is indeed the better plan. However, if taking on the mountain bike frame as a new product would lead to pressure to hire two more workers, more analysis is in order. It is still best to view direct labour as a fixed cost, but taking on the frames as a new product would lead to a jump in fixed costs of about $68,400 (1,900 hours × $18 per hour × 2). This must be covered by the additional contribution margin or the plan should be rejected. See the additional analysis on the next page.

Case 13-35 (continued)

Contribution margin from Plan 1:

Mountain bike frames produced (3,500 × $46.50)	$162,750
XSX Drums—make (1,625 × $107.60).................................	174,850
XSX Drums—buy (1,375 × $33.15).....................................	45,581
Total contribution margin	383,181
Less: Additional fixed labour costs..	68,400
Net effect of Plan 1 on net operating income	$314,781

Contribution margin from Plan 2: ....

XSX Drums—make (2,500 × $107.60).................................	$269,000
XSX Drums—buy (500 × $33.15)..	16,575
Net effect of Plan 2 on net operating income	$285,575
Net advantage of Plan 1	$ 29,206

Plan 1, introducing the new product, would still be optimal even if two more direct labour employees would have to be hired. The reason for this is subtle. If the company does not make the XSX drums itself, it can still buy them. Thus, using an hour of welding time to make the mountain bike frames does not mean giving up a contribution margin of $128.88 on drums (assuming direct labour is a variable cost). The opportunity cost of using the welding machine to produce mountain bike frames is less than this since a purchased drum can replace a manufactured drum. An amended analysis using the opportunity cost concept appears on the next page.

Managerial Accounting, 6th Canadian Edition

Case 13-35 (continued)

Amended solution assuming direct labour is fixed

	Manufactured	
	XSX Drums	Mountain Bike Frames
Contribution margin per unit (above) (a)	$74.45*	$46.50
Welding hours per unit (b).................................	0.8 hour	0.2 hour
Contribution margin per welding hour (a) ÷ (b)	$93.06 per hour	$232.50 per hour

Amended solution assuming direct labour is a variable cost

	Manufactured	
	XSX Drums	Mountain Bike Frames
Contribution margin per unit (above) (a)	$69.95*	$24.00
Welding hours per unit (b).................................	0.8 hour	0.2 hour
Contribution margin per welding hour (a) ÷ (b)	$87.44 per hour	$120.00 per hour

* Net of the $33.15 contribution margin of a purchased drum. If the company does not make a drum, it can purchase one, so the lost contribution from making bike frames rather than drums is less than it otherwise would be.

With this amended approach, assuming direct labour is variable points to the same solution as when direct labour is assumed to be fixed—place the highest priority on making mountain bike frames. This won't always happen.

Chapter 14
Capital Budgeting Decisions

Exercise 14-1 (30 minutes)

1.

Year(s)	Amount of Cash Flows X	Amount of Cash Flows Y	20% Factor	Present Value of Cash Flows X	Present Value of Cash Flows Y
1	$1,000	$4,000	0.833	$ 833	$3,332
2	2,000	3,000	0.694	1,388	2,082
3	3,000	2,000	0.579	1,737	1,158
4	4,000	1,000	0.482	1,928	482
				$5,886	$7,054

2. a. From Table 14C-3, the factor for 6% for 3 periods is 0.840. Therefore, the present value of the investment required is:

$$\$12,000 \times 0.840 = \$10,080.$$

b. From Table 14C-3, the factor for 10% for 3 periods is 0.751. Therefore, the present value of the investment required is:

$$\$12,000 \times 0.751 = \$9,012.$$

3.

Option	Year(s)	Amount of Cash Flows	10% Factor	Present Value of Cash Flows
A	Now	$500,000	1.000	$500,000
B	1-8	$ 60,000	5.335	$320,100
	8	200,000	0.467	93,400
				$413,500

Mark should accept option A. On the surface, option B appears to be a better choice since it promises a total cash inflow of $680,000 ($60,000 × 8 = $480,000; $480,000 + $200,000 = $680,000), whereas option A promises a cash inflow of only $500,000. However, the cash inflows under option B are spread out over eight years, whereas the cash flow under option A is received immediately. Since the $500,000 under option A can be invested at 10%, it would actually accumulate to more than

$680,000 at the end of eight years. Consequently, the present value of option A is higher than the present value of option B.

4. You should prefer option a:

Option a: $50,000 × 1.000 = $50,000.
Option b: $75,000 × 0.507 = $38,025. (From Table 14C-3)
Option c: $12,000 × 4.111 = $49,332. (From Table 14C-4)

Exercise 14-3 (30 minutes)

1. Annual savings over present method of delivery........... $5,400
   Added contribution margin from expanded deliveries
     (1,800 pizzas × $2 per pizza) .... <u>3,600</u>
   Annual cash inflows... <u>$9,000</u>

2. $\text{Factor of the internal rate of return} = \dfrac{\text{Investment required}}{\text{Annual cash inflow}}$

   $$= \dfrac{\$45,000}{\$9,000} = 5.000$$

   Looking in Table 14C-4, and scanning along the six-year line, we can see that the factor computed above, 5.000, is closest to 5.076, the factor for the 5% rate of return. Therefore, to the nearest whole percent, the internal rate of return is 5%.

3. The cash flows are not even over the six-year life of the truck because of the extra $13,000 cash inflow that occurs in the sixth year. Therefore, the approach used above cannot be used to compute the internal rate of return. Using trial-and-error or some other method, the internal rate of return turns out to be about 11%:

	Year(s)	Amount of Cash Flows	11% Factor	Present Value of Cash Flows
Initial investment	Now	$(45,000)	1.000	$(45,000)
Annual cash inflows...	1-6	9,000	4.231	38,079
Salvage value............	6	13,000	0.535	<u>6,955</u>
Net present value......				<u>$ 34</u>

As expected, the extra cash inflow in the sixth year increases the internal rate of return.

Exercise 14-5 (15 minutes)

1. The profitability index for each proposal would be:

Proposal	Present Value of Cash Inflows (a)	Investment Required (b)	Profitability Index (a) ÷ (b)
A	$119,000	$ 85,000	1.40
B	184,000	200,000	0.92
C	135,000	90,000	1.50
D	221,000	170,000	1.30

2. The ranking would be:

Proposal	Profitability Index
C	1.50
A	1.40
D	1.30
B	0.92

Two points should be noted about the ranking. First, proposal B is not an acceptable proposal at all, since it has a profitability index of less than 1.0 (negative net present value). Second, proposal D has the highest net present value, but it ranks lowest of the three acceptable proposals in terms of the profitability index.

Exercise 14-7 (15 minutes)

1. a. $400,000 × 0.794 (Table 14C-3) = $317,600.
   b. $400,000 × 0.712 (Table 14C-3) = $284,800.

2. a. $5,000 × 4.355 (Table 14C-4) = $21,775.
   b. $5,000 × 3.685 (Table 14C-4) = $18,425.

3. Looking in Table 14C-4, the factor for 10% for 20 years is 8.514. Thus, the present value of Sally's winnings would be:

   $50,000 × 8.514 = $425,700.

   Whether or not Sally really won a million dollars depends on your point of view. She will receive a million dollars over the next 20 years; however, in terms of its value *right now* she won much less than a million dollars as shown by the present value computation above.

Exercise 14-9 (15 minutes)

Item	Year(s)	Amount of Cash Flows	20% Factor	Present Value of Cash Flows
Project A:				
Cost of the equipment................	Now	$(300,000)	1.000	$(300,000)
Annual cash inflows....................	1-7	80,000	3.605	288,400
Salvage value of the equipment ..	7	20,000	0.279	5,580
Net present value.......................				$ (6,020)
Project B:				
Working capital investment.........	Now	$(300,000)	1.000	$(300,000)
Annual cash inflows....................	1-7	60,000	3.605	216,300
Working capital released.............	7	300,000	0.279	83,700
Net present value.......................				$ 0

The $300,000 should be invested in Project B rather than in Project A. Project B has a zero net present value, which means that it promises exactly a 20% rate of return. Project A is not acceptable at all, since it has a negative net present value.

Exercise 14-11 (15 minutes)

Item	Year(s)	Amount of Cash Flows	16% Factor	Present Value of Cash Flows
Project A:				
Investment required.....	Now	$(15,000)	1.000	$(15,000)
Annual cash inflows......	1-10	4,000	4.833	19,332
Net present value.........				$ 4,332
Project B:				
Investment..............	Now	$(15,000)	1.000	$(15,000)
Cash inflow.............	10	60,000	0.227	13,620
Net present value.........				$ (1,380)

Project A should be selected. Project B does not provide the required 16% return, as shown by its negative net present value.

Alternatively, the profitability indexes of the projects can be computed.

$$\text{Profitability index} = \frac{\text{Present value of cash inflows}}{\text{Investment required}}$$

Project A:

$$\text{Profitability index} = \frac{\$19,332}{\$15,000} = 1.289$$

Project B:

$$\text{Profitability}\atop\text{index} = \frac{\$13,620}{\$15,000} = 0.908$$

Project A is preferred since its profitability index is higher.

Exercise 14-13 (30 minutes)

1. $$\text{Factor of the internal}\atop\text{rate of return} = \frac{\text{Investment in the project}}{\text{Annual cash inflow}}$$

    $$= \frac{\$136,700}{\$25,000} = 5.468$$

Looking in Table 14C-4 and scanning along the 14-period line, a factor of 5.468 represents an internal rate of return of 16%.

2.

Item	Year(s)	Amount of Cash Flows	16% Factor	Present Value of Cash Flows
Initial investment	Now	$(136,700)	1.000	$(136,700)
Net annual cash inflows	1-14	25,000	5.468	136,700
Net present value.....				$ 0

The reason for the zero net present value is that 16% (the discount rate we have used) represents the machine's internal rate of return. The internal rate of return is the rate that causes the present value of a project's cash inflows to just equal the present value of the investment required.

3.

$$\frac{\text{Factor of the internal}}{\text{rate of return}} = \frac{\text{Investment in the project}}{\text{Annual cash inflow}}$$

$$= \frac{\$136,700}{\$20,000} = 6.835$$

Looking in Table 14C-4 and scanning along the 14-period line, the 6.835 factor is closest to 6.982, the factor for the 11% rate of return. Thus, to the nearest whole percent, the internal rate of return is 11%.

Exercise 14-15 (20 minutes)

1. Annual cost of student help in collating $60,000
   Annual cost of the new collating machine:
   Operator $18,000
   Maintenance 7,000   25,000
   Net annual cost savings (cash inflow) $35,000

2. The net present value analysis follows:

Items and Computations	Year(s)	(1) Amount	(2) Tax Effect	(1) × (2) After-Tax Cash Flows	14% Factor	Present Value of Cash Flows
Cost of the new collating machine	Now	$(170,000)		$(170,000)	1.000	$(170,000)
Net annual cost savings (above)	1-15	35,000	1 – 0.40	21,000	6.142	128,982
Salvage value of the new machine	15	40,000		40,000	0.140	5,600
Cost of the new roller pads	8	(20,000)	1 – 0.40	(12,000)	0.351	(4,212)
CCA tax shield:						41,990

$$\frac{Cdt}{d+k} \times \frac{1+.5k}{1+k} - \frac{Sdt}{d+k} \times (1+k)^{-n}$$

$$\frac{170,000 \times .3 \times .4}{.3+.14} \times \frac{1.07}{1.14} - \frac{40,000 \times .3 \times .4}{.3+.14} \times .14$$

$$= \$43,363.64 \times .9386) - (\$10,909.09 \times .14) = \$41,990$$

Net present value .... $ 2,360

Yes, the new collating machine should be purchased.

Managerial Accounting, 6th Canadian Edition

Problem 14-17 (30 minutes)

1. The net annual cost savings is computed as follows:

Reduction in labour costs	$240,000
Reduction in material costs	96,000
Total cost reductions	336,000
Less increased maintenance costs ($4,250 × 12)	51,000
Net annual cost savings	$285,000

2. Using this cost savings figure, and other data provided in the text, the net present value analysis is:

	Year(s)	Amount of Cash Flows	18% Factor	Present Value of Cash Flows
Cost of the machine	Now	$(900,000)	1.000	$ (900,000)
Installation and software	Now	(650,000)	1.000	(650,000)
Salvage of the old machine	Now	70,000	1.000	70,000
Annual cost savings	1-10	285,000	4.494	1,280,790
Overhaul required	6	(90,000)	0.370	(33,300)
Salvage of the new machine	10	210,000	0.191	40,110
Net present value				$ (192,400)

No, the etching machine should not be purchased. It has a negative net present value at an 18% discount rate.

3. The intangible benefits would have to be worth at least $42,813 per year as shown below:

$$\text{Required increase in net present value} = \frac{\$192,400}{4.494} = \$42,813$$

Factor for 10 years

Thus, the new etching machine should be purchased if management believes that the intangible benefits are worth at least $42,813 per year to the company.

Problem 14-19 (20 minutes)

Item	Year(s)	Amount of Cash Flows	14% Factor	Present Value of Cash Flows
Cost of equipment required......	Now	$(850,000)	1.000	$(850,000)
Working capital required..........	Now	(100,000)	1.000	(100,000)
Net annual cash receipts	1-5	230,000	3.433	789,590
Cost of road repairs	3	(60,000)	0.675	(40,500)
Salvage value of equipment......	5	200,000	0.519	103,800
Working capital released	5	100,000	0.519	51,900
Net present value...................				$ (45,210)

No, the project should not be accepted; it has a negative net present value. This means that the rate of return on the investment is less than the company's required rate of return of 14%.

Problem 14-21 (20 minutes)

Items and Computations	Year(s)	(1) Amount	(2) Tax Effect	(1) × (2) After-Tax Cash Flows	12% Factor	Present Value of Cash Flows
Investment in new trucks	Now	$(450,000)		$(450,000)	1.000	$(450,000)
Salvage from sale of the old trucks	Now	30,000		30,000	1.000	30,000
Net annual cash receipts	1-8	108,000	1 – 0.30	75,600	4.968	375,581
CCA tax shield:						83,445

$$PV = \frac{Cdt}{d+k} \times \frac{1+ .5k}{1+k} - \frac{Sdt}{d+k} \times (1+k)^{-n}$$

$$(450,000 - 30,000) \times \frac{.3 \times .3}{.3 + .12} \times \frac{1.06}{1.12} - 20,000 \times \frac{.3 .3}{.3 + .12} \times .404$$

$= \$90,000 \times .9464) - (\$4,285.71 \times .404) = \$83,445$

Overhaul of motors	5	(45,000)	1 – 0.30	(31,500)	0.567	(17,861)
Salvage from the new trucks	8	20,000		20,000	0.404	8,080
Net present value						$ 29,245

Since the project has a positive net present value, the contract should be accepted.

Problem 14-23 (continued)

3. a. 5-year life for the equipment:
   The factor for the internal rate of return would still be 3.812 [as computed in (1) above]. From Table 14C-4, reading this time along the 5-period line, a factor of 3.812 is closest to 3.791, the factor for 10%. Thus, to the nearest whole percent, the internal rate of return is 10%.

   b. 9-year life for the equipment:
   The factor of the internal rate of return would again be 3.812. From Table 14C-4, reading along the 9-period line, a factor of 3.812 is closest to 3.786, the factor for 22%. Thus, to the nearest whole percent, the internal rate of return is 22%.

   The 10% return in part (a) is less than the 14% minimum return that Dr. Black wants to earn on the project. Of equal or even greater importance, the following diagram should be pointed out to Dr. Black:

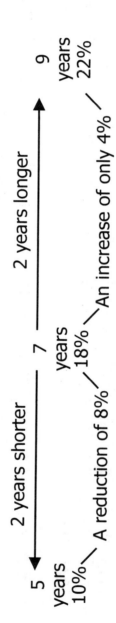

   As this illustration shows, a *decrease* in years has a much greater impact on the rate of return than an *increase* in years. This is because of the time value of money; added cash inflows far into the future do little to enhance the rate of return, but loss of cash inflows in the near term can do much to reduce it. Therefore, Dr. Black should be *very* concerned about any potential decrease in the life of the equipment, while at the same time realizing that any increase in the life of the equipment will do little to enhance her rate of return.

Managerial Accounting, 6th Canadian Edition

Problem 14-23 (continued)

4. a. The expected annual cash inflow would be:

$37,500 × 120% = $45,000

$$\frac{\$142,950}{\$45,000} = 3.177$$

From Table 14C-4 in Appendix 14C, reading along the 7-period line, a factor of 3.177 is closest to 3.161, the factor for 25%, and is between that factor and the factor for 24%. Thus, to the nearest whole percent, the internal rate of return is 25%.

b. The expected annual cash inflow would be:

$37,500 × 80% = $30,000

$$\frac{\$142,950}{\$30,000} = 4.765$$

From Table 14C-4 in Appendix 14C, reading along the 7-period line, a factor of 4.765 is closest to 4.712, the factor for 11%. Thus, to the nearest whole percent, the internal rate of return is 11%.

Unlike changes in time, increases and decreases in cash flows at a given point in time have basically the same impact on the rate of return, as shown below:

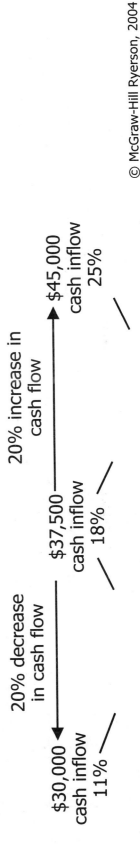

20% decrease in cash flow

20% increase in cash flow

$30,000 cash inflow 11%

$37,500 cash inflow 18%

$45,000 cash inflow 25%

Student Solutions Manual, Chapter 14

© McGraw-Hill Ryerson, 2004

14-15

A decrease of
7%

An increase of
7%

Problem 14-23 (continued)

5. Since the cash flows are not even over the five-year period (there is an extra $61,375 cash inflow from sale of the equipment at the end of the fifth year), some other method must be used to compute the internal rate of return. Using trial-and-error or more sophisticated methods, it turns out that the actual internal rate of return will be 12%:

Item	Year(s)	Amount of Cash Flows	12% Factor	Present Value of Cash Flows
Investment in the equipment...	Now	$(142,950)	1.000	$(142,950)
Annual cash inflow	1-5	30,000	3.605	108,150
Sale of the equipment	5	61,375	0.567	34,800
Net present value.................				$ 0

© McGraw-Hill Ryerson, 2004

Problem 14-25 (30 minutes)

1. The income statement would be:

Sales revenue		¥200,000
Less commissions (40% × ¥200,000)		80,000
Contribution margin		120,000
Less fixed expenses:		
Maintenance	¥50,000	
Insurance	10,000	
Depreciation*	36,000	
Total fixed expenses		96,000
Net operating income		¥ 24,000

*¥180,000 ÷ 5 years = ¥36,000 per year

2. The simple rate of return would be:

$$\text{Simple rate of return} = \frac{\text{Net operating income}}{\text{Initial investment - Salvage from old equipment}}$$

$$= \frac{¥24,000}{¥180,000 - ¥30,000} = \frac{¥24,000}{¥150,000} = 16\%$$

Yes, the games would be purchased. The return exceeds the 14% threshold set by the company.

3. The payback period would be:

$$\text{Payback period} = \frac{\text{Initial investment - Salvage from old equipment}}{\text{Net annual cash inflow}}$$

$$= \frac{¥180,000-¥30,000}{¥60,000^*} = \frac{¥150,000}{¥60,000} = 2.5 \text{ years}$$

*Net operating income, ¥24,000 + Depreciation, ¥36,000 = ¥60,000.

Yes, the games would be purchased. The payback period is less than the 3 years.

Problem 14-27 (45 minutes)

1.

Labour savings	€190,000	
Ground mulch savings	10,000	€200,000
Less out-of-pocket costs:		
Operator	70,000	
Insurance	1,000	
Fuel	9,000	
Maintenance contract	12,000	92,000
Annual savings in cash operating costs		€108,000

2. The formula for the simple rate of return when a cost reduction project is involved is as follows:

$$\text{Simple rate of return} = \frac{\text{Cost savings} - \text{Depreciation on new equipment}}{\text{Initial investment}}$$

$$= \frac{€108,000 - €40,000*}{€480,000} = 14.2\% \text{ (rounded)}$$

*Depreciation is calculated as follows: $\dfrac{€480,000}{12 \text{ years}} = €40,000 \text{ per year}$

3. The formula for the payback period is:

$$\text{Payback period} = \frac{\text{Investment required}}{\text{Net annual cash inflow}}$$

$$= \frac{€480,000}{108,000*} = 4.4 \text{ years (rounded)}$$

* In this case, the cash inflow is measured by the annual savings in

cash operating costs.

The harvester meets Mr. Despinoy's payback criterion since its payback period is less than 5 years.

Problem 14-27 (continued)

4. The formula for the internal rate of return is:

$$\text{Factor of the internal rate of return} = \frac{\text{Investment required}}{\text{Net annual cash inflow}}$$

$$= \frac{€480,000}{€108,000} = 4.4 \text{ (rounded)}$$

Looking at Table 14C-4 in Appendix 14C, and reading along the 12-period line, a factor of 4.4 would represent an internal rate of return of approximately 20%.

Note that the payback and internal rate of return methods would indicate that the investment should be made. The simple rate of return method indicates the opposite since the simple rate of return is less than 16%. The simple rate of return method generally is not an accurate guide in investment decisions.

Problem 14-29 (30 minutes)

1. The present value of cash flows would be:

Item	Year(s)	Amount of Cash Flows	18% Factor	Present Value of Cash Flows
Purchase alternative:				

Purchase cost of the plane	Now	$(850,000)	1.000	$(850,000)
Annual cost of servicing, etc...	1-5	(9,000)	3.127	(28,143)
Repairs:				
First three years...............	1-3	(3,000)	2.174	(6,522)
Fourth year......................	4	(5,000)	0.516	(2,580)
Fifth year........................	5	(10,000)	0.437	(4,370)
Resale value of the plane	5	425,000	0.437	185,725
Present value of cash flows				$(705,890)

Lease alternative:				
Damage deposit	Now	$ (50,000)	1.000	$ (50,000)
Annual lease payments	1-5	(200,000)	3.127	(625,400)
Refund of deposit	5	50,000	0.437	21,850
Present value of cash flows				$(653,550)

Net present value in favour of leasing the plane		$ 52,340

2. The company should accept the leasing alternative, since it has the lowest present value of total cost. When a company has a high cost of capital, such as the company in this problem, it is usually better to avoid tying up funds in equipment and facilities. Although the purchase of equipment and facilities allows a company to claim a resale value at the end of useful life, this resale value frequently has a very low present value if the company's cost of capital is high, as can be seen by the purchase alternative above. Moreover, leased equipment and facilities are often owned by pension funds and similar organizations that require a fairly low rate of return and thus can pass a savings on to the lessee. "You should lease whenever money is worth more to you than it is to the other person."

Problem 14-31 (45 minutes)

Alternative 1:

Items and Computations	Year(s)	(1) Amount	(2) Tax Effect	(1) × (2) After-Tax Cash Flows	8% Factor	Present Value of Cash Flows
Investment in the bonds...........	Now	$(200,000)		$(200,000)	1.000	$(200,000)
Interest on the bonds						
(8% × $200,000)	1-24*	8,000 *		8,000	15.247 **	121,976
Maturity of the bonds	24	200,000		200,000	0.390 **	78,000
Net present value						$ (24)***

* 24 six-month interest periods; $8,000 received each interest period.
** Factor for 4% for 24 periods.
*** This amount should be zero; the difference is due to rounding of the discount factors. (Since the bonds yield 8% after taxes, they would have a zero net present value at an 8% discount rate.)

Problem 14-31 (continued)

Items and Computations	Year(s)	(1) Amount	(2) Tax Effect	(1) × (2) After-Tax Cash Flows	8% Factor	Present Value of Cash Flows
Alternative 2:						
Investment in the business	Now	$(200,000)	—	$(200,000)	1.000	$(200,000)
Net annual cash receipts ($400,000 − $370,000 = $30,000)	1-12	30,000	1 − 0.35	19,500	7.536	146,952
CCA tax shield						19.260

$$\frac{Cdt}{D+k} \times \frac{1+.5k}{1+k} - Sdt \times (1+k)^{-n}$$

$$= \frac{\$80,000 \times .2 \times .35}{.2 + .08} \times \frac{1.04}{1.08} - \frac{\$0 \times .2 \times .35}{.2 + .08} \times .397$$

$$= \$20,000 \times .963) - \$0 = \$19,260$$

Items and Computations	Year(s)	(1) Amount	(2) Tax Effect	(1) × (2) After-Tax Cash Flows	8% Factor	Present Value of Cash Flows
Recovery of working capital ($200,000 − $80,000 = $120,000)...	12	120,000	—	120,000	0.397	47,640
Net present value................						$ 13,852

The net present value of Alternative 2 is higher than the net present value of Alternative 1. That certainly gives the edge to Alternative 2. However, the additional net present value is so small that it may be outweighed by the higher risk of Alternative 2 and the potential hassles of owning a store.

Case 14-33 (45 minutes)

1. As a member of the division budget committee that is conducting the postaudit review, Amy Kimbell will be implicitly lending her credibility to any report that is forwarded to the board of directors. If she were to implicitly accept the review by failing to call attention to its shortcomings, she would be violating several of management accounting ethical standards including:

   - Competence. Prepare complete and clear reports and recommendations after appropriate analysis of relevant and reliable information. The current postaudit review is incomplete—incremental service department costs have been excluded.

   - Integrity. Communicate unfavourable as well as favourable information and professional judgments or opinions. The current postaudit review suppresses unfavourable information.

   - Objectivity. Communicate information fairly and objectively. Disclose fully all relevant information that could reasonably be expected to influence an intended user's understanding of the reports, comments, and recommendations presented. The intent of the current postaudit review is clearly to justify the earlier decision to invest in the high-tech operation, rather than to present a fair and balanced view. Unfavourable information has been suppressed.

Amy is in a delicate situation if the other members of the budget committee are unwilling to heed her concerns. On the one hand, she cannot let the flawed postaudit review go to the board of directors. On the other hand, she needs to maintain good working relations with the other members of the budget committee. And her actions on this committee will likely become known throughout the company and influence her relations with just about everyone she comes into contact with. We suggest that, as diplomatically as she can, she should firmly state that she feels the postaudit review is an important document, but the current version is deeply flawed, and that she respects the opinions of the other members of the committee, but will feel obligated to file a minority report if the current version is sent to the board of directors. Quite often, the threat of such a report is enough to bring the other members of the committee to their senses. If it does not have this effect, then she should file the minority report.

Case 14-33 (continued)

2. Unfortunately, the situation that Amy faces is all too common. Rather than acknowledge mistakes and cut losses, managers (and people in general) too often remain committed to their failing courses of action. This commitment leads people into self-delusion, self-justification, and cover-ups—all of which sap time and energy as well as perpetuating the results of bad decisions. Postaudits, if conducted properly, provide an escape route from this self-defeating behaviour.

    The review process is flawed from the very beginning if the postaudit review is prepared by the same people who approved the original proposal. The people who approved the original proposal are probably going to be interested in justifying their original decision rather than in conducting an objective review. Therefore, the postaudit review should be conducted by an independent group—perhaps the company's internal audit office—rather than by the division budget committees.

Case 14-35 (60 minutes)

1. This is a least-cost problem; it can be worked either by the total-cost approach or by the incremental-cost approach. Regardless of which approach is used, we must first compute the annual production costs that would result from each of the machines. The computations are:

			Year		
		1	2	3	4-10
Units produced		20,000	30,000	40,000	45,000
Model 2600: Total cost at $0.90 per unit		$18,000	$27,000	$36,000	$40,500
Model 5200: Total cost at $0.70 per unit		$14,000	$21,000	$28,000	$31,500

Using these data, the solution by the total-cost approach would be:

Item	Year(s)	Amount of Cash Flows	18% Factor	Present Value of Cash Flows
Alternative 1: Purchase the model 2600 machine:				
Cost of new machine	Now	$(180,000)	1.000	$(180,000)
Cost of new machine	6	(200,000)	0.370	(74,000)
Market value of replacement machine	10	100,000	0.191	19,100
Production costs (above)	1	(18,000)	0.847	(15,246)
" " "	2	(27,000)	0.718	(19,386)
" " "	3	(36,000)	0.609	(21,924)
Repairs and maintenance	4-10	(40,500)	2.320 *	(93,960)
	1-10	(6,000)	4.494	(26,964)
Present value of cash outflows				$(412,380)

© McGraw-Hill Ryerson, 2004

14-26
                                                                   Managerial Accounting, 6th Canadian Edition

Case 14-35 (continued)

Alternative 2: Purchase the model 5200 machine:

Item	Year(s)	Amount of Cash Flows	18% Factor	Present Value of Cash Flows
Cost of new machine	Now	$(250,000)	1.000	$(250,000)
Production costs (above)	1	(14,000)	0.847	(11,858)
"	2	(21,000)	0.718	(15,078)
"	3	(28,000)	0.609	(17,052)
"	4-10	(31,500)	2.320 *	(73,080)
Repairs and maintenance	1-10	(4,600)	4.494	(20,672)
Present value of cash outflows				$(387,740)
Net present value in favour of Alternative 2				$ 24,640

* Present value factor for 10 periods 4.494
  Present value factor for 3 periods 2.174
  Present value factor for 7 periods starting 4 periods in the future 2.320

Case 14-35 (continued)

The solution by the incremental-cost approach would be:

Item	Year(s)	Amount of Cash Flows	18% Factor	Present Value of Cash Flows
Incremental cost of the model 5200 machine.............	Now	$ (70,000)	1.000	$ (70,000)
Cost avoided on a replacement model 2600 machine....	6	200,000	0.370	74,000
Salvage value forgone on the replacement machine............	10	(100,000)	0.191	(19,100)
Savings in production costs......	1	4,000	0.847	3,388
" " "	2	6,000	0.718	4,308
" " "	3	8,000	0.609	4,872
" " "	4-10	9,000	2.320	20,880
Savings on repairs, etc.	1-10	1,400	4.494	6,292
Net present value...................				$ 24,640

Thus, the company should purchase the model 5200 machine and keep the presently owned model 2600 machine on standby.

2. An increase in materials cost would make the model 5200 machine less desirable. The reason is that it uses more material per unit than does the model 2600 machine, as evidenced by the greater material cost per unit.

3. An increase in labour cost would make the model 5200 machine more desirable. The reason is that it uses less labour time per unit than does the model 2600 machine, as evidenced by the lower labour cost per unit.

Group Exercise 14-37
Students' answers will depend on the specific project they investigate at your local university or college.

Appendix A
Service Department Costing: An Activity Approach

Exercise A-1 (20 minutes)

	Service Departments			Operating Departments		
	Administrative	Janitorial	Maintenance	Prep	Finishing	Total
Overhead costs	$84,000	$67,800	$36,000	$256,100	$498,600	$942,500
Allocation:						
Administrative:(5%; 20%; 50%; 25%)*	(84,000)	4,200	16,800	42,000	21,000	
Janitorial: (1/10; 2/10; 7/10)		(72,000)	7,200	14,400	50,400	
Maintenance: (1/4; 3/4)			(60,000)	15,000	45,000	
Total overhead costs after allocations	$0	$0	$0	$327,500	$615,000	$942,500

* Allocations can be done using percentages, fractions, or a rate per unit of activity. Administrative allocations, for example, have been shown as percentages above, but they could have been shown as 1/20; 4/20; 10/20; and 5/20 or they could have been shown as $70 per employee. Fractions should be used if percentages result in rounding error.

Exercise A-1 (continued)

Supporting computations:

Administrative allocated to:

Janitorial............................	60 employees	5%
Equipment Maintenance........	240 employees	20
Prep	600 employees	50
Finishing	300 employees	25
Total..................................	1,200 employees	100%

Janitorial allocated to:

Equipment Maintenance........	1,000 sq. m.	1/10
Prep	2,000 sq. m.	2/10
Finishing	7,000 sq. m.	7/10
Total..................................	10,000 sq. m.	10/10

Equipment Maintenance allocated to:

Prep	10,000 MH	1/4
Finishing	30,000 MH	3/4
Total..................................	40,000 MH	4/4

Exercise A-3 (15 minutes)

	Arbon Refinery	Beck Refinery
Variable costs:		
$0.075 per litre × 1,080,000 litres.................	$ 81,000	
$0.075 per litre × 520,000 litres....................		$ 39,000
Fixed costs:		
60% × $200,000..	120,000	
40% × $200,000..		80,000
Total allocated costs...................................	$201,000	$119,000

Exercise A-5 (10 minutes)

The budgeted rate of $60 per employee should be multiplied by the actual number of employees in each operating department during the year for the end-of-year allocations.

	(1) Budgeted Rate	(2) Actual Number of Employees	(1) × (2) Total Allocation
Cutting Department...............	$60	500	$ 30,000
Milling Department	$60	400	24,000
Assembly Department............	$60	800	48,000
Total		1,700	$102,000

The difference between the budgeted and actual cost per employee is the responsibility of the Medical Services Department and will not be allocated to the operating departments. This variance totals $20,400 for the year.

1,700 employees × ($72 − $60 = $12 per employee) = $20,400.

Exercise A-7 (20 minutes)

1.

	Men's 8%	Women's 40%	Shoes 28%	House- wares 24%	Total 100%
Percentage of 2002 sales					
Allocation of 2002 fixed administrative expenses (based on the above percentages)	$ 72,000	$360,000	$252,000	$216,000	$900,000

2.

	Men's	Women's	Shoes	House- wares	Total
2002 allocation (above)	$ 72,000	$360,000	$252,000	$216,000	$900,000
2001 allocation	90,000	225,000	315,000	270,000	900,000
Increase (decrease) in allocation	$(18,000)	$135,000	$(63,000)	$(54,000)	$ 0

The manager of the Women's Department undoubtedly will be upset about the increased allocation to the department but will feel powerless to do anything about it. Such an increased allocation may be viewed as a penalty for an outstanding performance.

3. Sales dollars is not ordinarily a good base for allocating fixed costs. The costs allocated to a department will be affected by the sales in *other* departments. In our illustration above, the sales in three departments remained static and the sales in the fourth increased. As a result, less cost was allocated to the departments with static sales and more cost was allocated to the one department that showed improvement during the period.

Problem A-9 (45 minutes)

1.

	Machine Tools Division	Special Products Division
Variable costs:		
$0.50 per machine-hour × 90,000 machine-hours..	$45,000	
$0.50 per machine-hour × 60,000 machine-hours..		$30,000
Fixed costs:		
65% × $80,000..	52,000	
35% × $80,000..		28,000
Total cost allocated..	$97,000	$58,000

The variable costs are allocated by multiplying the budgeted rate per machine-hour by the budgeted number of machine-hours that will be worked in each division during the month. The fixed costs are allocated in predetermined, lump-sum amounts based on the peak-period maintenance needs in each division.

Managerial Accounting, 6th Canadian Edition

Problem A-9 (continued)

2.

	Machine Tools Division	Special Products Division
Variable costs:		
$0.50 per machine-hour × 60,000 machine-hours	$30,000	
$0.50 per machine-hour × 60,000 machine-hours		$30,000
Fixed costs:		
65% × $80,000	52,000	
35% × $80,000		28,000
Total cost allocated	$82,000	$58,000

The variable costs are allocated according to the budgeted rate per machine-hour and not according to the actual rate. Also notice that the fixed costs are again allocated in predetermined, lump-sum amounts based on budgeted fixed costs. Any difference between budgeted and actual costs is not allocated but rather is treated as a spending variance of the maintenance department:

	Variable	Fixed
Total actual costs for the month	$78,000	$85,000
Total cost allocated above	60,000	80,000
Spending variance—not allocated	$18,000	$ 5,000

Problem A-9 (continued)

3.
Actual variable costs...............	$ 78,000
Actual fixed costs...................	85,000
Total actual costs...................	$163,000

   One-half of the cost, or $81,500, would be allocated to each division, since an equal number of machine-hours was worked in each division during the month.

4. This method has two major problems. First, the spending variances should not be allocated because this forces the inefficiencies of the service department onto the using departments. Second, the fixed costs should *not* be allocated according to month-by-month usage of services, because this causes the allocation to one division to be affected by what happens in another division.

5. Their strategy probably will be to underestimate their peak-period needs in order to force a greater proportion of any allocation onto other departments. Top management can control such ploys by careful follow-up, with rewards being given to those managers who estimate accurately, and severe penalties assessed against those managers who underestimate long-run usage. For example, departments that exceed their estimated peak-period maintenance requirements may be forced to hire outside maintenance contractors, at market rates, to do their maintenance work during peak periods.

Problem A-11 (30 minutes)

1. Yes, there is merit to the complaint. The company is using a variable base (lines of print) to allocate costs that are largely fixed. Thus, the amount of cost that is charged to a division during a given month will depend to a large extent on usage in other divisions. A reduction in usage in one division can result in shifts of costs from it onto the other divisions, even though the other divisions receive no additional service.

2.

	Lines of Print	Total Cost
May activity...........	200,000	$182,000
June activity...........	150,000	179,000
Difference..............	50,000	$ 3,000

$$\text{Variable cost element} = \frac{\text{Change in cost}}{\text{Change in activity}}$$

$$= \frac{\$3,000}{50,000 \text{ lines}} = \$0.06 \text{ per line}$$

Fixed costs per month:

Total cost, May	$182,000
Less variable cost ($0.06 per line × 200,000 lines)	12,000
Fixed cost	$170,000

Problem A-11 (continued)

3.

	Lending	Retail	Commercial	Total
		Division		
May allocation:				
Variable cost at $0.06 per line:				
$0.06 × 80,000 lines	$ 4,800			
$0.06 × 20,000 lines		$ 1,200		
$0.06 × 100,000 lines			$ 6,000	
Fixed cost:				
40% × $170,000	68,000			
12% × $170,000		20,400		
48% × $170,000			81,600	
Total cost allocated	$72,800	$21,600	$87,600	$182,000
June allocation:				
Variable cost at $0.06 per line:				
$0.06 × 75,000 lines	$ 4,500			
$0.06 × 30,000 lines		$ 1,800		
$0.06 × 45,000 lines			$ 2,700	
Fixed cost:				
40% × $170,000	68,000			
12% × $170,000		20,400		
48% × $170,000			81,600	
Total cost allocated	$72,500	$22,200	$84,300	$179,000

Problem A-13 (60 minutes)

1. and 2.

	Medical Services	Mainte-nance	Metals	Plastics
Variable costs to be allocated.........	$3,630	$12,536		
Medical services allocation:				
$33 per employee × 8 employees......	(264)	264		
$33 per employee × 38 employees.....	(1,254)		$ 1,254	
$33 per employee × 64 employees.....	(2,112)			$ 2,112
Maintenance allocation:				
$0.80 per DLH × 6,000 DLH.............		(4,800)	4,800	
$0.80 per DLH × 10,000 DLH...........		(8,000)		8,000
Total variable costs	$ 0	$ 0	$ 6,054	$ 10,112

Problem A-13 (continued)

	Medical Services	Mainte- nance	Metals	Plastics
Fixed costs to be allocated	$7,500	$6,000		
Medical services allocation:				
6.67% × $7,500	(500)	500		
40.00% × $7,500	(3,000)		$ 3,000	
53.33% × $7,500	(4,000)			$ 4,000
Maintenance allocation:				
40% × $6,500		(2,600)	2,600	
60% × $6,500		(3,900)		3,900
Total fixed costs	$ 0	$ 0	$ 5,600	$ 7,900
Total allocated costs	$ 0	$ 0	$ 11,654	$ 18,012
Other budgeted overhead costs			104,000	155,000
Total overhead costs (a)			$115,654	$173,012
Direct labour-hours (b)			6,000	10,000
Predetermined overhead rate (a) ÷ (b) ..			$19.28	$17.30

Problem A-13 (continued)

Supporting computations:
Variable medical services allocation:

Maintenance	8 employees
Metals	38 employees
Plastics	64 employees
Total	110 employees

$3,630 ÷ 110 employees = $33 per employee

Variable maintenance allocation:

Metals	6,000 DLH
Plastics	10,000 DLH
Total	16,000 DLH

$12,800 ÷ 16,000 DLHs = $0.80 per DLH

Fixed medical services allocation:

Long-run employee needs:

Maintenance	10	6.67%
Metals	60	40.00
Plastics	80	53.33
Total	150	100.00%

Fixed maintenance allocation:

Square metres occupied:

Metals	800 sq. m.	40%
Plastics	1,200 sq. m.	60
Total	2,000 sq. m.	100%

Problem A-13 (continued)

3. Direct labour cost per unit:

$$\frac{10{,}000 \text{ DLHs}}{20{,}000 \text{ units}} = 0.5 \text{ DLH per unit}$$

$$\frac{\text{Direct labour cost}}{\text{Direct labour-hours}} = \frac{\$40{,}000}{10{,}000 \text{ DLHs}} = \$4.00 \text{ per DLH}$$

0.5 DLH per unit × $4.00 per DLH = $2 per unit

Direct materials cost per unit:

$$\frac{\$80{,}000}{20{,}000 \text{ units}} = \$4.00 \text{ per unit}$$

Overhead cost per unit:

0.5 DLH per unit (above) × $17.30 per DLH = $8.65 per unit

Total cost per unit:

Direct labour	$ 2.00
Direct material..............	4.00
Overhead	8.65
Total	$14.65

Case A-15 (75 minutes)

1. Step method:

	Cafeteria	Custodial Services	Machinery Maintenance	Milling	Finishing
Total costs before allocations	$320,000	$65,400	$ 93,600	$416,000	$166,000
Allocations:					
Cafeteria (@ $640 per employee)*	(320,000)	25,600	38,400	64,000	192,000
Custodial Services (@ $13.00 per sq. m.)**		(91,000)	13,000	52,000	26,000
Machinery Maintenance (4/5; 1/5)			(145,000)	116,000	29,000
Total overhead after allocations	$ 0	$ 0	$ 0	$648,000	$413,000
Divide by machine-hours				÷160,000	
Divide by direct labour-hours					÷ 70,000
Predetermined overhead rate				$ 4.05	$ 5.90

* Based on 40 + 60 + 100 + 300 = 500 employees.
** Based on 1,000 + 4,000 + 2,000 = 7,000 sq. m.

Case A-15 (continued)

2. Direct method:

	Cafeteria	Custodial Services	Machinery Maintenance	Milling	Finishing
Total costs before allocations	$320,000	$65,400	$93,600	$416,000	$166,000
Allocations:					
Cafeteria (1/4; 3/4)*	(320,000)			80,000	240,000
Custodial Services (2/3; 1/3)**		(65,400)		43,600	21,800
Machinery Maintenance (4/5; 1/5)			(93,600)	74,880	18,720
Total overhead after allocations	$ 0	$ 0	$ 0	$614,480	$446,520
Divide by machine-hours				÷160,000	
Divide by direct labour-hours					÷70,000
Predetermined overhead rate				$ 3.84	$ 6.38

* Based on 100 + 300 = 400 employees.
** Based on 4,000 + 2,000 = 6,000 sq. m.

Managerial Accounting, 6th Canadian Edition

Case A-15 (continued)

3. a. The amount of overhead cost assigned to the job would be:

Step method:
  Milling Department:
    $4.05 per machine-hour × 2,000 machine-hours .... $ 8,100
  Finishing Department:
    $5.90 per DLH × 13,000 DLHs 76,700
  Total overhead cost $84,800

Direct method:
  Milling Department:
    $3.84 per machine-hour × 2,000 machine-hours .... $ 7,680
  Finishing Department:
    $6.38 per DLH × 13,000 DLHs 82,940
  Total overhead cost $90,620

b. The step method provides a better basis for computing predetermined overhead rates than the direct method because it gives recognition to services provided between service departments. If this interdepartmental service is not recognized, then either too much or too little of a service department's costs may be allocated to a producing department. The result will be an inaccuracy in the producing department's predetermined overhead rate.

For example, notice from the computations in (2) above that using the direct method and ignoring interdepartmental services causes the predetermined overhead rate in the Milling Department to fall to only $3.84 per MH (from $4.05 per MH when the step method is used), and causes the predetermined overhead rate in the Finishing Department to rise to $6.38 (from $5.90 when the step method is used). These inaccuracies in the predetermined overhead rate can cause corresponding inaccuracies in bids for jobs. Since the direct method in this case understates the rate in the Milling Department and overstates the rate in the Finishing Department, it is not surprising that the company tends to bid low on jobs requiring a lot of milling work and tends to bid too high on jobs that require a lot of finishing work.

Group Exercise A-17

1. The answer to this part will depend on the industry the group selects.

2. The answer to this part will depend on the industry the group selects.

3. The answer to this part will depend on the industry the group selects.

4. & 5.
   Generally speaking, the wider the range of products made or services offered, the greater the support costs. More products and services require additional support resources for scheduling, planning, billing, shipping, and so on. As the resources demanded of the support departments increase, their costs increase as well.

6. Service department costs are reduced by decreasing spending on the resources the service departments consume. This can be accomplished by: (1) decreasing the activities the service departments are required to perform—perhaps by reducing the range and complexity of products and services offered by the company; (2) improving the business processes in the service departments so that fewer resources are required to carry out those activities; or (3) spending less on the resources—perhaps by negotiating for better prices from suppliers.